Sexuality and Social Control

Scotland 1660–1780

FAMILY,
SEXUALITY AND SOCIAL RELATIONS
IN PAST TIMES

GENERAL EDITORS:
Peter Laslett, Michael Anderson and Keith Wrightson

Sexuality and Social Control
Scotland 1660–1780

Rosalind Mitchison
and
Leah Leneman

Basil Blackwell

Copyright © Rosalind Mitchison and Leah Leneman 1989

First published 1989

Basil Blackwell Ltd
108 Cowley Road, Oxford, OX4 1JF, UK

Basil Blackwell Inc.
432 Park Avenue South, Suite 1503
New York, NY 10016, USA

British Library Cataloguing in Publication Data

Mitchison, Rosalind
Sexuality and Social Control, Scotland 1660–1780.
1. Scotland. Society. Historical role of Christian church.
I. Title II. Leneman, Leah III. Series 261.1'09411.
ISBN 0-631-15028-5

Library of Congress Cataloging in Publication Data

Mitchison, Rosalind.
Sexuality and Social Control, Scotland 1660–1780
Rosalind Mitchison and Leah Leneman.
p. cm. -- (Family, sexuality, and social relations in past times)
Includes index.
ISBN 0-631-15028-5
1. Family – Scotland – History. 2. Family – Religious aspects – Protestant churches.
3. Marriage – Scotland – History. 4. Marriage – Religious aspects – Protestant churches.
5. Illegitimacy – Scotland – History. 6. Church and state – Scotland – History.
I. Leneman, Leah. II. Title. III. Series.
HQ617.M58 1989
306.8'5'09411 – dc19

Typeset in 11/13pt Garamond
by Hope Services, Abingdon
Printed in Great Britain by
T.J. Press Ltd, Padstow, Cornwall

Contents

List of Figures

Acknowledgements

The research on which this book is based has been supported by the Economic and Social Research Council (at that time the Social Science Research Council), the British Academy and the Leverhulme Trust. We are grateful to these organizations for making the study possible, and to the Department of Economic and Social History of Edinburgh University which has provided us with space, secretarial aid and the miscellaneous support and encouragement which counts for a great deal in the carrying on of a research project. Most of the material used was located in the Scottish Record Office, and we have benefited from the courtesy and expertise of the staff. We are also grateful for the help of the staffs of the National Library of Scotland and of the regional achives in Forres, Dundee, Stirling and Glasgow. Individuals to whom we owe ideas, suggestions, information and general help include Michael Anderson, R. H. Campbell, Tristram Clarke, Michael Lynch, Rosalind Marshall, Rory Paddock, Geoffrey Parker, Alasdair Roberts, David Sellar, T. C. Smout, I. A. Whyte and E. A. Wrigley.

Abbreviations

APS	*Acts of the Parliaments of Scotland*, 12 vols (London, 1814–75)
KSR	Kirk Session Register
NLS	National Library of Scotland
NSA	*New Statistical Account of Scotland*, 15 vols (Edinburgh, 1845)
OPR	Old Parish Register
OSA	*The Statistical Account of Scotland*, Sir John Sinclair (ed.), 21 vols (Edinburgh, 1791–7): revised in a regional arrangement with introductions in 20 vols, Donald J. Withrington and Ian R. Grant (eds), (Wakefield, 1973–84)
RPCS	*Register of the Privy Council of Scotland*, third series, 1660–91, 16 vols, various editors (Edinburgh, 1908–80)
SRO	Scottish Record Office

Introduction

The original research project which sustains this book was to explore and measure illegitimacy in Scotland in the seventeenth and eighteenth centuries, with particular attention to variations between regions and over time, using the evidence available in the records of the presbyterian system of church courts. The project widened for various reasons. Illegitimacy, that is births out of wedlock, can be assessed only with a clear understanding of the definitions of marriage in law and opinion. The changing social and economic scene had to be understood; the theology which sustained church discipline, and the court structure which applied it were also clearly fundamental to the research. We came to see a need to look at other forms of misbehaviour in the eyes of the Church, and their implications: thus bridal pregnancy, the support of bastard children, the eighteenth-century fashion for irregular marriage and the levels of repeated bastard bearing also came into our scope. These developments were the result of recognition that illegitimacy is only one indicator, though an important one, of the response of individuals to social norms. Our book has become a study of the adjustment of the normal sexual urges of people to social and religious convention.

Why study illegitimacy? Further, why study it for Scotland? If the answer is allowed to go beyond the Everest concept of 'because it is there', it will be seen that these two questions interact. Illegitimacy is of importance because it is an indicator of rule breaking. Its existence is proof that the generally accepted Christian principle which confined sexual activity to marriage has been disregarded; it also shows a breach of the social conventions which supported this rule and by which society regulated population in accordance with the economic openings, so that marriage in early modern Britain was restricted to those who could expect to support a family in an accepted way. In particular it was held at all levels of society that servants and apprentices living in other people's houses and working at industry or on the land were not free to marry. These rules, which conflicted with natural biological impulses, were important, and breach of them is likely to produce comments worth overhearing from the past.

A further important feature of illegitimacy is that where the records are suitable it can be quantified. Once quantified it can be used to show time-based and geographical variations in the level of rule breaking. This is not to claim an absolute numerical correlation between unmarried sexual intercourse and illegitimate births. Many features may affect the relationship. Fecundity is related to age, and also to the state of nutrition. There are various natural ways in which a foetus may come to be aborted early, and some unnatural ones; some pregnancies which start out of wedlock may be followed by marriage, not necessarily with the father. But in a society where the mass of the people did not have techniques of contraception, and only occasionally showed signs of interest in drugs which might lead to abortion, there is likely to have been a roughly proportional relationship between sexual intercourse among the unmarried and illegitimate births. It is the assumption of this study that where the records are complete this relationship can be used to quantify rule breaking.

Some historians have found reasons for using illegitimacy study as a route to the understanding of the views of the common people, and particularly to those of women. Sex is too important a matter to be left solely to the concern of the moralists. The pressures exerted by those who felt obliged to tell the world how it should behave, though they cannot be taken as the only significant aspect of sexual matters, have all the same some importance. In particular, two studies of church attitudes to sex have set the scene for this our study, and we are particularly grateful to the authors.[1] From the late 1960s an outbreak of books and papers appeared on the subject of sexuality in the past and its regulation. Some of these were produced in the *Journal of Interdisciplinary History* in articles later formed into a book.[2] One of the reasons for this outbreak was the work of Edward Shorter, at once both provocative and

---

1 J. R. Hardy, 'The Attitudes of Church and State in Scotland to Sex and Marriage, 1500–1707' (unpublished M.Phil. thesis, Edinburgh University, 1978); K. H. Boyd, *Scottish Church Attitudes to Sex, Marriage and the Family* (Edinburgh, 1980).

2 Robert I. Rotberg and Theodore K. Rabb (eds), *Marriage and the Family* (Princeton, NJ, 1980).

stimulating.[3] But Shorter merely encouraged attention to what was coming to be seen as a necessary area of concern for historians who wished either to study the social structure or to examine the personal experience of ordinary people.

This outbreak of work, and the various hypotheses put forward to explain variations in the level of illegitimacy, provide good evidence that our concern for this topic is in no way eccentric. Some of the theories advanced have had little basis in evidence. One popular theory, not particularly fashionable in academic circles today, is that of fertility testing: that a man would be unwilling to marry a woman until he knew for certain that she was capable of bearing a child. Implicit in this view is the idea that childlessness was in some way either materially disadvantageous or humiliating. It would obviously seem disadvantageous for a peasant with hereditary landholding rights, but otherwise it seems difficult to evaluate the pressure of such a need. In any case, the theory would be supported not so much by high illegitimacy as by a high level of premarital pregnancy. Yet, for instance, in England in the seventeenth century, when many of the rural population held land by relatively secure tenures, pre-marital pregnancy is considered to have been low.

Among other theories which have been advanced to explain illegitimacy, often for countries overseas, there is the argument advanced with reference to the north-east of Scotland in the nineteenth century that the official definition of marriage, and hence of children born outside it, was not the same as the popular one. Such a system can, for instance, be seen in eighteenth century Sweden,[4] though there the definition of legitimacy appears to have relied on the popular concept. Though the civil courts in Scotland had different rules on marriage from those of the Church, it was very easy for people uncertain of their marital status there to have it defined or reaffirmed.

Another reason for illegitimacy may be government regulations. For instance, the government prevented marriages by young men in Norway until they had completed their military service, an action which might well account for illegitimate births. In some parts of south Germany the States adopted Malthusian dogmas in

3 Edward Shorter, 'Female Emancipation, Birth Control and Fertility in European History', *American Historical Review* 78 (1973), pp. 605–40.

4 David Gaunt, 'Illegitimacy in Seventeenth- and Eighteenth-Century East Sweden', in Peter Laslett, Karla Oosterveen and Richard M. Smith (eds), *Bastardy and its Comparative History* (London, 1980), pp. 313–26.

the nineteenth century, and denied marriage to the poor, with consequent high illegitimacy ratios.[5] In late nineteenth century Banffshire it was also frequently alleged that the deliberate restrictions on cottage building by the farmers had an important role in the high level of illegitimacy.[6]

Where a specific ruling or practice is alleged as the explanation for illegitimacy the argument is clear and its efficacy can easily be evaluated. It is harder to assess some of the more theoretical arguments. An important concept which has been introduced to the topic by Peter Laslett is that of interrupted or frustrated courtship. It is likely that in societies with a relatively late age of marriage, as was the case in Western Europe, the young adults and teenagers will spend such recreation time as is available in single sex groupings. Only as these young people approach the normal age of marriage will they start looking for companionship of the other sex, and enter into courtship. In such courtship, intercourse before marriage would not be unusual. Expectations of some of the couples of being able to marry could be destroyed by social or economic events, and the result would be the pregnancy of an unmarried woman. Support for this idea is claimed in early modern England in the fact that the age at which an unmarried mother gave birth corresponded closely to that of married women at the birth of their first child.[7] Frustrated courtship may be suggested by such a correlation, but hardly proved without direct evidence as to the motivation of the unmarried mothers. The main weakness of the theory is that it would imply a much higher level of pre-marital pregnancy than appears to have existed before the eighteenth century. In Scotland we have some evidence from the late nineteenth century which opposes the theory, but in any case there is no reason to look for a similarity in the pattern of courtship and the expectation of marriage across the gulf of industrialization and the introduction of capitalized farming.

Theories attempting to explain the marked rise in illegitimacy in the eighteenth century, particularly the rapid acceleration of the rise after 1780 in England, are divided between those which assert a

5 Patricia James (ed.), *The Travel Diaries of Thomas Robert Malthus* (Cambridge, 1966), pp. 153, 277; J. Knodel, 'Law, Marriage and Illegitimacy in Nineteenth Century Germany', *Population Studies* xx (1966–7), pp. 279–94.

6 T. C. Smout, 'Sexual Behaviour in Nineteenth-Century Scotland', in Laslett et al. (eds), *Bastardy and its Comparative History*, p. 202.

7 Peter Laslett, 'Introduction', in Laslett et al. (eds), *Bastardy and its Comparative History*, pp. 1–60. But the work of David Levine, in *Family Formation in an Age of Nascent Capitalism* (New York, 1977) ch. 9 suggests that this was not general.

new pattern of sexual behaviour and those which claim an increase in the size of the section of the population already likely to have unmarried intercourse. There is agreement that the eighteenth century might anyway have seen a weakening in the control mechanisms used by the older members of families, the local social elites or the ecclesiastical authorities, over the behaviour of young people. Edward Shorter is the main adherent writing in English to expound the view of a drastic change in sexual behaviour, and he puts forward his conclusions as relevant not only to England but to France and Germany. His claim is that women were liberated by the wider prospects of paid work from control by either their families or by the local community, and expressed their liberation in a search for pleasure, sexual activity being a major element in this search. The weakness of this theory is the lack of specific links between rising illegitimacy and the women who experienced new forms of work. More profound as an argument is the wider claim that he makes, engagingly with the admission that there is no direct evidence supporting it, that there was a change from 'manipulative' to 'expressionist' sexual activity, that is from activity engaged in in the hope of securing marriage to activity for enjoyment.[8]

Of those who see the causative changes as enhancing the share of a particular form of deviance, David Levine has been an important contributor. In a chapter committed by its title to this view, 'Illegitimacy, Marriage Frustrated not Promiscuity Rampant',[9] he has looked at four villages and argued that the unsettling effects of price changes and of variations in the demand for specific textile products after 1750 led to postponement of marriage but not the postponement of sexual activity. His conclusion, that 'the interaction of personal experience and material trends' must be examined if we are to understand illegitimacy, seems inescapable, and not very profound, for it is what is to be discovered when the examination is made that will determine the validity of the theories. Another proponent of the alternative view to Shorter's, Cissie Fairchilds, has asserted that women were too submissive and too heavily involved in the family economy, both before and after industrial development, to have asserted themselves in the way that Shorter has claimed.[10] The arguments by which women were kept

8 Edward Shorter, 'Illegitimacy, Sexual Revolution and Social Change in Modern Europe', in Rotberg and Rabb (eds), *Marriage and the Family*, pp. 148–84.

9 David Levine, *Family Formation in an Age of Nascent Capitalism*, ch. 9.

10 Cissie Fairchilds, 'Female Sexual Attitudes and the Rise of Illegitimacy: A Case Study' in Rotberg and Rabb (eds), *Marriage and the Family*, pp. 163–204.

in a state of dependence and subordination were certainly taking a new turn and gaining strong religious sanction in the late eighteenth century.[11] But the concept of women as committed to the family home and family economy does not fit the British scene until after industrialization, for the system of farm service took them away from home before puberty. Such wages as they acquired in service would, presumably, be saved towards their own needs, for marriage or security, rather than taken to their parents. The family economy was manifest in the growing industrial sector, but that appears to have been still small before 1800. A more effective rebuttal of Shorter's theory comes from Louise A. Tilly, J. W. Scott and Miriam Cohen, who have argued that the economic changes of industrial expansion and innovation would increase the section of the population not restrained from sexual activity by the expectation of property, and so bring more people into risk of bastard bearing. The changes also might widen the group living in insecurity. They see the uncertainties produced by the new economic system as contributing to illegitimacy, and also the fact that migration might move young adults away from existing systems of control.[12]

Lawrence Stone has advanced a time scheme and explanation for illegitimacy in England over two and a half centuries. He holds that there was a period of puritanism in the seventeenth century, imposed on a population which had hitherto paid little attention to Christian regulation of sex. In the eighteenth century this gave way to secularization. Stone argues that increased severance of the bulk of the population from land rights and inheritance meant that there was a large population of landless labourers, not only without any desire to protect their lineage but also insecure.[13] Here again, as with most of those who stress insecurity, there is the assumption that much sexual activity usually preceded marriage, and that the task of the explanation of rising illegitimacy is to explain why pre-marital intercourse increasingly led to illegitimacy.

It has been claimed that illegitimacy and bridal pregnancy both followed a particular 'S' shaped graph, moving downwards to the early seventeenth century, and rising from the later decades of that century, and more sharply from the mid-eighteenth century. This

11 Leonore Davidoff and Catherine Hall, *Family Fortunes: Men and Women of the English Middle Class, 1780–1850* (London, 1987).

12 Louise A. Tilly, Joan W. Scott and Miriam Cohen, 'Women's Work and European Fertility Patterns' in Rotberg and Rabb (eds), *Marriage and the Family*, pp. 219–48.

13 Lawrence Stone, *The Family, Sex and Marriage* (London, 1977).

is the pattern put forward separately by Laslett and his associates and by Stone for England, and by Shorter for Europe.[14] Anderson claims that both illegitimate births and antenuptial conceptions rose almost everywhere in the eighteenth and early nineteenth centuries, but he points to variation earlier on.[15] For instance, both stood high in France in the sixteenth century, whereas in England both were low. In spite of Laslett's claim that there is a general pattern of similar movement between general and illegitimate fertility, which he sustains with the concept of an intensification of courtship activity, this does not find support in the evidence from France in the late eighteenth century. Laslett's contention that there is no general correlation between urbanization and illegitimacy stands up better. It is our view that these assertions, parallelisms and divergences are a good reason for the search for further evidence.

There are some studies of illegitimacy which relate it to specific local or familial features. In the early nineteenth century many moralists argued that the existence of Foundling Hospitals had a pernicious effect on sexual morals. In the later nineteenth century it was often asserted for north-east Scotland that the feeing market (the fair where farm servants were hired) was a cause of extra-marital sexual activity. The idea that illegitimacy had its specific and hereditary location is expressed in the work of Laslett, claiming that 'a bastardy prone sub-society' can be seen emerging from the late seventeenth century in England.[16] There is a strong risk that in studying a community in sufficient depth to ascertain the familial links the researcher may be making deductions on a very narrow base.

The basis of much of the theorizing on the social explanations of changes in illegitimacy levels is the estimate or calculation offered for pre-marital pregnancy in the pre-industrial age. It is on such estimates that the arguments of, for instance, Tilly and Scott depend. In 1967 P. E. H. Hair made an attempt to quantify this, using information from 77 English parishes, and also from four Scottish ones. His conclusion was that between the late sixteenth

14 Peter Laslett, *Family Life and Illicit Love in Earlier Generations* (Cambridge, 1977), ch. 3; Lawrence Stone, *The Family, Sex and Marriage*; Edward Shorter in Rotberg and Rabb (eds), *Marriage and the Family*; and also *The Making of the Modern Family* (London, 1976), ch. 3.

15 Michael Anderson, *Approaches to the History of the Western Family, 1500–1914* (London, 1980), pp. 21–2.

16 Peter Laslett, 'The Bastardy Prone Sub-Society', in Laslett et al. (eds), *Bastardy and its Comparative History*, pp. 217–46.

and the early nineteenth centuries certainly a sixth of brides in England were pregnant, and probably more than 40 per cent at the end of his survey period. Later, in a wider study he paid more attention to periodization, and claimed that the level of bridal pregnancy changed from approximately 20 per cent before 1700 to 40 per cent in the late eighteenth century. He also thought that many of these pregnancies were recent.[17] In 1981, in a very careful study, E. A. Wrigley offered still more precise figures, 17 per cent for the late seventeenth century, 28 per cent for the mid-eighteenth century, and over 35 per cent by 1800, at this final point, and with 4.5 per cent of births illegitimate.[18] If we assume that somewhere between a fifth and a quarter of all births are first births, this last period has nearly 60 per cent of all first births to women being conceived out of wedlock, and in such a state of affairs the idea of intercourse as normally a part of courtship is entirely reasonable. But this does not mean that it had been so a hundred years earlier, when somewhere between a quarter and a fifth of first births were conceived out of wedlock. In that period intercourse during courtship was clearly a minority activity. Studies of pre-marital pregnancy levels are an important way of gaining insight into the *mentalités* of bastard bearers.

To the second question 'why Scotland?', it should be pointed out that this country has already figured in the study of illegitimacy. Dr Laslett, in his comparative review of European illegitimacy,[19] has called Scotland 'the classic country for illegitimacy', though since the information on which this remark was based relates only to the later half of the nineteenth century, the label seems exaggerated. Certainly Scotland from the 1850s had a remarkably differentiated regional pattern of illegitimacy. Those who know the country will be more aware than Dr Laslett of the continuing sharp differences in culture and economy which survive in the country, and yet Scotland historically has displayed a remarkable level of homogeneity in religious belief, law, education and aspirations. The gradual fragmentation of church structure in the later eighteenth century involved very little dissent from

17 P. E. H. Hair, 'Bridal Pregnancy in Rural England in Earlier Centuries', *Population Studies* xx (1966–7), pp. 233–43; and also 'Bridal Pregnancy in Earlier Rural England Re-examined', *Population Studies* xxiv (1970), pp. 59–70.

18 E. A. Wrigley, 'Marriage, Fertility and Population Growth in Eighteenth-Century England', in R. B. Outhwaite (ed.), *Marriage and Society* (London, 1981), pp. 137–85.

19 Peter Laslett, 'Introduction', in Laslett et al., *Bastardy and its Comparative History*, p. 41.

Calvinism, and the established Church, which controlled the social provision of welfare and education in the eighteenth century, continued to dominate in the administration of these services right through the nineteenth century.[20] It is also the case that lowland Scotland had exceptionally well co-ordinated mechanisms of control of rural society before the industrial revolution.[21] On the other hand, the pattern of landholding displayed very marked variations, and, partly because of this, the agricultural systems of the nineteenth century involved almost every possible type of farming unit, from the small holdings of Galloway, where an enterprising man might rise from the status of labourer to the tenancy of a dairy farm, through the mixture of crofts and large farms characteristic of Aberdeenshire and the north-east, to the highly capitalized great farms of East and Mid Lothian.[22]

The Scottish Church in the early modern period displayed extreme distaste for physical intimacy between the sexes: it usually labelled any such demonstration 'scandalous carriage', and penalized it. In the nineteenth century the middle class held to a puritanical outlook on sexual matters, and regarded extra-marital sexual activity as the clearest indicator of the moral state of society. There was a profound belief in this class of the particular soundness and worthiness of Scottish institutions: at intervals Scots would lecture the English, wrestling with social problems, to point out, for instance, that it was a special mark of the superiority of Scottish education that poor relief could be managed at much less cost there than in England. There was also the common British belief, expressed in many novels and sermons, in the relative virtue of rural society in contrast to urban. These tenets led to an embarrassing debate, which went on for the rest of the century, when the results of the setting up of civil registration in 1855 became public. It was painful to discover that, for instance, for the years around 1861 the illegitimacy ratio for Scotland as a whole was 9.37 per cent; for rural Scotland, which the local basis of registration made it possible to identify, 9.51 per cent; and for urban Scotland, 9.22 per cent.[23] It was still more shame-making

20 Callum G. Brown, *The Social History of Religion in Scotland Since 1730* (London, 1987), ch. 6.

21 T. M. Devine, 'Unrest and Stability in Rural Ireland and Scotland, 1760–1840', in Rosalind Mitchison and Peter Roebuck (eds), *Economy and Society in Scotland and Ireland, 1500–1939* (Edinburgh, 1988), pp. 126–39.

22 T. M. Devine (ed.), *Farm Servants and Labour in Lowland Scotland, 1770–1914* (Edinburgh, 1984).

23 T. C. Smout, 'Sexual Behaviour in Nineteenth-Century Scotland'.

to know that in the south-west, particularly identified with presbyterianism by a somewhat dubious historiography, it was over 13 per cent and in the north-east over 15 per cent. If the illegitimacy ratio was to be accepted as the inverse of a morality indicator, morality stood lower in the Scottish countryside than in the towns, and was thought to stand nationally lower than for many countries in Europe. Though this last belief was the result of a failure to appreciate the inadequacies of the ratio as an index, and also to understand the role in some states of official definitions, there was no escaping the fact that illegitimacy was higher in Scotland than in England where the ratio was between 6 and 7 per cent.

It is true that a better understanding of the weakness of the ratio as a measure (since it does not allow for the different size of the unmarried female population, and of the hurdles put up in some states to marriage) modified the national embarrassment, but there still remained for Scots the linked problems of the need to understand what social and economic forces lay behind some of the very high local ratios, and how to modify them. As T. C. Smout has pointed out, a teenage girl in Banffshire was twenty times more likely to have an illegitimate child than one in Ross and Cromarty.[24] In individual parishes where the ratio might stand at over 30 per cent, illegitimacy was clearly not simply a matter of a single out of wedlock birth. Much effort was put into trying to bring the errant population to a chaster way of life, and with little success. This outcome appears to have been because nobody was prepared to put forward policies which would interfere with the rights of property, and oblige farmers to make more provision, in jobs and housing, for married workers, and partly because the church increasingly adopted the view that the moral deviance was located totally in the girls who became pregnant, and not in the men with whom they liaised.[25] Illegitimacy figures for the north-east and south-west stayed high into the interwar period, while they remained much lower, for instance, in the Highlands. In terms of nineteenth century persistence in regional variation, Scotland was indeed the classic country.

Our interest in this project stemmed partly from this nineteenth century regional pattern. We wished to find out whether the

24 Ibid.

25 J. R. D. Blaikie, 'Illegitimacy in Nineteenth-Century North-east Scotland' (unpublished Ph.D. thesis, Queen Mary College, London, 1987).

remarkably high figures in some areas could be found before the development of capitalized agriculture. We also wanted to see to what degree Scotland participated in the rising trend of illegitimacy and pre-marital pregnancy in the eighteenth century, and in the proportion of births conceived several months before marriage. Edward Shorter has pointed out that illegitimacy ratios were rising so fast in Europe and in the American colonies that the illegitimacy rate, the level of illegitimacy among unmarried women, must also have been rising.[26] Since in the period since 1870 there has been considerable parallelism in the movements of both legitimate and illegitimate fertility within the developed world, it seemed worth enquiring whether the Scottish figures would give similar results.[27] There was also the validity of popular assumptions about the definitions of marriage in the Scottish past to be tested. Recent controversy has shown that such assumptions can survive with no factual base, but this was an area needing exploration.[28] We had to ascertain whether the popular conception of what was marriage agreed with the official definitions.

We were encouraged to further research by the independent discovery on both our parts of the excellent quality of the Scottish material. This enabled us to plan a project which would use a large number of parishes and cover most of what we defined as distinct cultural regions in Scotland. Though we were not able to cover all possible regions, we still had the advantage of choosing our parishes to illustrate particular areas, instead of having to rely on parishes on which local work had already been done. We were also enabled not to be misled by the erratic behaviour of individual parishes. There are studies of illegitimacy in particular parishes, both in Scotland and elsewhere, in some cases made with very sophisticated reference to the local economy,[29] which seem to us not to appreciate – what was soon brought home to us – how a single parish may differ markedly and persistently in its

---

26 Edward Shorter, 'Female Emancipation, Birth Control and Fertility in European History', *American Historical Review* 78 (1973), pp. 605–40.

27 Ansley J. Coale and Susan Cotts Watkins (eds), *The Decline of Fertility in Europe* (Princeton, NJ, 1986).

28 Ian Carter, 'Illegitimate Births and Illegitimate Inferences', *Scottish Journal of Sociology* I (1977), pp. 125–35.

29 e.g. P. P. Viaggio, 'Illegitimacy and the European Marriage Pattern: Comparative Evidence from the Alpine Area', in Lloyd Bonfield, Richard M. Smith and Keith Wrightson (eds), *The World We Have Gained* (Oxford, 1986), pp. 100–21; Donna L. Baker, 'A Demographic Study of Illegitimacy in Ceres Parish, Fife, 1841–61', *The Scottish Genealogist* xxx (1983), pp. 113–20.

illegitimacy levels from the region in which it is situated. For this reason we think that studies of small parishes, not widened by regional scrutiny, should be accepted only with great caution. Minor social circumstances, a few jobs within the capacity of unsupported mothers, spare labour for child care, a relatively generous level of poor relief, etc., can enormously reduce the economic problems faced by unmarried mothers.

Much abuse, and much of it justified, has been thrown at the obvious demographic material of early modern Scotland, the Old Parish Registers (OPRs).[30] The material on which this study is based is from the parishes, but different. It comes from the records of the lowest court of the system of the established Church, the kirk session. Several hundred parishes have left carefully kept kirk session registers (KSRs) for the eighteenth century, and there are over 200 even for the later years of the seventeenth century. For doctrinal reasons, which are set out in chapter 1, discipline by these courts had to be comprehensive of the common people. It is our claim that it is sounder to rely on figures from this discipline record than on whether a parish clerk did or did not record the legal status of children at baptism. Though it is clear that not all Scottish OPRs are as bad as has been alleged (some indeed were kept very carefully and can be relied on for various matters), they were not subject to regular inspection by the higher courts of the church system as were the KSRs.

Of course, the Scottish Church was not the only one in the seventeenth century to attempt to control sexual activity by discipline. There are interesting studies based on such attempts in southern England, for Oxfordshire, for Wiltshire and for Somerset, the first two being for the first half of the seventeenth century, the last for the central decades.[31] The policy of control was imposed from above, and how far it met with popular support is not clear. In Oxfordshire there seems to have been a scale of penalties deliberately kept low, and with personal penance commutable for cash. In Wiltshire it seems to have been relatively easy for the offender to slip away and not be traced. Here again, and because of this, the formal penalties were frequently imposed

30 M. W. Flinn (ed.), *Scottish Population History from the Seventeenth Century to the 1930s* (Cambridge, 1977), pp. 45–51.

31 S. A. Peyton, 'Churchwardens' Presentments', *Oxfordshire Record Society* x (1928), pp. xiv–v; M. J. Ingram, 'Ecclesiastical Justice in Wiltshire, 1600–1641' (unpublished D.Phil. thesis, Oxford University, 1976); G. R. Quaife, *Wanton Wenches and Wayward Wives* (London, 1979).

only in reduced form – for instance in the ordering of penitential appearance when congregations would be small. In Somerset, though discipline was based on both Quarter Sessions and the Consistory Court, i.e. on the arms of both Church and State, it does not appear to have impinged on all sinners. Many men, and even some women, were able to ignore it completely, so that the figure of 50 per cent evasion has been suggested. Evasion was made easier by rogue clergy offering clandestine marriage to some couples. The whole system of enquiry in England was more haphazard than in Scotland, so that the likelihood of evasion may have prevented even the initial presentation of cases. The cost of the proceedings may have also discouraged the prosecution of the impecunious. It was obviously unjust that a man accused of fathering a bastard would have to pay costs equivalent to two weeks' earnings even if he established his innocence. In only a minority of cases were the courts ruling the arrangements for the illegitimate child's support, a fact which suggests that these courts were of less significance in social controls than the activities of local landowners or the families involved. There was also a discipline system, which later excited the enthusiasm of the early Oxford Movement, in the Isle of Man, which carried on, with fairly mild penalties, until the eighteenth century.[32] It was run by the bishop, and seems to have been enabled to be effective by the relative difficulty found by the sinners of moving elsewhere. The relative weakness of the disciplinary system in England is a strong argument for trying to get figures from a country where discipline could not easily be evaded.

A further reason for studying illegitimacy in Scotland is that in many ways society there was similar to that in England, and became more so. The Union of 1707 made a state of the two kingdoms which already had a great deal in common in social structure, and which came to approximate closely to each other in aspects of the economy, at least for Scotland in the Lowlands. If there had been no such common basis, it is unlikely that Scottish nationalism, as it became articulate, would for the most part have been accompanied by a wish to remain integrally joined with England. This fact means that, at least in a negative way, a study of society in Scotland may give indicators to possible motivation and practices in England.

It is our claim that for a considerable period the system of

---

32 E. H. Stenning, 'Manx Spiritual Laws', *Isle of Man Natural History and Antiquarian Society Proceedings* v (1942–50), pp. 287–97.

discipline in Scotland has left records which show investigation into all unmarried pregnancies once they reached a fairly advanced stage, and also into pregnancies preceding marriage. The dogma that sustained this discipline was held by the great bulk of the population. Those who deliberately repudiated Calvinism appear to have been only a few hundred Quakers, at their highest level (though the historian of Quakerism in Scotland evades the issue of numbers), and some Roman Catholics. The established Church launched regular inquiries into the number of Catholics in the various parts of Scotland, and it is on these that the figure of 16,490 Catholics in Webster's census of 1755 is based.[33] This was 1.3 per cent of the total population. All but 1,059 of these were located in the counties of Argyll, Banffshire, Inverness-shire and Aberdeenshire. Though the figures submitted for remote parishes in the Highlands resemble in reliability those used for counting sheep in Lewis Carroll's *Sylvie and Bruno*, for the areas used by this enquiry they were so small as to show that doctrinal divergence would not have weakened the Church's practical authority. We are confident that the material on which we have based our study is comprehensive for the period covered. However, we have not extended our study outwith the years 1660–1780. Before 1660 political events – the wars against England, participation in the English Civil War, civil war within Scotland, eventually conquest by England – created so much disturbance that we have no confidence in the capacity of local churches to maintain control over their flocks. We have been obliged to stop our work in 1780 because by then many parishes were abandoning the system of discipline, and study of their records convinced us that we could no longer be sure that their record of cases would be comprehensive.

Stopping in 1780 is, of course, a great pity. It means that there persists a large gap between our work and that of Professor Smout – a gap which covers the industrial revolution in Scotland and the transformation of agriculture. It is true that there are some individual studies of value which can give glimpses of trends between these two periods, but any systematic and large-scale study would have to use some other basic material.[34]

We had hoped to see whether the pattern of regional variation, so conspicuous after 1855, was of long standing, and whether

33 George R. Burnet, *The Story of Quakerism in Scotland, 1650–1850* (London, 1952); J. G. Kyd (ed.), *Scottish Population Statistics* (Scottish History Society, Edinburgh, 1951).
34 Blaikie, 'Illegitimacy in Nineteenth-century North-east Scotland'.

Scotland shared the European upward trend. What we have discovered is that there was no clear, national trend upwards before 1780, but that one region, the south-west, did experience steadily rising illegitimacy from the 1750s. Our negative discovery means that the upward movement in Scotland must, for the most part, be placed not in the period of extraordinarily rapid economic growth which preceded the industrial revolution, but in or after that revolution.

A further justification of this study is that in pursuing it we have been able to hear the response of ordinary people to the particular stresses involved in the repression of normal sexual impulses. In few other records can the voices of the common and fallible citizens of both sexes be heard.

1

Scotland: the Church and the Regions

The accepted ethic of post-reformation Scotland and the formal system of social control by which parts of it were enforced were both based on Calvinist dogma, only partly subverted by older values. Calvinism held to the sinfulness of man, and the uselessness of any form of good works for the achievement of salvation. Its central feature was the total gulf between God and man. God was almighty and the creator of the world: man his creation was corrupted in all his activities by the taint of original sin. There could be no merit or virtue in man except that attributed to him by God, though God was capable of working for his own ends through varied kinds of causation. From this central distinction of power of the two classes of being stemmed determinism. Everything that happened, including the salvation or damnation of an individual, was settled by God. In the fully fledged 'supralapsarian' theology, which took hold in the early seventeenth century, the division of mankind into the company of the elect, those to whom God had allotted salvation, and the reprobate, those destined to damnation, had been made before the Fall. This doctrine required the arguing away or ignoring of the numerous texts in the New Testament which asserted that Christ had died for all men. It was taken for granted that the number of the elect was small compared with that of the reprobate. The elect would receive some sort of assurance of their status.

Calvin nevertheless put great stress on the organization of the Church and its relationship to secular power: his follower, John Knox, who put his stamp on Scotland's Reformation, stressed even further the importance of the individual congregation. Within the congregation the sacrament of the eucharist held a central place, and the priest or minister, who could alone administer this, had great prestige, enhanced by his exclusive duty of also preaching the Word, that is of expounding doctrine. Only one other sacrament was recognized, that of baptism, but this, it was expressly stated in the Confession of Faith, was not necessary for salvation.[1] It was still considered of great importance as a sign of membership of the Christian church. Justification, that is the attribution of righteousness, was by faith alone, and was not linked to any action on the part of the justified. This did not mean that those who assented to the dogmas of the Church were necessarily among those to be saved.

That all man's faculties and actions were corrupted by sin did not mean that all were equally sinful, any more than that the difference between real numbers and infinity in mathematics makes all numbers equal. Those convinced that they were members of the elect, and assurance of this was an essential feature of such membership, were expected to show this fact in their daily life by abstaining from gross sins and by repentance after sinning. Calvinism thus called on all claiming to be Christians not only to hold the right beliefs but also to keep the commandments and the moral laws, and in this way to further God's will.

As a means of securing and encouraging the believers in acting in accordance with God's commands there developed covenant theology. This postulated the covenant of grace, an agreement between Christ and his flock by which redemption was promised to the elect. The elect would receive the gift of the Holy Ghost and be sustained in faith by the Church and the sacraments. This theology would counter any suggestion that those assured could ignore the commandments, since it tied election to the fulfilment of God's will, not to membership of the Church. In Scotland covenant theology led to formal renewals of the National Confession of Faith, and subscription to it. Since the original protestant confession of 1560 declared that a godly discipline was one of the signs of the true church, the renewal of the confession reaffirmed the necessity of membership of the Church and subjection to its rules. The true church was the body of the elect: the 1560 Confession defined the church as a 'company and multitude of men chosen by God', a congregation would not consider itself part of this company unless it sustained discipline. So the system of regular discipline enforced by the church courts in Scotland in the early modern period was an essential part of the affirmation by the community of its membership of the elect.[2]

1 W. C. Dickinson (ed.), *John Knox's History of the Reformation in Scotland* (Edinburgh, 1949), vol. 2, Appendix 6.

2 We are grateful to Professor R. H. Campbell for our understanding of the doctrinal significance of discipline.

There was a further argument for the enforcement of discipline which extended to denominations not Calvinist, as well as to Calvinists. God was seen as likely to intervene directly in human affairs: such interventions did not contradict the concepts of predestination, for God had many ways of achieving his aims. His intervention was likely if He were affronted by the behaviour of mankind, and would lead to chastisement. In other words, a nation in which sinful behaviour was tolerated, and therefore proliferated, was very likely to suffer some general disaster – a deadly epidemic, an unusual and devastating climatic change, a defeat in war. Plagues, famines, riots and rebellions were all signs of divine displeasure. Morality was therefore an important element in national security. The Scottish Church showed its acceptance of this view not only in sermons from all colours of ecclesiastical opinion during the 1745 Jacobite rising,[3] but also by the general habit of imposing a day of fasting and humiliation when the physical or political climate experienced unpleasant developments.

Despite the fact that all individuals were expected to make a positive adherence to the Church – that is, to understand its theology, to obey its rules and to aim all the time at a godly life, for to fail to do so was to declare oneself reprobate – these ideas were accepted by a society highly unequal in wealth and authority. The protestant reformers, even if they had not been in alliance with the nobility to achieve the Reformation, would not have considered that Christianity made all men equal, still less that equality extended to women. When a congregation affirmed its covenant, very noticeably in the National Covenant of 1637, the affirmation was by men only. Naturally landowners expected those of lesser rank to be under their authority. In June 1656 the laird of Brodie had a verbal exchange with his sister:

She said, thes that should be heirs of glori with us, we oght not to compt the less of them for outward thing. I replied, Heirs of glori did not exeem them from al civil duties and subjection on earth. He might have more grace then I, and sit above me in heaven, that wer not to goe befor me, nay, nor be considerd besid me on earth.

Landowner authority did not confine itself to wordly matters. In 1654 the males of this family had renewed their covenants by pledging their souls and bodies, lands and houses, wives, children

3 Richard B. Sher, *Church and University in the Scottish Enlightenment* (Edinburgh, 1985), pp. 43–4.

and servants to God.[4] Their women folk confirmed this pledge: the assent of the servants seems to have been taken for granted.

From soon after the Reformation, in some cases even before it was politically achieved, the structure of the Church's government was being built up. By the early seventeenth century it was agreed that ministers were nominally equal in status and function, even though the Crown had planted an episcopal structure on the Church. There was a hierarchy of church courts, the kirk session for parish business, above it the presbytery, then the synod, with the General Assembly, a meeting ground for the whole Church and the source of ecclesiastical legislation, at the top.[5]

Reformation Scotland was a country with little real power in the hands of the central authority, the Crown. In many areas great feudatories exercised the functions of government, in the form of justice and military authority; nominally as delegates of the monarch, but in practice near to independence. Such great lords also intercepted parts of the royal revenue. The Crown had, in many areas, no officials directly responsible to it alone. The establishment in such a state of the hierarchy of church courts and the settling of ministers responsible to these courts in the parishes, meant that the Church had a far more effective system of government than had the State. The ministry of the Church was professionally trained, and held by a professional ethos, whereas the local instruments of royal authority which were set up by the Crown during the seventeenth century to provide a system of civil government, for instance the Justices of the Peace introduced by James VI or the Commissioners of Supply established by Charles II, were qualified by being landowners, and held to an ethic appropriate to the owners of inherited property. Only gradually did they exempt themselves from the dominance of the great feudatories. By the mid-seventeenth century the Church had a minister of religion in almost every parish (in some areas of the Highlands endemic disorder prevented this), and a kirk session, that is a permanent committee made up of minister and elders, in most. By becoming an elder, nominally at the election of the existing session, a man entered into an office for life:[6] in the eyes of the Church he ceased to be a layman, but in the eyes of the general

---

4 David Laing (ed.), *Diary of Alexander Brodie of Brodie MDCLII–MDCLIX and his son James Brodie of Brodie MDCLXXI–MDCLXXXV* (Spalding Club, Aberdeen, 1863), pp. 180, 113.

5 W. R. Foster, *The Church before the Covenants* (Edinburgh, 1975), chs 4–6.

6 G. D. Henderson, *The Scottish Ruling Elder* (London, 1935).

public he remained one. Elders were the men of local note or distinction, but such distinction did not have to be great, for it was usual for the session to select at least one elder from every settlement in the parish. In the seventeenth century many of the elders were unable to read, but by the mid-eighteenth century, the school system these men had helped to create meant that such a disability was rare. Some of the elders were landowners, but the session needed more elders than the landowning class could provide, and tenants and merchants supplied these. In the towns the sessions drew on merchants, craftsmen and members of the professions.

The court above the kirk session was the presbytery, where the authority of the presbyterian system had come to lie. It was the presbyteries that moved topics into discussion by the General Assembly and the presbyteries which selected which parishes should send representatives to the Assembly. Presbyteries contained all the ministers within their areas. In the Restoration period the elders were not included in the membership of presbyteries, or of synods, but they were restored to these in 1689. But it is clear from the minutes of these courts that attendance by elders was rare in the eighteenth century, even though only one elder from each parish was expected to attend. There were problems of distance, for travel to the presbytery might involve time and expense, and of the technical nature of some of the business. Such meetings were not seen as regular assignments by which a man could meet friends and do other business, but as a specific appointment for each occasion with people with whom an individual elder might have no other links. If elders did attend these courts, they were usually men of the upper class.

The presbytery was a key point in the authority of the Church, for after 1697 proposals and rulings could not be moved in the General Assembly without having been referred to all the presbyteries. It also held a key position in the system of discipline, for the penalty of the lesser excommunication, which cut an offender off from communion, was under its control. Lesser excommunication could, until 1712, lead to referral of an offender for imprisonment by the sheriff. Greater excommunication, which cut an offender off from all contact with anyone outside his household and prohibited movement away from the parish, was under the control of the bishop (after 1689 of the synod), but this was a sentence too drastic to be used except very occasionally.

In the episcopal period, that is before 1690, the induction of new ministers was by presbytery and bishop; after 1690 by presbytery alone, though in certain tendentious cases the presbytery might be reinforced by outside ministers. Presbyteries heard candidates for the ministry go through their trials, appointed ministers when the rights of patrons had lapsed, and between 1690 and 1712 'cognosed', or arbitrated, in disputes when appointments were by heritors and elders but also to be approved by heads of households, supervised the records of the kirk sessions (though their instructions on the detailed presentation of information were not always followed), provided some level of services during vacancies, put pressure, where necessary, on landowners to perform their duties in building and maintaining church, manse and school, inspected the equipment and management of parish and churches and the conduct and doctrine of ministers, dealt with disciplinary cases which were beyond the competence of the session, and intervened in quarrels between landowners and their ministers in attempts to compromise the issues.

There were somewhat more than 900 parishes, and 62 presbyteries, in Scotland at the start of the eighteenth century. New units were carved out of older ones, or older units were combined, according to the sense of the General Assembly of religious, financial or administrative need, and for this reason there can be no fixed number asserted for our period as a whole. The rough figures mean that parishes were usually substantial in population: most comprised between 600 and 3,000 inhabitants, and often covered a large geographical area. A minister would not have considered anything under 80 square miles as exceptionally large, and the population of a parish was normally not grouped in any nuclear village but was scattered in smaller settlements, farm towns, or wherever there was a stretch of good farm land. Parishes were even larger in the Highlands, where their limited number reflected the difficulty of recruiting ecclesiastical manpower equipped with Gaelic. In the Lowlands a conscientious minister could, and would, get round all the settlements regularly in his annual catechising, but in the Highlands his contact was less, particularly since there were often no roads. Even in the Lowlands the size of many parishes made it unlikely that all parishioners could attend church regularly. The system of elders meant, however, that all settlements were in touch with the kirk session.

The presbytery was a committee small enough to be effective

and, to make sure that it was effective, regular attendance by the ministers was insisted on. It had no fixed base, being able to vary its meeting from parish to parish. This meant that it normally met in one fairly central location, but visited different parishes at intervals, inspecting the records and equipment. Many ministers could walk or ride to and from the meeting within the day, but even where a longer absence was involved the presbyteries insisted on punctual attendance. Under episcopacy the moderator or chairman was appointed by the bishop, often for six months or more at a time, but later was elected by the presbytery.

The presbyteries met several times a year, often monthly in the summer. A kirk session met as often as business required. That is, it might meet weekly or even more frequently; rarely did more than a month go by without a meeting. In some parishes, though, the meetings were sparser. Session business involved poor relief, and money might be doled out monthly, quarterly or even by the half year. It also involved arrangements for church repairs and for the purchase of equipment; the arrangements for fees for the use of church equipment at funerals, for the communion service which came to be normally an annual event, for collections for good causes commended by the higher courts, which later would check on whether the recommendations had been followed; supervision of the school; and arrangements for the material needs of visiting ministers during vacancies. Some session registers record the text of the weekly sermons. It is clear from the quality of surviving record that the members of sessions were conscientious men who took their duties seriously. A session could manage most business effectively without a resident and active minister for about six months, but if a vacancy or serious illness went on for longer than that the conduct of business would become disorganized. But on discipline matters, cases were sometimes left ready for action when a minister should be appointed, rather than dealt with by the elders without their moderator.

Above the presbytery came the synod. A synod approximated in size to a medieval diocese. It met twice a year for two or three days, in spring and autumn, with a good deal of formality and an opening sermon with some pretensions to authority. Not much in the way of disciplinary matters came to these courts, unless there were particular difficulties preventing the lower courts being effective, as for instance in disturbed parts of the Highlands. They had an influence on political and local government matters. Their records contain a great deal of formality, but at times show that their role in discipline could be a significant reinforcement to the authority of the lower courts.[7]

Elders seem to have been more regular attenders at synod than at presbytery, probably because of the higher status of this court and its involvement in politics. The synod had some legislative significance under episcopacy, since, with the refusal of the government to call the General Assembly, it was the highest level of church court. Inevitably rulings about discipline and worship had to be made, and were, by synods. Synods also usually appointed days of fasting and humiliation, called for subscriptions to good causes, not all of which had a religious component, and played a part in the workings of local government. Synods were particularly important in the Highlands after 1689, because of the weakness of presbyteries and sessions there, and because the large size of the parishes meant that the ministers needed more support and control than elsewhere. The lack of ministers of presbyterian allegiance able to command Gaelic led to the synods pursuing a policy over selection very different from that of the General Assembly, and to the retention of many episcopal ministers in this area. A court of stature was also needed for negotiation with powerful chiefs and for sustaining the parish clergy against the pressures of Catholicism. All this enhanced the political dimension of the synod of Argyll and, once it was formed, that of Glenelg. After the defeat of the 1745 rising and the forced incorporation of the highland area into the normal government structure of Scotland the political role of the highland synods was reduced, even though difficulties in co-operation between church and lay courts continued, but they continued to have to represent to the General Assembly the special problems of finding and controlling ecclesiastical manpower in their areas.[8]

At the top of the structure of church courts stood, when it was allowed to meet, the General Assembly. This met annually, in the early summer, but also had a committee, the Commission, which carried on business between meetings and which convened three times a year. Parishes were selected for Assembly representation, except in the case of the General Session of Edinburgh, which was

7 W. R. Foster, *Bishop and Presbytery* (London, 1958), ch. 4; G. D. Henderson, *Religious Life in Seventeenth-Century Scotland* (Cambridge, 1937), ch. 7.

8 James Kirk (ed.), *The Records of the Synod of Lothian and Tweeddale* (Stair Society, Edinburgh, 1977), pp. ix–xxix; W. Ferguson, 'The Problems of the Established Church in the Western Highlands and Islands in the Eighteenth Century', *Records of the Scottish Church History Society* 17 (1970), pp. 15–31.

regularly represented. The General Assembly was considered politically dangerous in the Restoration period, and though an Act was passed defining its membership, it was not called till 1689, when a highly unrepresentative presbyterian group claimed this status.[9] In spite of the continually changing nature of its membership the Assembly in the eighteenth century had a strong party structure, at first being divided between those of episcopal and those of presbyterian sympathies, later between the so-called evangelical or popular party and the moderates. The Assembly was not normally a place to which discipline cases came, except where ministers were accused of heresy or misbehaviour, but the surviving correspondence of the Commission carries a certain amount of discipline material, since some individuals appealed there against the decision of their presbytery.

It is commonplace to call the Scottish presbyterian system democratic, but this is not the correct adjective for what was basically an oligarchy, open to selected social groups. The activity of the laity was most conspicuous in the lowest and the highest courts, but the laymen involved in these two courts were of widely different rank and performed different functions. In the kirk session the laity were the greater part of the membership, and played a vital part in the working of all aspects of the sessions' business, though they did not fill the post of moderator. Membership was for life, though an elder might take periods of retirement. It carried considerable responsibility, not only for the making of decisions but also for the handling of the parish's money. The laymen who attended the General Assembly did so only occasionally, and had no political organisation in it. Assembly time was, for those selected by the presbyteries to attend, mainly an occasion for social life, but also, in the case of lawyers, an opportunity to pick up useful business. Since the input to Assembly business came from the presbyteries, the impact of the laity was often of a negative kind, preventing outbursts of clericalism, but the lay membership was the mechanism by which the small moderate party maintained dominance in the late eighteenth century.[10]

The two intermediate courts were predominantly of clergy, and were places for the exercise of professional expertise. Presbyteries insisted on regular attendance by ministers, saw to it that church

9 A. L. Drummond and J. Bulloch, *The Scottish Church 1688–1843* (Edinburgh, 1973), ch. 1.

10 Sher, *Church and University in the Scottish Enlightenment*, pp. 124–8.

buildings were maintained, and discipline sustained. They were also the place where discipline of ministers, if called for, would be initiated, and they carried out the more difficult aspects of the discipline of ordinary parishioners. It is clear that the members of presbyteries were aware of the distinction of ranks and knew that it was not usually productive to quarrel with the landowning class.

The strength of this court structure must strike anyone who works in its records. The courts suffered no lapse by death. Regular record keeping was imposed by their superiors. A uniformity in policy permeated the whole system, unusual in a country with so much regional diversity as Scotland, for the meetings of the courts not only provided formal regulation and definitions, but also opportunities for the exchange of ideas about how to handle particular types of issue. The result was that a kirk session in Easter Ross would be making disciplinary decisions in exactly the same way as one in Wigtownshire. Occasional translation of a minister from a parish in one synod to a distant alternative also helped to maintain uniformity. As judiciaries the courts of the Church had a great advantage over the whole system of secular justice, in that they were worked free of charge by salaried people. If a woman brought a complaint against her husband to her session, or a session called on a man named as father of a bastard child to answer the accusation, the entire business involved no payment of costs. Only when a member of the upper class was embarrassed by an allegation and wished to repel it with legal support would lawyers appear in these courts. The ministers were sustained by their stipends, and the officials of the court who called on people to appear and the clerks who kept the records were recipients of small salaries funded out of the church collections. It seems that the ministers paid for the cost of using the postal services to enquire about missing offenders and to check upon the documentation submitted to the session.

Since even by the early seventeenth century the Church was an institution equipped with a far more modern system of government than the State, it is not surprising that it tended to intrude into matters of political and penal policy. Religion was, after all, an important political issue: nobody could ignore this fact after the events of 1637–8 when the aristocratic opposition to the policy of Charles I successfully managed the popular hostility to the new Prayer Book and so provoked revolution. Ever since the Reformation the Church had tended to see major decisions on policy as within its sphere of influence. It assented to the idea of a separation of Church and State, but interpreted this as a system in which the Church governed itself but expected the Crown to be merely the practical administrator of the wishes of God, which would, if necessary, be defined for it by the Church. So the early General Assemblies called for specific penalties on what it saw as sins, and expected these to be passed into legislation and imposed by the State. An example of this is the post-Reformation view that the death penalty was the suitable treatment for adultery, a view which the Crown, conscious of the sexual failings of many of the aristocracy, was not prepared to enact.[11] The Church felt at liberty to denounce the behaviour of the great, including the monarch himself, either in general terms as lacking in Christian zeal, or for particular shortcomings, and to close its eyes to moral failures on the part of those whom it saw as promoting the interests of the Church. All moral failures were, in its eyes, its sphere of action, but it also recognized that God might choose to work in mysterious ways and by dubious instruments. It also saw moral offences as objectionable to God in absolute terms, and was not particularly concerned over the mental state and the intentions of the offender, or the social desirability of penalties. An example of its pressure on criminal law is its persistent hostility to the system of compensation for murder. The Crown used this system in the early seventeenth century because it saw it as the shortest way to end feuds, but the Church regarded it as a way of imposing different penalties for the offence on different ranks. It was the Church's view which prevailed eventually.[12]

The Church had, of necessity, to carry out functions of government which, in the modern world, are regarded as secular. Until the mid-nineteenth century it was in charge of education and poor relief. In the latter case this role came from the incoherence and inefficiency of such lay local government as existed in the seventeenth century. The lay system of government was interrupted by great feudal franchises, and in any case had no regional structure. When we find a synod promoting a secular cause, such as the raising of funds for bridges or harbours, we can see the Church stepping into a gap in the lay State.

---

11 J. R. Hardy, 'The attitudes of Church and State in Scotland to Sex and Marriage, 1560–1707' (unpublished M.Phil. thesis, Edinburgh University, 1978).

12 Jenny Wormald, 'Bloodfeud, Kindred and Government in early modern Scotland', *Past and Present* 87 (1980), pp. 54–97.

From 1661 to 1689 the Church of Scotland had not only a presbyterian system of government but also an episcopal one. The dioceses of the bishops were coterminous with the synods. Bishops had their own administrative staff. They were involved in the disciplining of ministers, where necessary, for misbehaviour or inadequate doctrinal conformity, acted as permanent moderators of synods, might associate with presbyteries for particular activities, in which case they would also be moderators, and would otherwise appoint the moderators of presbyteries.[13] But they seem to have had very little effect on the actual working of the system at parish level. The political pressures of this period in Scotland and the waywardness of Crown policy brought about a situation in which the episcopate was closely associated with the monarchy. Bishops had no strong territorial base, and were not linked to the major surnames. So, when the direct Stewart line was forced out in the Revolution of 1688–9 the episcopate could not accept the intrusion of William III and Mary as monarchs, and became 'Jacobite'. The new monarchy, with no core of bishops prepared to accept and support it, was forced to allow the establishment of a totally presbyterian system. The self-selected General Assembly, made up entirely of ministers who had not compromised with the Restoration church system, ruthlessly purged over two-thirds of the ministry over the next few years and intruded its own candidates into the parishes so vacated.

This drastic change in the officiating ministry, and the concealing verbiage put up at the time and accepted by later historians, might have been expected to have had effect on the activities of the Church at parish level. In some parishes, mostly in the north-east, where it was difficult for the Assembly to get in its candidates and so create an intruded presbytery because of the popular support for the existing men, there were riots and disturbances; in some parishes almost a state of organized disruption for many years.[14] In some areas the new ministers were anxious to display zeal. In Cramond, Midlothian, for instance, the new minister's policy is shown in a sudden surge of prosecutions for Sabbath breach. But the discipline of sex offences does not seem to have been affected by discontinuity and disturbance. The elders might postpone action if there was a vacancy, until a new minister had been installed. But the resulting surge in cases gives a distorted picture

13 W. R. Foster, *Bishop and Presbytery*, ch. 3.
14 For instance the parish of Newtyle, Angus, seems from its KSR to have been the scene of near civil war for many years.

of normal parish life, and for this reason this study has omitted years in which there was clearly a break in kirk session business. There was no change in the general policy regarding such cases. The Episcopalian Church, as it came to be called, and the Presbyterian agreed on doctrine and discipline, and carried on the same policy through the Revolution.

Union with England in 1707 brought considerable changes in the administration of secular justice, but seems to have had little direct effect on the Church. Ministers continued to treat England as a foreign country, and the receipt of English ministrations for marriage or baptism as a church offence. But the ensuing Toleration Act of 1712 left its mark on the Scottish system of church courts. By this Act the Episcopalian Church was allowed to hold its own services and use its own service book, so that though the established Church continued to hold that its parochial system included everybody resident there, it was not always easy for it to exercise discipline over episcopalians without the co-operation of the episcopal clergy. The outcome of the 1715 Jacobite rising, in which the episcopal clergy was clearly shown as disaffected to the government, made services in meeting houses legally dependent on the minister having taken the oaths of allegiance and assurance, and this reduced the level of official toleration promised by the Toleration Act. The Act had also removed the right of the Church to call on the sheriff to imprison those under excommunication, but this had been so rarely executed that it was not of importance.

There were, from 1689 and even before, some minor sectarian bodies, such as the Quakers, and there was also a small, scattered organization of covenanters, who were not prepared to follow the main body of covenanting opinion into the Presbyterian Church, but dissent within protestantism played a very small role in early eighteenth century Scotland. The Original Secession of 1733 was a small and local affair of an extremely scrupulous and puritanical group, as the surviving session records of the body show. But the Relief Church, which came into existence in the 1750s, was wider in its support, and ready to accept a wide range of opinion. It is thus only in the 1760s that dissent became significant, and involved a considerable minority of the people in communions organized outwith the establishment.[15]

The Church's system of government underwent remarkably little change in the period of this study. The disappearance of

15 Drummond and Bulloch, *The Scottish Church 1688–1843*, ch. 2.

episcopacy left the system working in practice much as before. More important was the simultaneous re-establishment of the General Assembly, which gradually became representative of the Church as a whole, and which, by its existence, reduced the importance of the synods. The other change of long-term significance was the break in presbyterian unity, which allowed the establishment of dissenting communions and their eventual proliferation. The civil government of Scotland experienced much greater changes. It expanded not only by institutional change but also by a general increase in efficacy and authority. The new central criminal court, the Court of Justiciary, is important in this connection, and so is the creation, in the Commissioners of Supply, of a mechanism for local valuation and taxation.[16]

But the major change in civil government was the enhanced authority of the State in and from the Restoration period. In the period of the Great Rebellion the Scottish aristocracy had met political defeat, had been disciplined by the Church and had been shown as dispensable in government. Eventually the country had been conquered by England. English success in suppressing a major rising in the Highlands had shown that even in that area armies from the low country could penetrate and exert control. All these events showed that no area of Scotland could regard itself as immune from control, and that Scotland as a whole could not afford to quarrel with England. In the Restoration the aristocracy had been restored along with the monarchy, but even when noblemen had cleared their estates of the debts produced by the wars and by fines, the lessons of the Rebellion period were not lost. Even the greatest men in the land recognized that a moderate degree of co-operation with the policy of the central government and obedience to the law were essential for survival. Though large territorial franchises continued to exist until the 1740s, and so excluded parts of the country from the authority of the Crown's courts, law and order had become firmly established in the Lowlands. In the Highlands, though endemic warfare continued until the 1690s, it was on a much smaller scale than in the past. Highland chiefs found it necessary to maintain some sort of contact with the central government, and for this reason had to restrain some of the more lawless tendencies of their clansmen.[17]

Union with England in 1707 provided a further strength for the

16 Ann E. Whetstone, *Scottish county government in the eighteenth and nineteenth centuries* (Edinburgh, 1981), ch. 3.

17 Paul Hopkins, *Glencoe and the end of the Highland War* (Edinburgh, 1986).

forces of order. It led to the enhancement of the functions of the central courts, and also to a surreptitious policy of intrusion by these courts into the areas of the franchises.[18] The membership of the Court of Session gradually shifted from appointments simply by political patronage to one of patronage modified by the recognition of professional ability. This change led to the great age of the development of Scots law and to the establishment of authoritative works on it. Some of this law must seem to inexperienced students the arbitrary improvisation of judges, inspired mainly by the interest and ethos of landed society, but these features did not damage the authority of the works.

The judges and advocates who worked the legal system were almost exclusively of the gentry, that is they were owners of moderate sized estates. The same section of society provided the sheriffs, Justices of the Peace and Commissioners of Supply. Whereas in the seventeenth century this section of society had been overshadowed and bullied by the great lords, it now became a secure and independent layer in society. The aristocracy, already tamed by the Great Rebellion, now was deflected in its ambitions to London based opportunities.[19] These changes meant that the government of Scotland in the eighteenth century approximated closely to that of England in lay matters, with local administration and justice in the hands of the gentry. The difference between the systems in the two countries was that in Scotland the lay system provided only part of the arrangements for social control, the other part coming in the form of the church courts. The peasantry was under the law, and this included not only the law of the land but also the law of the Church. There was also another element of control, the baron court, in which problems of intermixed farming were settled and the landowners' orders and interests promoted. Scotland had never been a country with long-established peasant rights, and though it now suited some landowners to promote longer tenancies the security of any peasant household was limited.

The combined systems of authority, ecclesiastical and lay, and the tenurial system, all meant that the population of Scotland was held to obedience by a strong and interlaced set of bonds.[20] There

18 S. J. Davies, 'The courts and the Scottish legal system 1660–1747: the case of Stirlingshire', in V. A. C. Gatrell, Bruce Lenman and Geoffrey Parker (eds), *Crime and the Law* (Cambridge, 1980), pp. 120–54.

19 J. S. Shaw, *The Management of Scottish Society* (Edinburgh, 1983), ch. 1.

20 T. M. Devine, 'Unrest and Stability in Rural Ireland and Scotland, 1760–1840', in Rosalind Mitchison and Peter Roebuck (eds), *Economy and Society in Scotland and Ireland, 1500–1939* (Edinburgh, 1988), pp. 126–39.

is no reason for thinking that this was distasteful to those controlled by it. There were, certainly, groups with much greater liberty than that experienced by the peasantry: recent work has shown, for instance, that the miners, nominally serfs, had an effective trade union system which enabled them to resist the efforts of the mineowners to increase output.[21] There were also vestigial occasions in the year when disorder or misrule were accepted. Saints days were supposed to have disappeared at the Reformation, but New Year replaced Christmas as a festival and became an occasion for heavy drinking, and Shrove Tuesday was observed with orgiastic enthusiasm. Other days of celebration and disorder were the occasions of fairs, particularly of hiring fairs, and weddings supplied opportunities for boisterousness and drink. But in spite of these occasions for breach of order, or perhaps because of them, it seems that most people of both sexes accepted the systems of control under which they lived, and actively co-operated with that of the Church. The abolition of the sanction of imprisonment by the sheriff for those incurring the lesser excommunication in 1712 had no effect on the level of obedience to the courts of the Church.

The continuation of Church discipline by the Scottish Kirk marks that country out from the rest of the British Isles in the eighteenth century. It was a manifestation of the sort of discipline aimed at by all the reformed churches in the seventeenth century. There have been recent studies of the activity of the English Church in this way. Ingram has examined the treatment of sexual misconduct in Wiltshire in the early seventeenth century by the Church of England, and Quaife has displayed it in the Quarter Session records for Somerset and particularly for the Cromwellian period.[22] Neither of these areas had particularly effective discipline, largely because those accused could move away, and often would not be traced. Anglican church discipline survived in the Isle of Man until the mid-eighteenth century. Its success there may have been based on the fact that it was difficult for miscreants to disappear from its jurisdiction.[23] The penalties in

---

21 Christopher A. Whatley, 'The Fettering Bonds of Brotherhood: Combination and Labour Relations in the Scottish Coal Mining Industry, 1690–1775', *Social History* XII (1987), pp. 139–54.

22 M. J. Ingram, 'Church courts and neighbourhood: aspects of social control in Wiltshire, 1600–1641' (unpublished D.Phil. thesis, Oxford University, 1976); G. R. Quaife, *Wanton Wenches and Wayward Wives* (London, 1978), chs 8 and 9.

23 E. H. Stenning, 'Manx Spiritual Laws', *Isle of Man Natural History and Antiquarian Society Proceedings* V (1942–56), p. 287.

Man were mild, compared with those in Scotland, and that for
fornication was waived if the couple subsequently married. That
this was common is suggested by the phrase used to describe the
process, 'going from the sheet to the ring'. In Man, as in Scotland,
there was a hierarchy of penalties for different degrees of offence;
for instance, adulterers paid a heavier fine and made more
appearances for every 'relapse', in other words for repeats of the
original offence, but even at the most severe these penalties did not
approach those of the Scottish code.

Clearly the efficacy of any system of discipline depends on its
comprehensiveness. In England the refusal by the gentry of control
or censure by the Church was one reason for the weakness of
discipline even in the early seventeenth century. Later the
proliferation of dissent meant that the Established Church could
not be seen, and did not see itself, as responsible for the entire
populace. Yet in the early seventeenth century illegitimacy in
England appears to have been low. Though the nadir of the
illegitimacy ratio was achieved at a time when it was difficult to
claim that all births were being registered, for this was the period
of civil registration imposed by the Commonwealth government,
objected to by many people, the levels calculated for other decades
are still strikingly low, and the number of parishes used as a base is
large. Before the Civil War the material comes from a period when
the unity of the Church had not been seriously refuted. The figures
are based on parish registration: one study used the registers of 24
parishes, distributed across much of the country, another a
registration and family reconstitution in eight mainly southern
parishes.[24]

The research in England has, in some cases, been able to enlarge
the illegitimacy numbers recorded in the parish register by other
information, particularly that in burial registers, and this is a
warning against taking the baptismal registration as a full record.
In any case parish registration does not carry information about
children dying unbaptized, and it is likely that in the seventeenth
and early eighteenth centuries higher perinatal mortality of the
illegitimate child over the legitimate was a fact, as it has been in the
nineteenth and twentieth centuries. It is, of course, possible that

---

24 Peter Laslett and Karla Oosterveen, 'Long-term trends in bastardy in England',
Population Studies XXVII (1973), pp. 255–86; Karla Oosterveen, Richard M. Smith and Susan
Stewart, 'Family reconstitution and the study of bastardy: evidence from certain English
parishes', in Peter Laslett, Karla Oosterveen and Richard M. Smith (eds), *Bastardy and its
Comparative History* (London, 1980), pp. 86–140.

parish clerks did not enter as illegitimate all children who were so, but the trends of the figures is remarkably consistent, suggesting that the level of omission was not great. The law imposing parish registration was effective in England and the age of baptism in the seventeenth century very low.[25] Even though the fact that the Church as a whole had a less effective discipline over its ministers than did the Scottish Church, and that ministers were allowed a certain amount of non-residence and plurality, which might prevent them being fully familiar with the population of the parish, we should accept the English figures as a convincingly stable understatement of the level of illegitimacy.

In Scotland parish registration, though ordered in 1616 for baptisms and burials, was, as in many other areas of statutory regulation, effectively optional. A reasonably representative case is the parish of Tranent, East Lothian, where, with all deliberate speed, a register of burials was opened only in 1753, and kept for less than 30 years.[26] There was no very strong pressure to get children to the font immediately after birth since baptism was not regarded as necessary for salvation.

English parish recording might allow some cases of illegitimacy not to be described as such, but the concern of the parish ratepayers was that the parish should not be saddled with the support of bastards. The English Poor Law led to a secular motive for the repression of unmarried sexual activity, and also meant that illegitimate births were likely to be noted in other places than the parish register. This fact, combined with the proliferation of local record keeping and the smallness of many English parishes, means that often more information about the social setting of illegitimacy cases can be elicited for England than is possible for Scotland. Even so, we should accept the statement of Keith Wrightson, made relevant to the Interregnum but of a more general impact, that there was 'no simple pattern of moral regulation'.[27] The established Church in England never had the disciplinary authority that distinguished the Church of Scotland.

The Scottish system of control of individuals by the Church was not only much more effective than the English, it also extended for

25 E. A. Wrigley and R. Schofield, *The Population History of England* (London, 1981), p. 289.

26 SRO CH2/357/21. Rosalind Mitchison, 'Death in Tranent', *Transactions of the East Lothian Antiquarian and Field Naturalists' Society* xvi (1979), pp. 37–48.

27 K. Wrightson, 'The nadir of English illegitimacy in the seventeenth century', in Laslett et al. (eds), *Bastardy and its Comparative History*, pp. 176–91.

a longer time, continuing through the third quarter of the eighteenth century, only to end abruptly after that. There were not the pockets of resistant dissent comparable to those in seventeenth century England. Doctrinal and ecclesiastical unity meant that the most likely cause of resistance to the mechanisms of control would come from laziness or inefficiency rather than from basic disagreement, and the higher courts of the Church did their best to prevent such faults persisting. Men and women were not, for much of our period, allowed to move from one parish to another without a certificate of good behaviour, a 'testificat', from their past parish, and these documents were not issued as a matter of course. Because of this practice, one of the main reasons for the ineffectiveness of moral discipline in England, the disappearance to some other area of the offender, did not happen in Scotland. The kirk session receiving a testificat would, through the minister, examine it carefully, as it would certificates of marriage from outwith the parish. If there were any doubt of authenticity, the documentation would be checked. Errors in terminology or handwriting would be perceived, and the minister would then write to the minister of the parish from which it was supposed to have emanated, and enquire about its authenticity. In the case of parishes within the same presbytery, the information needed could easily be obtained at the next meeting of the presbytery, otherwise the post would be used. Enquiries about offenders who had fled from discipline to one of the cities would often elicit accurate information as to where they were. There were even instances of sessions advertising in newspapers for information about missing suspects. The handwriting of those people of whom the Church disapproved, who made an income by selling irregular marriages, was well known to many sessions. Study of kirk session registers sometimes gives the impression that the espionage system of the Kirk was an important element in the financial success of the postal service.

Offenders could thus be traced so long as they were within the area of effective church organization. But fugitives might go further than this. In central and northern Scotland people might run away to the Highlands, though they usually did not stay there long. In the south-east they might go to the Netherlands, in the Border area to England, in Galloway to Ulster. Such flight certainly put people beyond the authority of the Kirk, but it might place a heavy strain on them, and it did not expunge the record. Return after many years would lead to the re-opening of the enquiry.

The Kirk treated England as a foreign country. Claims of marriage or baptism there would be treated with considerable scepticism, but were not automatically ignored – support and proof would be asked for. The Scottish Kirk had a low opinion of Anglican discipline and was sceptical of claims of marriage by English divines, which, in the absence in England of a system of 'testificats' might not be easy to check.

There were still groups that the church system in Scotland could not fully control. At the head of these came the landowning class. Only for a brief period after the political change of 1649 was the Church in a position to extend discipline to such people. A session would, however, note a claim that paternity of a child was to be attributed to a landowner, though sometimes it was unreasonably anxious to preserve the reputation of such a man (see chapter 7), and if the accusation was sustained and given support the session would at least enquire of the landowner if he agreed in its truth. Discipline could not be brought to bear on such men, but they might make penitential payment to the parish's poor fund. Discipline also could not be brought home to the servants of the upper class.

Another group enjoying immunity was the army. Soldiers were not under the discipline of the parish, though if named, they might agree to meet with members of the session and give an account of their actions. Sometimes the military authority would co-operate with a session in helping a girl to get married to her lover, but by contrast some superior officers prevented their men marrying. An officer could refuse a man a certificate that he was not married, and almost force a soldier into an extra-marital liaison. For the most part, when it was alleged that a soldier was the father of an illegitimate child all that a session could do was to record the statement and make the girl do her penance.

A final area of doubt may remain – the question of whether all the people were firmly attached to one or another parish. Andrew Fletcher of Saltoun asserted in 1698 that in normal times 100,000 people in Scotland were vagrants living wild in the hills, spurning Christian ordinances, and that in times of dearth the number went up to 200,000. 'In all time', he wrote, 'there have been about 100,000 of them Vagabond who have lived without any regard or subjection either to the Laws of the Land, or even those of God and Nature.' And he accused these people of incest, murder and coercive begging. 'In years of Plenty many thousands of these meet together in the Mountains, where they feast and riot for many days

. . . at country Weddings, Burials and other the like publick occasions they are to be seen both Men and Women perpetually drunk.'[28]

Two hundred and twenty nine KSRs survive for the period, the 1680s, when this was written, a time of severe food shortage, and these give more than simply account book information. Of these we have studied 225, and these give no grounds whatever for believing in such a horde of people outwith the normal, parochial system, though the registers do show that more people than usual were on the roads looking for some form of support in these years. Fletcher's statement must be seen as a manifestation of class prejudice enlarged by total innumeracy. He suffered from a failing still prevalent today, a tendency to use numbers to convey emotions and colour rather than in any way to be numerical. A few extra noughts on a number to this sort of person is merely a form of emphasis. He also was experiencing a type of panic of which there have been modern examples – the reaction of settled and propertied rural society to the existence of small numbers of relatively mobile people who do not conform to the norms of settled society. A characteristic of this hostility is to accuse the dissenting population of sexual offences, living on welfare and evading honest work. Fletcher's relatively savage proposal for the management of this sub-culture was that it should be forcibly enserfed to the tenant population and lend its labour to the transformation of the Scottish economy. His remarks do nothing to enhance his intellectual reputation, which seems to be largely based on a lack of other thinkers displaying his variety of patriotism and class thinking.

That there were some people living by travelling was true. The label 'vagrant' would be used not only to describe the throwouts of the economy but also the valuable group of chapmen (roving pedlars and storytellers) and their families. It would sometimes also include old women collecting rags for the newly started paper industry, families migrating to and from England, demobilized and injured soldiers, and, particularly in the 1690s, dispossessed episcopal ministers and their families.[29] But such people appear in the records of almsgiving by the kirk sessions only in ones or twos.

---

28 *Two Discourses Concerning the Affairs of Scotland* (1698), Second Discourse, pp. 24–9.

29 Rosalind Mitchison, 'Who were the poor in eighteenth century Scotland?', in Mitchison and Roebuck (eds), *Economy and Society in Scotland and Ireland, 1500–1939*, pp. 140–8.

At communions and at 'publick occasions', where indiscriminate almsgiving was a common practice, people would flock in from neighbouring parishes, but these were not permanent vagrants, merely poor people keen to pick up some small sums. The vagrancy element was not large, and many of the people who occur occasionally as 'stranger beggars' had firm parochial settlements and indulged in the various vices listed by Fletcher no more than did any other sample of the population.

The effectiveness of the parochial system can therefore be asserted, except that in Galloway in the later seventeenth century there was a widespread repudiation of the ministry of the established Church, and that in the Highlands chronic disorder in some areas made it impossible for some ministers to reside in their parishes; more often, they were unable to do parish visiting. Occasionally there are gaps in the session record; this was supplied by men of relatively weak literacy who might omit a particular case at some stage. Sometimes during a vacancy in the ministry the slips of paper on which records were kept before they were inserted in the session register became confused or duplicated. But since each of our illegitimacy cases would normally appear in the register at least half a dozen times, starting with the allegation that an unmarried girl was pregnant, recording her statements and those of her named associate, their confessions when and if made, and ending with at least three recorded appearances in church by each, an occasional lapse does not prevent cases being noted. There might also be requests to have the child baptized. More serious offences produced an even higher level of paper work, since the number of appearances escalated: whereas the sentence was three appearances for simple fornication, it was six for a 'relapse', that is a second offence, 26 for 'trilapse' or for adultery, 39 for 'quadrilapse' or relapse in adultery, and a whole year for incest.[30] These appearances were supposed to be made in sackcloth: a fine on each partner of ten pound Scots (16 shillings and eightpence sterling) was also exacted, though sometimes omitted in cases of poverty. The literal minded approach to sin and to God's wrath imposed these high levels of penalty, without any discussion as to whether 39 appearances on the penitential pillar might not be counter-productive in terms of true penitence. Our research project has depended on the almost automatic insistence on the penalties and on the careful recording of every stage in the

---

30 Hardy, 'The attitudes of Church and State in Scotland to Sex and Marriage, 1560–1707', p. 416.

investigation. The outstanding quality of the record is responsible for the fact that we have been able to quantify illegitimacy, and to relate it to other forms of rule-breaking, and also for the fact that in this record there can be heard the response of people, including the accused, to the prospect of a birth out of wedlock. Whereas it has been pointed out that there is, for eighteenth century England, a lack of information on the views of the lower orders on sexual matters,[31] we have for Scotland some examples of their voices, at least on this particular aspect.

Our study begins in 1660, by which time the presbyterian court system in the Church was well established, and the planting of ministers even in the remoter areas had made considerable progress. Apart from areas of surviving Roman Catholicism, which the Church frequently inquired into and for which the adherents were listed, and in spite of the survival of pagan rites in some areas, the Church had by 1660 achieved a near monopoly of religious organization in Scotland, an effective government, a trained ministry and a generally accepted theology.[32] We did not try to take the study before 1660, for the combined effects of revolution, war and conquest made it likely that for some of the years before that date the system of church government was unlikely to be working smoothly. As a sample of this there is the gap in the kirk session register for Yester parish over the period covering the battle of Dunbar, followed by the note 'No session was kept in our church betwixt the 22 of July 1650 and the 3 of August 1651 because of our troubles and absence of our minister.' We stopped the study in 1780 because of the obvious sudden deterioration in the system of church discipline. Possible reasons for this are discussed in chapter 2. It is enough here to say that the change is unmistakable in most session registers at some point in the 1770s.

Those who know Scotland today are well aware of its marked internal regional differences. Probably these stem from the variety of ethnic and linguistic groups which have settled in the country in the distant past, namely the various Celtic societies, the Norse and the Anglo-Saxon. Diversity has been sustained by the problems of

31 Lawrence Stone, *The Family, Sex and Marriage in England 1500–1800*, ch. 12.
32 Martin Martin, *A description of the Western Isles of Scotland circa 1695* (London, 1703); W. McKay (ed.), *Extracts from the presbytery records of Inverness and Dingwall* (Scottish History Society, Edinburgh, 1896); G. D. Henderson, *Religious Life* (Cambridge, 1937).

communication created by mountainous terrain, major rivers and inlets of the sea, and enhanced by the different levels of accommodation to royal authority achieved in different areas. The original research project aimed at discovering whether the relatively high national level of illegitimacy, and the marked regional differences, shown in the later nineteenth century, obtained at an earlier period, and also whether there was an upward trend in illegitimacy as has been found in both England and France in the later eighteenth century.

Avoiding the period of revolutionary disturbance in the mid-seventeenth century, we opened our project in 1660 with the restoration of monarchy and aristocracy. But parts of Scotland continued to be subject to chronic disturbance and could not render material for this study for several decades. After an initial survey of the records we selected 78 parishes as suitable for our study, and separated them into ten regions which seemed to us to reflect most of the major regional differences surviving to the present. There are other good runs of parish material beside these 78 in the 900 odd parishes of early modern Scotland; our selection was made to ensure a sizeable base population in each region. Three areas were, with regret, omitted from our regions, the Northern and the Western Isles, through lack of enough early material, and the Borders, where massive depopulation at some point or points in the eighteenth century meant that we could make no reasonable guess as to the size of a parish's population at the start of our period. We have used this area only, therefore, for its experience of irregular marriage, which was made easy by its nearness to England.

Otherwise the main regions that we have defined will probably seem obvious to a modern Scot. We took five of the ten from south of the Highland geographic fault, the line from Dumbarton to Stonehaven. These were the Lothians, conspicuous all through our period for its relatively prosperous farming, its pattern of large landowning units and its relative accessibility to government; Fife, also near to government but agriculturally poor, isolated by the two great firths to the north and west, an important area for industry in the form of mining, salt works and fisheries; the Central Lowlands of Stirlingshire and southern Perthshire, prosperous in its farming but suffering both the advantages and the disadvantages of being adjacent to the Highlands; Ayrshire in the west, with an economy based on good farm lands, ports and, later, coal and salt; and finally Dumfries and Galloway in the south-west, an area of decaying ports, hilly terrain and mild climate. Galloway was a region with very high illegitimacy in the nineteenth century, and had been conspicuous through many centuries for separate laws, and notable in the seventeenth century for being the area of most persistent resistance to the ecclesiastical policy of the Crown. In northern Scotland an obvious region to take was the north-east, that is Moray, Banffshire and Nairnshire, for this was the other area in the later nineteenth century showing high illegitimacy. It is economically a mixed area, a coastal string of ports backed by a narrow strip of rich farm land experiencing an unusually mild climatie, and giving way to a highland belt. The adjacent area of Aberdeenshire formed another necessary region, the biggest single agricultural base of modern Scotland with, as in the north-east, a long tradition of adherence to the Episcopal Church and some enclaves of Roman Catholicism. Then there was, inescapably, Caithness, a lowland economy placed beyond the bulk of the Highlands, predominantly English-speaking as early as the eighteenth century, but in origin an area deriving its culture from the Norse. Finally there were two areas of highland culture, the western Highlands, and the central and eastern. These were Gaelic-speaking areas in which, at the beginning of our period, the government had only limited ability to make its wishes felt. The geographical boundaries of our regions are, in many cases, sharp, created either by some conspicuous geographic barrier or by a linguistic change. In all the regions, once their records had started on a regular basis we were able to select enough parishes to make sure that we have always a population base of several thousand.

The choice of regions, and the need to limit the total of records studied, mean that there are some counties for which we have collected no material – Angus, Mearns (Kincardineshire) and Lanarkshire for instance. We acknowledge that a greater sensitivity to local variations might have produced evidence that these counties did not fit into our rough divisions. Nevertheless we feel confident that a study drawn from 78 parishes out of approximately 900 gives a picture much more complete for Scotland than that as yet drawn for other countries in which illegitimacy has been studied.

It is a pity that the closing date of this study, 1780, lies only just within the period when agriculture was being reorganized and improved, the work experience of the rural population undergoing sharp changes and the factory system being introduced. The social changes of the last decades of the eighteenth century were considerable, but the deterioration in the quality of parish discipline in the 1770s made it impossible to go on. We could no longer be confident that a session would reliably deal with and record all cases of illegitimacy arising within its bounds. In the next chapter we discuss the influences which made for this change.

Scotland's rural population, at least in the Lowlands, in the early modern period was mobile. Young people left home early in their 'teens to go into service, and then moved from farm settlement to settlement as their labour developed in value. Where this has been studied for the nineteenth century it is clear that they stayed within an area where the same farm techniques and agricultural conditions obtained.[33] The range of surnames in any parish in the surviving poll tax records of the 1690s gives good grounds for seeing this retention of people within a region as established by then. In the Highlands geographical difficulties and hostility between clans prevented the same degree of mobility. But from the mid-eighteenth century the highland population developed a pattern of temporary seasonal migration to the Lowlands for young adults. These people, however, remained part of the population under the control of their own kirk sessions. Our study does not touch on the larger cities for we, mistakenly we now think, did not expect the Church to be able to keep up with the movements of parishioners in these places as it could in the countryside, but it includes several smaller towns or semi-urban settlements: Dumfries, Thurso, Dysart, Dalkeith, St Ninians. People migrated to these places, but mostly from fairly near at hand. We think it reasonable to take our parishes as containing populations which predominantly truly belonged to the region in which the parish lay.

Our procedure is set out in detail in chapter 5. It involved making estimates of birth rates in the relevant parishes. The sources of possible error described in chapter 5 mean that, though our knowledge of the total number of unmarried pregnancies is extremely reliable – better than that obtainable from other countries of this period except Scandinavia – our illegitimacy ratios are only approximate. But there is a consistency and rationality in their levels and trends which make them worth serious attention.

The problems which we met in assessing the number of births each year in a parish before the introduction of civil registration, or of gaining a figure of the total population year by year, are not

---

33 Ian Carter, *Farmlife in Northeast Scotland, 1840–1914* (Edinburgh, 1979), ch. 5.

peculiar to Scotland. English and French historical demography, though its techniques of family reconstitution and back projection can arrive at good information on birth rates and infant mortality, cannot be sure of the size of local population to which these pertain, and therefore can be sure of the illegitimacy ratio only when there is a contemporary parish listing or when there is good reason to see the Old Parish Register as a complete record. The OPRs available for these countries are a source immensely different in quality from those of Scotland, but it is still not clear that all parish clerks held identical standards of professional routine. There was no special doctrinal reason imposing this on them, and, indeed, the fact that in the English work parts of the records of the 'master sample' of 24 parishes had to be disregarded shows that the clerks did not achieve a guaranteed standard.[34] French figures may be sound for rural areas, but the wide use of abandonment to foundling hospitals of both illegitimate and legitimate children in the larger cities in the eighteenth century must weaken the authority of figures from areas within reach of these cities. In both France and England there are reasons therefore to think that the calculated illegitimacy ratios are too low – for England it has been admitted that this may be by 20 per cent.[35] By contrast for Scotland, where the doubtful figures are not so much the illegitimate births as the total births, the errors run the other way. But we have no reason to see Scotland as ever having achieved the very low levels of illegitimacy found in some individual parishes in other countries, the 1.1 per cent for Chalons sur Marne from 1660–1793 for instance or the 1 per cent for Terling in the 1700s. But our material shows, as pointed out in the Introduction, that an individual parish may consistently deviate from the region within which it lies and that there should be considerable reservations over the acceptance of studies of individual parishes as having general significance.

Another weakness of this study is that it concerns itself only with illegitimacy ratios, never with the illegitimacy rate. The rate is a calculation of the level of illegitimacy relative to the proportion of unmarried women of fertile age in a population. The English studies can offer illegitimacy rates only when civil registration had started. For Scotland in our period we have no direct information about the level of spinsterdom; such figures as have been found

---

34 Peter Laslett, *Family Life and Illicit Love in Earlier Generations* (Cambridge, 1977), ch. 3.
35 Ibid., p. 112.

show considerable variation. The age of marriage has been calculated for a short period in one parish only, for it was only in this parish that the OPR was of a reliable quality and gave enough information for women to be identified from baptism to marriage.[36] Illegitimacy rates are a better register than illegitimacy ratios, but in a period when contraception and deliberate abortion do not appear to have been available to the mass of the people, the ratio is still of considerable significance.

36 M. W. Flinn (ed.), *Scottish Population History from the Seventeenth Century to the 1930s* (Cambridge, 1977), p. 277.

2

The Changing Economic and Social Setting

In Kilmartin parish, in July 1693, Katrin McGillivhide 'was rebuked for her sin of uncleanness, for defiling her body and soul that should be the pure temple of the Holy Ghost'. In January 1761, Elizabeth Downie 'acknowledged her having had the misfortune to be got with child upon the Hill of Southfarthing'. Both these statements epitomize the periods in which they were uttered and indicate how greatly attitudes – on the part of both Church and the people – changed in the course of our period ending with the disintegration of discipline in the 1780s. The aim of this chapter is both to chart the changes which took place and to attempt some explanation of why they happened.

The years between the two unmarried pregnancies here referred to saw great changes in the economy, society and governing institutions of Scotland. This does not mean that our inquiry opens in a static economy and society. It is the view of a distinguished economic historian that the first quarter of the seventeenth century saw genuine economic growth, though on a small scale, and growth probably carried on into the 1630s.[1] However, there is no doubt that the period of revolution, war and conquest from 1638 to 1660 caused great destruction and dislocation. There was direct expenditure on war materials (a loss to the economy), interruption of trade, the permanent loss of young male manpower in emigration or death, and war taxation. Paradoxically the political and economic stresses had a long-term effect in speeding up the modernization of the country, for they reduced the economic strength of the aristocracy and the role of lordship.

The 1660s saw a remarkable recovery, which was sustained for three decades in spite of the setbacks of the Dutch wars. A striking sign of this is the sharp drop in grain prices, approximately of

1 S. G. E. Lythe, *The Economy of Scotland in its European Setting, 1550–1625* (Edinburgh, 1960, pp. 248–54.

20 per cent, which occurred in the early 1660s, and which suggests an easier relationship between food supply and population.[2] The new price levels discouraged landowners from investment in agricultural improvement, but with their acquisitive instincts sharpened by their recent distresses, many men showed an interest, simple-minded but not unwise, in developing new trading centres on their estates. The 1670s was a great period for the founding of new burghs and markets, and even though many of these never got off paper, there were some of social and economic significance, particularly in encouraging mobility. Hopes of material gain were presumably part of the inspiration of statutes attempting to turn vagrants into a labour force for new manufactories, none of which led to action. In the 1680s, though, an attempt by the government to create new industries sheltered by some privileges in regulations and taxation from the chill winds of international competition had limited success.[3] There was no general famine in these decades, and transport was able to reduce local shortages to manageable proportions.

The industrial side of these developments was fragile, and of greater significance in intention than achievement. The expanding commercial interest of the upper class did not solve the basic economic problem of the country, but over time did much to provide better outlets for farm produce and better purchasing opportunities.

The later seventeenth century saw a series of Acts of Parliament which could, in the right circumstances, have done much to encourage more effective use of the land. They were passed in the interests of the landowning class in a Parliament dominated by that class, but this does not mean that they were in opposition to the interests of those who worked the land. These people, the tenants and subtenants, at least in the Lowlands, appear to have accepted an individualistic ethos even though they had to work communally. They were not tied to the land by legal bonds, rights or affection: their relationship with their landowners was by lease or by tenancy at will, if they were tenants. Less formal agreements between tenants and subtenants or cottars gave the latter some access to land, and the former some part of their labour input. The system of farm service sent the children of the families from home

---

2 Rosalind Mitchison, *Lordship to Patronage: Scotland 1603–1745* (London, 1983), p. 94.

3 W. R. Scott, *The Constitution of English, Scottish and Irish Joint Stock Companies* (London, 1912), vol. III, pp. 121–95.

early in their teens, if not before, to live in the houses of other families and to move from one farming household to another over an area of common agricultural practice for many years.

There is a customary image of a peasant society, with the whole of each household committed to the exploitation of an inherited holding, in some cases in collaboration with other households, and with the land and its main crops regarded not as commercial assets but as inalienable. If this image had ever been appropriate to lowland Scotland, it had ceased to be so before the seventeenth century. There were still areas where the joint farm, occupied by several tenants with intermixed but individually possessed arable units, dominated the landscape, but this type of settlement had become rare in the most advanced region, the Lothians. More and more tenancies tended to be held by written lease rather than by word of mouth or established local tradition. Labour services were an important part of the rent, and these still bound the tenant and his labour force to make frequent contact with the landowner or his representative, but in the Highlands as much as in the Lowlands landowners were trying to enlarge the proportion of the rent due in money.[4] Money had become the means of settling agreements for all classes in the Lowlands, and even relatively humble families were used to handling it, and might well, at one time or another, have surprisingly large sums pass through their hands. This is revealed by occasional large 'voluntary' charitable collections which the Church could extract in times of economic tranquillity (though this fact must be seen in the light of the somewhat specialized meaning of the word 'voluntary' in the statements of the Church) and also by the considerable body of lending by tenants to the economic enterprises of their landowners.[5] There is every reason to see the Lowlands as holding a 'peasantry' thoroughly monetized and with no particular devotion to any individual unit of land.

The peasantry was fully open to the idea of monetary gain. Pressure both by landowners and tenants for better land exploitation was to lead in the eighteenth century to the process of enclosure, that is the walling off of individual fields and the separating of holdings. There was also pressure on the cottars to become full-time hired labour, pressure which during the century led to the

    4 R. A. Dodgshon, *Land and Society in Early Scotland* (Oxford, 1981), pp. 254–5, 281–4.

    5 Ian Whyte, *Agriculture and Society in Seventeenth Century Scotland* (Edinburgh, 1979), pp. 192–4.

gradual disappearance of this group of people in the Lowlands and their replacement with long-term hired farm servants or temporary labourers. The existence of cottar holdings had enabled these people and their children to avoid hirings which appeared unattractive, and they were likely to be more independent than suited the interest of their employers, the tenants. As the single tenancy farm became the norm, it increased the gulf between tenants on the one hand and cottars and labourers on the other, encouraged the movement to a more effective use of manpower, and weakened the coherence of rural society. Already in the seventeenth century the gulf between the two farming groups was considerable. The burden of economic insecurity lay almost entirely on the cottars, even though in the eighteenth century insecurity no longer meant exposure to famine. It was, for instance, very rare for a tenant to become so destitute as to need poor relief. Besides the long established gulf between the class of lairds and the actual tillers of the soil, the new economic system of the eighteenth century was opening a gulf between the tenants and the less privileged group who made up most of the labour force.

The changes, which took more than a century to complete, met and enhanced the sense of individualism of those in relatively strong economic positions. Landowners ceased to have to maintain personal contact with their tenants or to put pressure on them to fulfil the complex series of obligations laid down in rentals and tacks, and the tenantry when it came to pay its rent entirely in money, was able to exploit the land as best fitted the market economy. It was in the interests of landowners, both for profit and for convenience, to have large farms, and of the tenants selected to occupy these to control as much land as possible. The labourers did not have the link with the land which had given some element of independence to subtenants, nor did they need to retain some part of the labour of their children. It is relevant to the study of sexual irregularity to see that the complex economic linkages of early modern society were becoming much simpler and dominated by money in the late eighteenth century.

Agricultural change was promoted by the enhanced rate of population growth after 1750, which stimulated food prices, but since improved agriculture needed no more labour than unimproved, and in some areas needed less, there was a surplus population to be taken up by urban life and by industry. There was thus a rapid increase in the mobility of people – a mobility encouraged by the expansion of marketing. Economic and demographic changes were, by 1770, transforming the way of life and the priorities of many in the Lowlands.

Development had not proceeded so fast in the Highlands but the tendencies were similar. The combination of rivalry or hostility between clans, and the localization of settlement in the small areas of fertile valley, meant that the movement of people had been even more restricted than was normal in upland areas. The level of monetization was low, though clan chiefs in the later seventeenth century were copying lowland landlords in trying to obtain more of their revenue in cash. We cannot be certain that the desire, so conspicuous in the nineteenth century highland community, for retention of a foothold on land in the area to which people were accustomed was as strongly developed in the previous two centuries:[6] it may have gained in force from cultural isolation, religious extremism and economic collapse. Certainly the readiness of some highland groups to migrate, either to the cities or overseas, when in the later eighteenth century they were free to do so suggests that by then economic prosperity mattered more to such people than retention of a plot of land.

We have no grounds for attributing to the highlanders of the later seventeenth century the same economic motivation as appears in the lowland community, but in any case the motivation of highlanders is obscured to us by the acceptance of the need for obedience to the orders of the clan chief. This necessity was destroyed in the attack on clanship after the 1745 Jacobite rising. It seems that by the later eighteenth century neither highlander nor lowlander considered his relationship to his landlord, for that is what chiefs had become, as involving personal loyalty. There are even signs that the desire for independence was creating exasperation at the continuation of services to landowners as part of the tenurial bargain.[7] But lordship continued, even in the Lowlands into the early eighteenth century, to have aspects of authority and obligation not solely based on tenurial relationships, and in the Highlands chiefly dominance, even if resented, remained a conspicuous feature until the changes forced by the events of 1745.

The main change of the early eighteenth century was the 1707 decision to accept a treaty of union with England. The motivation for this bargain was the Scottish sense of the weakness of the economy, which had been revealed in the difficulties of the 1690s.

6 T. C. Smout, *A Century of the Scottish People, 1830–1950* (London, 1986), ch. 3.
7 Bernard Bailyn, *Voyagers to the West* (London, 1987), ch. 14.

The treaty left the Scottish Church and the Scottish legal system apparently untouched. In reality, however, the Church was not immune to interference: one of the early actions of the new Parliament of Great Britain was to establish some level of religious toleration for protestant dissent in Scotland, and to accompany this by the reintroduction of lay patronage over church appointments. The legal system was affected more gradually by the introduction of a system of appeals to the House of Lords as supreme court. Scots law at the time of union needed new features which would recognize the enhanced political significance of the gentry in opposition to the powers of the aristocracy, and economic development brought out the need for expansion of the content of mercantile law. Union hastened on these developments.

The trend towards individualism was apparent in other areas of life. Modernization of the criminal law was one of these. As in other parts of Europe, law in Scotland had combined popular practices and traditions with the more modern concept of specific orders emanating from the central government. Offences might well be absorbed by the local community without penalty, since overt action could lead to revenge either by the offender or by his kin. In the Crown's courts different principles controlled the procedures and penalties for people of wealth and status from those applicable to the common people, for the payment of compensation by offenders with suitable resources or their kin was a swifter and more sure way to end a feud than was any State-imposed penalty. Increasing professionalism among lawyers and judges and the influence of the Church combined to expedite the change towards the modern concept of crime as a breach of an explicit rule, and that penalties should be the same for all classes. The idea of crime as an offence, the offensiveness of which did not lie in the wickedness of the intent behind it, was encouraged by the Church. Criminal acts were, to the Church, a direct offence to God and, unpunished, a menace to society. Law thus became more uniform and penalties harsher in the seventeenth century. At the same time a more professional lawyers' code of what was and what was not admissible evidence provided some protection for the accused.

The trend towards individualism necessarily weakened lordship. In any case the power of the aristocracy never recovered after the period of revolution. In 1647 the Church had showed that it could prevent the tenantry supporting its lords. In the Restoration period there were occasions when landowners claimed that they could not control their tenants in matters such as church attendance and other issues of conscience. By the late seventeenth century even a highland chief could not assume that his clansmen would automatically follow him with arms in every alliance he might make. In the Jacobite risings of the eighteenth century men followed their chiefs, but often only after threats, and many deserted whenever opportunity showed.

An important legal change of the seventeenth century which can be seen as a further aspect of individualism was the criminalization of women. It seems that responsibility for any offences committed by women had lain with their governing menfolk – with the father of an unmarried woman, the husband of a wife, and with the son if she was a widow. This situation indicates group rather than individual responsibility, and suggests that women were seen as chattels. In a system where a widespread kin could be called upon to make compensation for crime, it was of no particular interest that the criminal was a woman. It is likely that the enhanced emphasis on personal responsibility which the Reformation and Counter Reformation cultivated, was one strand in the acceptance of the existence of women by the criminal law, but this acceptance was for a long time patchy.[8] In one area, that of witchcraft, in spite of the dubious theology on which the legal concept of this crime was based, women were 'more equal' than men, for some 80 per cent of the victims of witchcraft accusations and trials were women, a proportion high enough to suggest that the gender element was significant, even if not exclusive, in the motivation of such events. The total number of victims of these trials has been set lower by recent scholars than had previously been assumed, but it still stands in four figures for known executions in the seventeeth century,[9] and since accusations were likely to flare in any place which had already experienced the witchcraft craze, there were lowland areas where any sharp-tongued woman who did not have influential relations was at real risk. At the same time both the criminal and the civil law had difficulty in accepting women as witnesses. A surprising amount of the time of educated legal manpower in court was spent in arguing this issue.[10] A common

8 Christina Larner, 'Crimen Exceptum? The Crime of Witchcraft in Europe', in V. A. C. Gatrell, Bruce Lenman and Geoffrey Parker (eds), *Crime and the Law* (London, 1980), pp. 68–71.

9 Christina Larner, *Enemies of God* (London, 1981), ch. 14.

10 John Burnett, *A Treatise on various branches of the Criminal Law of Scotland* (Edinburgh, 1811), p. 389; W. G. Scott-Moncrieff (ed.), *The Records of the proceedings of the*

compromise was that women could bear witness only on events for which it was unlikely that there would be male witnesses.[11] This brought them into trials involving sexual irregularity, for instance adultery cases and the naming of the man by the woman in childbirth in fornication cases. They might also give evidence in church courts over 'scandalous carriage' or unusual and disapproved bedding arrangments. When concealed pregnancy was taken to raise a presumption of infanticide in cases where an illegitimate infant died, it was women who were questioned in the criminal courts.

Dogma made it clear that women had souls of equal concern to God as those of men, but they were still second-class citizens in the eyes of both Church and State. The revulsion shown in the 1560 Confession of Faith over the Roman Catholic practice of allowing women to baptize extended further than the conveying of the sacrament, for baptism was available only to infants whom a male sponsor would present. If a woman was in trouble with her kirk session her husband might be included in the reproof, presumably on the grounds that he had not adequately controlled her. A husband was expected to rule his household, and authority was normally expressed by violence. The Church acquiesced in the idea of male superiority, but made attempts to modify the violence. A minister would reprove a man for exceeding the accepted level of marital violence if the occasion had been public, or if the reaction of the woman made it public by her screaming or running away, and severe violence would bring such behaviour under the head of scandal. In June 1695, in Dumbarton, Duncan Campbell had added to his offences of slander and drunkenness on the sabbath, hitting his wife when out of doors with such force that she thought her hearing had been damaged, and he was ordered by the presbytery to do penance. In Cameron, November 1697, Andrew Robertson was called to the session for striking his wife and setting his foot upon her. He stated that he only 'drew a foot out under her because she arose not soon enough at his bidding' and added, 'will you deny me that obedience due to me by my wife?'. He was recommended to bear with his wife with meekness and exhorted to behave more circumspectly. A man would also be reproved if chastisement took place on Sunday. Usually, though, any reproof

Justiciary Court, Edinburgh, 1661–78 (Scottish History Society, Edinburgh, 1905), vol. 1, p. 196, vol. 2, p. xiv.
    11 David Hume, *Commentaries on the law of Scotland respecting crimes* (Edinburgh, 1986), pp. 339–46.

of a husband would be accompanied by a reproof of the wife for having provoked him. If a man retorted angrily to inquiry by a kirk session into his behaviour, or refused to carry out its orders, the session would maintain its pressure but without further reproof; whereas if a woman did the same she would receive a strongly worded reproof. In Arbuthnot, in November 1696, Elizabeth Myres was reproved for not having risen from a bed of sickness to prevent a neighbour and her servant moving grain on a Sunday. She answered 'presumptuously, like unto one altogether ignorant of a deity that albeit she knew of it yet being sickly she neither could nor would hinder them for she was not partaker of their sin neither would she submit herself to censure for the same'. The minister, 'greatly offended', threatened to hand her over to a civil judge for 'contumacy'. Clearly he was not used to being answered back by a woman. In Caithness sexual offences in the seventeenth century and early years of the eighteenth often led to the woman involved being beaten, but this penalty was not imposed on the men. In burghs in the eighteenth century a kirk session might stimulate the Burgh Council to force a woman alleged to be a prostitute to leave. No action would be taken against her customers. The same differential in values was shown in the language used; women might be labelled whores or common strumpets, but there was no derogatory word available for a man whose offences had repeatedly brought him before the session.

Yet women were not seen as surplus to the economy. They were a vital part of the work force. Even though they could not provide the important element of male muscle power, they were hired as individuals and set to tasks, outdoors as well as indoors, for which they had the strength and skill. Such tasks included most work that involved stooping, and much of what was wet or messy. They did not usually form part of the group ploughing, nor did they often act as herds, but they worked in the sowing and harrowing. In harvest they were the reapers, using sickles.[12] They did the pulling of flax, the carrying of peats, the whole range of dairy work, the spinning, cooking and such minimal cleaning and washing as was expected, and collaborated with men in winnowing, malting and brewing, and retting the flax. In mining they went underground along with the men to carry up the coal, and in other industries they did much of the unskilled but tiring work.

The poverty and lack of possessions of the peasantry forced the

12 C. H. Firth, *Scotland and the Protectorate* (Scottish History Society, Edinburgh, 1899), pp. 407–9; A. Fenton, *Scottish Country Life* (Edinburgh, 1976), pp. 52–6.

sexes into close contact. Most houses were of one room, measuring not more than 20 by 14 feet,[13] and at least until well into the eighteenth century these were undivided rooms. The 'domestic revolution' diagnosed by Dr Hoskins in England, in which a sudden change of life style occurred, with the purchase of good furniture, the improvement of house structure, the achievement of some minimal level of privacy by the creation of extra rooms, and the making of window curtains,[14] does not appear to have come to Scotland until the eighteenth century. Among the few household inventories which survive from tenants and cottars it is clear that even in the early decades of the eighteenth century reasonably sized farm holdings would be held by farmers who possessed almost no place of comfort except their beds, and almost no change of linen.[15] The box beds, frequently commented on in the nineteenth century, which made a division in the room, seem to have been a feature starting only in the mid-eighteenth century. So were luxury purchases, such as oak tables, chests of drawers and mirrors. For most of the period of our study these features did not obtain. The people we have been studying lived in a world in which privacy and cleanliness were impossible.

By contrast a luxury level of accommodation, handsome equipment in furniture and elegance in houses and gardens were a marked feature of the life of the better off lairds from the late seventeenth century on. The gentry gave up living in tower houses, for the most part in the Restoration period, since law and order made for less need of verticality and more ease. The Scottish upper classes had been rather slow, by European standards, to abandon their medieval military functions. In the seventeenth century most of the aristocracy seem to have thought it normal that they should command troops on occasion, though some had had no technical education in weapons handling, and few had benefited by study of the art of war. By the 1680s the situation had changed in the Lowlands. Military activity had become a specific career, in which only a few were engaged. The sword might still be worn: it was a sign of gentility, an indicator that the wearer was entitled to settle disputes by its use. The change was not simply a matter of greater selectivity in careers; it reflected the much greater level of law and

13 Rosalind Mitchison, *Life in Scotland* (London, 1978), pp. 67–8.
14 W. G. Hoskins, *The Midland Peasant* (London, 1957), ch. 10; 'The Rebuilding of Rural England', *Provincial England* (London, 1963), pp. 131–48.
15 E.g. the inventory of William McGuffog, SRO, Commissariot of Wigtown, 1705.

order, and was one of the signs of the eighteenth century dominance of the class of lairds.

Promotion of the lairds had been the aim of James VI, who had not managed to achieve it, though he had created the office of Justice of the Peace, which was to become one of the instruments by which these men controlled society. Charles I had had a similar aim, and his settlement of teind became a major element in the security of these men. Probably it was the defeat and disciplining of the aristocracy by the church party in the central decades of the seventeenth century which created a gap in the power structure which they were able to occupy. The upper range of the lairds, those who were tenants in chief of the Crown, played an important part in the assertion of the independence of Parliament from 1688, even though the political groups within which they worked were controlled by the great magnates and wielded in the interests of the great houses. Union with England completed the emancipation of the lairds by turning the ambitions of the aristocracy to London. Political and military careers had to be pursued there, and even some legal ones. It was in London that whatever spoils the government had to distribute were to be sought. The attention of those of the aristocracy who were capable of an important role (and not all were) moved from Scotland and left effective power there to the lairds.

The word 'laird' covers a wide range of landowning income. At the top were men of estates equivalent in size and wealth to those of the lesser aristocracy, and indeed such men might move into the ranks of the aristocracy. Examples of such transfer were the Murrays of Scone, ennobled in 1757, or the Elliots of Minto, who had benefited by marriage with an heiress and reached the House of Lords in 1797. In some cases a laird in this group might have become the only landowner in a parish, which gave him a very powerful voice in its affairs. Then there were the owners of moderate estates, which would provide, unimproved, an income of between £100 and £1,000 a year. Finally there were the men to whom Sir Walter Scott gave the label of 'bonnet laird', and who were more officially referred to as 'proprietors of single farms', a group of economic standing no higher than some of the greater tenants. These men were under economic pressure, and becoming fewer in the later eighteenth century, but were still of considerable social significance. Often they had a taste for a larger income than a single farm could provide, and would rent out their land and move into the professions. The particular career chosen by men of this sort, and their more affluent brethren, was the law. The advocates and judges of late seventeenth and eighteenth century Scotland were almost entirely drawn from the ranks of the medium and small landowners.

In spite of differences in wealth the class of landowners had a unity, arising from its status as acknowledged by the other ranks of society. A common feature throughout the class was the aspiration for gracious living. Intermarriage within the class enhanced this unity. Altogether, according to Sir John Sinclair, there were, at the end of the eighteenth century, almost 400 large estates worth over £2,500 a year, just over a thousand middling ones and over 6,000 giving less than £600 a year. Dr Timperley, who is probably a more accurate source, confirms these figures as nearly true for 1770: her numbers are 336 large estates, 1,100 middling and over 6,100 small.[16] These figures cannot be directly translated into landed families, for such families might hold land units in different counties, but they give some idea of the numbers in the class.

The different types of estate were unevenly distributed. Large estates dominated the scene in the Borders and in East Lothian. 'Bonnet lairds', even though they did not control much of the total acreage, were numerous in Lanarkshire, Galloway and Ayrshire, Banffshire, Bute and the central Lowlands, and fairly common in Fife and Caithness.[17] Since our material suggests an unusual approach to the authority of the Church in Galloway and Ayrshire, this social difference may have been of significance.

Some members of the landed class were involved in the expanding commerce of the eighteenth century, or in its important associate activity, banking. The payment of rents in kind had presented many landowners with the need to organize marketing of surplus grain, and some among these men in all areas developed contacts and skills in this activity which kept them actively involved in buying and selling. Social prestige in Scotland differed in its basis from the English system of values. It was not the absence of a link with trade which made for respectability, but the reality of the link, however slight, with landowning. Younger sons also might be sent into trade as an alternative to the army or to government service, and the professional posts which expanded rapidly in the eighteenth century, in medicine, the navy, and the

16 John Sinclair, *Analysis of the Statistical Account* (London, 1826), p. 244; L. Timperley, 'The pattern of landholding in eighteenth century Scotland', in M. L. Parry and T. R. Slater (eds), *The Making of the Scottish Countryside* (London, 1980), pp. 137–54.
17 Timperley, 'The pattern of landholding in eighteenth century Scotland'.

universities, were frequently held by men linked to land. The Church ministry might receive some recruitment from the landed classes, but for the most part was self-sustaining, a hereditary caste.[18] Merchant houses and craftsmen's workshops also kept as much family continuity as the risks of bankruptcy allowed. These closed, or nearly closed, groups made for a society in which people knew their place well, and held to it without any discomfort in the consciousness of the social superiority and the reality of power in the landowning class.

The landed gentry thus dominated the law, the economy, culture and society. The eighteenth century could be called the century of the lairds. These men did not rest idle in their position. It was they who transformed Scotland from a country backward in economy, dominated by territorial magnates and bullied by a dogmatic and intransigent clergy, into an active participator in social change and economic growth, contributing significantly to the industrial revolution and to the eighteenth century intellectual movement which we call the Enlightenment.[19]

The landed class came, somewhat grudgingly, to co-operate with the Church in making the poor law of Scotland into a working system, at least in the Lowlands. Much of what was in the statute book on the support of the needy and the disciplining of vagrants was never put into practice, and so ceased, through the Scottish legal principle of 'desuetude', to have any authority, but in the period of Whig dominance in the mid-seventeenth century the Church had secured an Act of Parliament handing the management of relief to its courts,[20] and this Act marks the start of all practices which could be called a poor law. The aristocracy was then politically in eclipse, and in many lowland parishes the ministers were able to make the requirement that assessment should be laid on landowners work for a short while. From then on lowland parishes regularly worked some system of support for the infirm and indigent, and received legacies to sustain this work, to which also the fines for misbehaviour went. The funds of a parish were normally known as the poor's money, even though they were used also to support the parish officer and clerk, the clerks of the higher courts, and to provide for necessities such as communion

18 This is clear from the biographical details in Hew Scott, *Fasti Ecclesiae Scoticanae*, 7 vols (Edinburgh, 1915–28).

19 N. T. Phillipson and Rosalind Mitchison (eds), *Scotland in the Age of Improvement* (Edinburgh, 1970).

20 *APS* VI ii 220, *Act anent the poore* (1649).

equipment, and minor conveniences such as a church porch. In the famine of the 1690s pressure from the Privy Council through the system of county government supported ministers in gaining help from landowners, and a substantial scatter of parishes were able to impose assessment on landowners. They were aided in this by an Act of Parliament which shared the landowners' burden with the tenantry.[21] This was one of the few enactments on poor relief which took effect. On the whole the system should be seen as developing under the authority of the Church, rather than of the State.

In the eighteenth century the relief system in the Lowlands was capable of supporting the obvious cases of need, but at a low level. There were outbreaks of pressure from county governing groups to make it adequate, and also to force parishes to control vagrancy. In the south and south-east of Scotland these pressures led to most parishes being assessed (i.e. rated) on a permanent basis by the end of the century, but assessment was rare and occasional in the north and north-east. However, in these areas the needs of those severely destitute were often partly met by special collections. In periods of crop failure, notably the very bad harvests of 1740 and 1782, landowners in both north and south made generous gifts and collected subscriptions which made possible a system of subsidy for grain purchases and kept the population from starvation. In 1782 the Highlands were bailed out by grain left over from the War of the American Revolution, but in normal times the weakness of parish structure there, and the relative immunity of this area from government control until the mid-century, meant that poor relief barely existed. Parishes might make an occasional dole of a few shillings, but were not able to support those with no resources.

We can thus see lowland Scotland as developing a system of effective relief in the eighteenth century, but one with limitations. Landowners liked to think of it as a matter of generous giving rather than legal obligation, and in the north came to view assessment with hostility.[22] There was a struggle for control of parish funds in the mid-eighteenth century between landowners and the Church, but in practice the legal victory of the landowners made little difference. Since relief funds were never lavish, there were no major policy decisions for landowners to influence, and

21 *APS* x 64, *Act for the better provideing the Poor, and repressing of Beggars* (1696, confirmed 1701), in *APS* x Appendix 99b, *Act anent the Poor*.

22 Rosalind Mitchison, 'North and South: the development of the gulf in poor law practice', in R. A. Houston and Ian Whyte (eds), *Scottish Society 1500–1800*, forthcoming.

they were not interested in the detailed work of distribution. The allowances given in a parish would keep an elderly and infirm person from starvation, care for orphans and foundlings until they were ready for service or apprenticeship (and even provide medical aid for them after they had entered service), sustain the insane in some comfort, give partial help to men whose losses put their earning power at risk and bury pensioners with seemly rites. But the poor law never established a right to relief in a claimant. Occasionally lawyers might, indeed, bring a case for a claimant in the sheriff court, and the decision might order a specified level of parish support, but the general principle was that the kirk session accepted an obligation to support the poor of which it was the judge.[23] This absence of paupers' rights, while it meant that Scotland did not have to develop the structure of settlement law which attempted to control labour movement in England, also meant that there was no particular obligation on a Scottish parish to support illegitimate children. A parish might well give an allowance to a nursing mother of a legitimate or illegitimate child who had no other resource while her nursing prevented her from employment, but this was merely a temporary aid. This absence of support for bastards, other than foundlings, meant that the moral control which the Church exercised over sexual affairs had little mercenary motivation: it was based simply on Calvinist dogma.

Already in the seventeenth century both lairds and nobility were concerned to increase the yield of their estates. They were involved together in the drive for more market outlets in the 1670s, supported the attempts of Privy Council and Parliament to expand the range of industries in the 1680s, and participated in the encouragement of the linen manufacture on their estates and the marketing of cattle in England. Linen was to become the dominant industry in Scotland. It often provided the money with which tenants paid their rent, increased the resources of many poor households by giving profitable work to women and children and, since it was an industry aimed at export, had a marked influence on the improvement of roads and the expansion of market activity. Between the 1720s and the 1770s the value of linen reaching the open market, and much was done to private contract, went up over five times. Much of the effect of this change can only be guessed at, for the firms who organized its transport or sale were often too small to leave records. But it clearly caused a major change in the

---

23 *Paton vs Adamson*, in W. Wallace (ed.), *Decisions of the Court of Session for the Years 1772, 1773 and 1774* (Edinburgh, 1784).

availability of markets, although in the eighteenth, not the seventeenth century. In the 1670s and 1680s this was not foreseeable.

Many of the new burghs created in and after the 1670s never had anything which could be called urban life, and new industries did not take root. The idea, expressed in an Act of 1672, that vagrants could be made into an effective labour force for new industries was, understandably, nothing but a mirage. What is of importance in the various plans and schemes is the evidence they give of strong motivation for economic gain. New ideas had more effect in agriculture, and several Acts of the newly independent parliament at the end of the century gave landowners a freer hand in the management of their estates. They show that, though landowners were not ready yet to undertake the drastic reorganization which would really send up output, yet they were prepared to weaken traditional relationships in the search for economic gain.[24]

It was thus only in the eighteenth century that the agricultural revolution came about in Scotland. Well into that century landowners continued to receive much of their rents in kind and in services. Rents in kind dictated the cultivation pattern that could be used by tenants, and so reminded them of their dependent status. Services, such as labour in harvest, or 'carriages', which meant the application of labour and carts for carrying goods as required by the landowner, carried the same reminder, and were an obstacle to any system by which a tenant might be left free to decide how to use his resources to his own best advantage.

The difficulties in the way of seeing that a freer use of the tenants' time could enhance their productivity is shown by the comment made by the first member of landed society to put forward a written argument for 'improvement', that is for changes in the method of production. In this case the proposals were very limited. William Mackintosh of Borlum in his *An Essay on Ways and Means for Inclosing, Fallowing, Planting etc. . . . Scotland* of 1729 was claiming that the introduction of fences and the separation of farms would be an expenditure which would lead rapidly to profit. He also went on to argue against 'services', but in doing so had to admit that he could not see how landowners would ever manage without having their peats cut and brought in by their tenants. Where the most adventurous thinker could not see that paid labour would become available to fill this gap, agricultural

24 Ian Whyte, *Agriculture and Society in Seventeenth Century Scotland*, ch. 4.

reorganization was bound to be delayed. Borlum was, in fact, in advance of most of landed society in perceiving that some of the economic rights which seemed advantageous to landowners, particularly the right to labour services, might be holding back productivity from which landowners might gain more markedly. Another early 'improver', John Cockburn of Ormiston, shows his limited appreciation of this point, for though he did much to promote the security of his more successful tenants, he still insisted on using his right to have and use a dovecote, in other words to provide himself with meat at the expense of his tenants' seed corn.

The most striking area of economic development in the first half of the eighteenth century, and one with impact on the whole of society, was in the economic infrastructure, that is in transport, communications and financial services. This ground work was responsible for the remarkable growth of the third quarter. A rough indication of this growth can be seen in the figure of a 40 per cent increase in Scotland's home manufactured exports,[25] but more significant in social terms was the corresponding growth in internal trade, which cannot be easily measured. Both these areas of expansion were based on small scale cottage production, and so indicate a transformation of domestic life for many households. But also, the change in the quality of transport facilities, and the use made of them, had great impact on the lives of the people. Towns, which expanded at a faster rate in population in eighteenth century Scotland than anywhere else in Europe, grew in scale and changed markedly in the services which they offered. People moved from place to place, sometimes of necessity but also often of choice, and their movements could no longer be controlled by the system of 'testificats', certificates of good behaviour given by the kirk session of the parish from which someone was moving, and without which the parish of his proposed stay would not receive him. In the second half of the century kirk sessions cease to refer to these documents except for the purpose of verifying marriages. An important element in the control of the people had been abandoned, of necessity.

The increased mobility of the mass of the people, whether for work or for purchasing, necessarily lessened the influence of the landowning class, even if it did not affect its legal rights. If evicted from a farm a tenant had knowledge that there were openings

---

25 T. C. Smout, 'Where had the Scottish economy got to by the third quarter of the eighteenth century?', in Istvan Hont and Michael Ignatieff (eds), *Wealth and Virtue* (Cambridge, 1983), pp. 45–72.

elsewhere: the towns needed more and more labour. The transport system itself, the roads and bridges, the carting system, the inns and stage coaches, all needed hands. Later came wider prospects for the dissatisfied and adventurous in the expansion of the American colonies. Scotland provided much of the surge of emigration to America in the 1770s, sending whole farming families into the unknown. One of the motives which inspired this movement was the desire to be free of the burdens of rent and services and gain control of the management of a piece of land. A marked streak of individualism sustained this movement.

Another result of increased mobility was the increase in irregular marriage. This facility had for some time been available in some larger towns: suddenly it became available to much of the rural population, who turned to it in the 1750s and later.[26] Since the practice was in defiance of rules of the Church its expansion indicates a weakening of that body's authority.

Individualism produced a different response in the upper class. The intellectual fashion of the day was to become known as the Enlightenment: its basic theory was a development from the work of writers of the seventeenth century which has become known as civic humanism. This theory laid down secular principles of moral action for the citizen. Its definition of the citizen as an independent man meant that this status was confined to those who did not need to rely on decisions about employment or tenure made by others, in other words to those who owned land. A recent definition is clear: 'to qualify for . . . citizenship the individual must be master of his own household, proprietor along with his own equals of the only arms permitted to be borne in wars . . . and possessor of property.'[27] Citizenship was exclusively the possession of adult male landowner heads of households. Civic humanism confirmed the widely held belief that the function of the State was to protect landed property, a belief actively used by the landed class at this time since it alone had representation in Parliament and it also supplied the judiciary. Using the theory of civic humanism men were able to discuss morals without reference to Calvinist dogma. It was not so much that dogma was denied or refuted: most of the discussants of humanist issues would have

26 See ch. 4.

27 J. G. A. Pocock, 'Cambridge paradigms and Scotch philosophers: a study of the relations between the civic humanist and the civil jurisprudential interpretation of eighteenth century social thought', in Istvan Hont and Michael Ignatieff (eds), *Wealth and Virtue*, p. 236.

assented to Calvinism. But the whole body of argument was bypassed in much the same way as it was in the world of the late nineteenth and early twentieth century universities. Christian morality subsumed many of the historical and political judgements of academics then, but was not necessarily expressed.

Landed society did not make the Enlightenment on its own. There was a powerful current entering it from the world of the professions, particularly the professoriate and the clergy. Early in the century a transformation of the universities of Scotland began with the creation of the Edinburgh medical school and the placing of Alexander Monro as the first professor of anatomy. Monro has left us a book-sized document of advice, claiming to be a letter to his daughter, which, though it discusses many aspects of behaviour, makes no explicit reference to revealed religion.[28] For working purposes the professional theorizing of the great men in the medical schools was conceived entirely in terms of natural philosophy, not of dogma. The 1740s saw the emergence of a powerful though small group of young clergy concerned to promote freedom in artistic and intellectual culture, who were to be known as the leaders of the Moderate party in the Church.[29] At the same time the powerful intellect of David Hume was moving to a position of religious scepticism, and to this was added personal hostility to the claims of organized religion.

The conspicuous figures of the Enlightenment, other than Hume, did not oppose Calvinism, but most of them avoided expatiating on it. It was feasible for Adam Smith in his analysis of the working of the economy to speak of an 'invisible hand' without regarding it as part of an anthropomorphic God. The achievement of the Enlightenment was to develop various areas of natural and social science in their own terms, as subject to their own discoverable laws. In this way the students of society saw it as having stages of development, and Hutton's pioneer work in geology saw the natural forces which impinged on the earth's crust, in current as well as in past terms, as responsible for the existing scenery. The Moderate clerics then, and sometimes since, were accused of not holding to Calvinist dogma, and of refusing to preach on it; this was an important part of an anonymous attack launched on them by John Witherspoon in the 1750s.[30] It would be

28 NLS MS 6658, dated 1738 or 9, 'Essay on Female conduct'.

29 Richard B. Sher, *Church and University in the Scottish Enlightenment* (Edinburgh, 1985), part 1.

30 *Ecclesiastical Characteristics* (1753) and *A Serious Apology for the Ecclesiastical Characteristics* (Edinburgh, 1763).

truer to say that they did not see sermons on predestination as a means of helping their flocks to lead more Christian lives.

These intellectual and economic changes did not come about painlessly, or with harmony of opinion. Even in the late seventeenth century there are clear signs that some elements in landed society strongly resented the political and moral claims of the clergy. A sign of this was the unwillingness of the professional lawyers, almost all landowning, to aid in prosecutions for witchcraft and in general for ecclesiastical cases. In 1696 the Court of Justiciary had sentenced a young man of undistinguished birth, one Thomas Aikenhead, to death for blasphemy: it was said that the court would move for a reprieve only if urged to by the Edinburgh clergy, but almost all of these ministers not only would not intervene for mercy, but urged that there be an exceptionally prompt carrying out of the sentence to prevent any intervention from the Crown in London.[31] In 1704 a group of Pittenweem women was accused of witchcraft: correspondence about this alleges that a local minister had obtained a confession by beating one of them.[32] At this interval of time it is not possible to sort out the full details of this sordid and violent case, which ended with a lynching, but the tone of the letter, with its criticism of 'barbarous severitys' by ministers, shows strong upper class hostility to the clergy. Anticlericalism, in the seventeenth century usually directed only at clerical influence on political matters, was becoming more widespread and openly voiced because of the intolerant behaviour of the remnant of 'outed' ministers which had gained control of the General Assembly and was purging the Church of all who had accepted episcopacy, and was now shown in those areas where Church and State interlocked. The Act of Union and the 1712 Toleration Act, opposed by the clergy on the sound grounds that these would, and did, reduce clerical power, made possible greater openness of resistance to clerical demands, but it is striking that the lawyers, though they were able to frustrate most witchcraft prosecutions, never denounced the legal basis of the offence until it had been abolished by statute in 1736.

There were new as well as old grounds for friction between landowners and clergy. Presbyteries were taking as a standard for

31 Hugh Arnot, *A Collection and Abridgement of Celebrated Criminal Trials in Scotland from AD 1536 to 1784* (Edinburgh, 1785), pp. 322–7.
32 State Papers, Ireland, Letters and Papers, PRO SP 63/364, anonymous letter from Edinburgh, 19 November 1704, to Edward Southwell, Dublin. We owe it as a reference to the kindness of T. C. Smout.

manses, which the landowners would have to pay for, a much larger and more solidly built house than in the past. There were often parish issues over grazing for the minister's horse. In 1749 various presbyteries and synods put before the General Assembly their view that the incomes of many ministers were inadequate. It was claimed that the cost of living had risen since stipends had been fixed in the first half of the seventeenth century. It is difficult to sustain this in crude terms, for stipends had been fixed in grain, but grain prices had stepped down in the 1660s, and as a result stipends ran less well to meet the cost of the things that clergy needed to buy which were not food. The century or so which had elapsed had seen the production of more types of goods, and a rise in the wages of labourers and servants. There was now an established middle class life style to which the clergy naturally aspired. But stipends were levied off rents, and landowners in many counties held meetings to oppose and denounce what was called the Augmentation scheme. When the General Assembly ignored these hostilities and went ahead with the scheme the landed members of Parliament secured its consignation to the category of indefinite postponment in 1751, but not before a good deal of intemperate language on both sides had been aired in the Assembly and the press.[33]

This was not the only mid-century clash between lay and clerical. A series of law suits over the handling of the parish funds for poor relief, which appear to have had a linked organization, led to judicial decisions in 1751 which surprised even some judges with the freedom with which they handled the law and accepted new principles. These led to the decision that the landowners of a parish had by natural right complete control over all its funds. They also laid down restrictions on what could be done with parish money which proved impractical. In the long run little was changed, because it was in the interests of landed as well as unlanded society that the existing pattern of activity to support the poor should continue, but the decisions caused dismay to many ministers at the time.[34]

Dictionaries contain no counterpart for the sentiment of anti-clericalism to cover how the clergy may feel about lay society, but it is clear that in the 1750s and 1760s there was much heat about the

33 N. Morren, *Annals of the General Assembly of the Church of Scotland* (Edinburgh, 1838), vol. 1, pp. 158–67, 280.

34 Rosalind Michison, 'The Making of the Old Scottish Poor Law', *Past and Present* 63 (1974), pp. 58–93.

powers and behaviour of landowners in sections of the clergy. It was a new experience for the Scottish Church to discover that lay society might not, even outwardly, conform to its views. There are sermons and pamphlets from this period, often interpreted at their face value, which allege a serious fall off in moral standards and in church attendance on the part of the gentry.[35] When the writings are examined more closely they give more evidence of ecclesiastical pique than of deterioration in lay behaviour. The protection of the known sceptic, David Hume, from ecclesiastical censure or worse is usually one of the grievances, but the frustration of the Augmentation scheme ranks larger, though it is less openly expressed. For instance, Patrick Bannerman's sermon preached to the synod at Stirling in 1751 states that 'Infidelity, Scepticism, or an absolute Indifference about all Religion, prevail so much among Persons of Rank and Fashion, that these have become the Characteristics by which Men would distinguish themselves from the Vulgar', and James Oswald, preaching at the opening of the General Assembly in 1766, specifically attacked men of high rank, and accused them of 'contemptuous neglect of religious duties'. It is worth noting, in contradiction to these claims, that William Creech in his 'Letters to Sir John Sinclair' specifically stated that 'In 1763 – It was fashionable to go to church . . . Sunday was strictly observed by all ranks.'[36]

The literature brings out the gulf between clerics and landed society, and also reveals divisions within the Church. The political Revolution of 1688–9 had forced those who held by episcopal church government into the position of dissenters, and since this body included most of the ministry of Aberdeenshire and the north-east, there was considerable confusion and disorder in that region. The Episcopalian Church, which these dissenters formed, did not dissent from the Calvinism of the establishment but its political links with Jacobitism put it under difficulties, and after the 1715 rebellion some proscription. There was also surviving a small extremist covenanting communion, mainly in the south-west. But still, for the first third of the eighteenth century, the established

---

35 D. Withrington, 'Non-Church Going, *c.*1750–*c.*1850: A Preliminary Study', *Records of the Scottish Church History Society* XVII (1972), pp. 91–113.

36 Patrick Bannerman, *Sermon upon Reformation and Revolution Principles preached in the Church of Stirling April 10 1751 by appointment of the Synod* (Edinburgh, 1751), pp. 19–20; James Oswald, *Sermon at the opening of the General Assembly May 1766, to which are annexed Letters* (Edinburgh, 1766), p. 29; *OSA* VI (1793), p. 609, Appendix, 'Letters addressed to Sir John Sinclair by William Creed'.

Presbyterian Church was very nearly national in its scope, and hard line Calvinism prevailed.

There were, however, some rumblings of doctrinal differences, mainly associated with an English book of seventeenth century origin, *The Marrow of Modern Divinity*, republished in 1718. The emphasis of the dialogues in this book lay in the efficacy of free grace, that is in a denial of supralapsarianism. Grace could be made available to any sinner who sincerely sought it, and was not limited to a predetermined minority. The book was condemned by the General assembly in 1720, but there was always a party from then on uneasy over the official expression of the Church's theology, the Westminster Confession.

The Marrow controversy was one of the strands which led to the first open secession of a prebysterian group from the Church in the 1730s, but this group's protest was not over free grace: it was on the relative ways in which suppression of *The Marrow* and of other forms of deviant opinion had been treated, and, behind that, the readiness of the Assembly to accept lay patronage in appointments imposed by the State.[37] Patronage had been reintroduced, after its abolition in 1690, by the British Parliament in an Act which was not only offensive to the Church but also a violation of the accepted terms of the Union of 1707, which had included a Scottish statute affirming the independence of the Church. Patronage issues could create great local heat, rituals of protest and sometimes serious resistance to imposed ministers and continuing rifts within congregations. They enhanced the hostility between the landed class, which supported patronage, and the 'popular' party in the Church. The existence of even the small, but tightly organized and excessively self-righteous 'Original Secession', an alternative presbyterian church, was bound to weaken the authority of the Established Church. The Original Secession's pronouncements contain a distinct element of 'holier than thou', so that though it denounced 'sapless and lifeless descanting upon the moral virtues', there was no likelihood of it becoming a refuge for those who could not take the discipline of the Establishment. It had no appeal to moral deviants.

It was the second secession, that of the 1750s, again taking its start on the topic of patronage and the insistence of the Assembly in overriding presbyteries, which created a communion, the Relief

37 Andrew L. Drummond and James Bulloch, *The Scottish Church 1688–1843* (Edinburgh, 1973), pp. 35–44; W. Ferguson, *Scotland, 1689 to the Present* (Edinburgh, 1968), pp. 118–23.

Church, in 1761, open to those who were not happy with hard line Calvinism. No doctrinal requirements were placed on attendance at this Church's communion. Even before this the issue of free grace had been raised through a series of revival meetings. The first of these was held in the open at Cambuslang in 1742. The revivals became associated with the visit of George Whitefield, a leading preacher of the eighteenth-century evangelical movement. These revivals brought various converts to accept a serious commitment to religion; in so doing they accentuated the gulf between the upper class and popular religion. It should not surprise that Cambuslang was one of the parishes in which there had been persistent bad relations between the heritors, many of them episcopalian in loyalty, and the kirk session, relations which were revealed when it became one of the parishes picked on for a court case over the relative rights of the two groups. Landowners regarded the prospect of a religious revival on their land – and the 'Great Wark' of Cambuslang was repeated annually – in much the same way as a modern landowner would consider having a pop festival on his. There would be thousands of people gathered together, noise, emotional scenes, damage to fences, insanitary manifestations of population density, probably petty theft, and the general distraction of the workforce from its duties.[38]

The various secessions and revivals were evidence of genuine popular religious enthusiasm, in both the modern and the eighteenth century sense of the word. We do not know the numbers affected, but they were considerable. It has been alleged that as many as 100,000 adhered to the Relief Church in 1765, but this figure is one achieved by guesswork, not by counting.[39] In any case, it is the existence of the communion, rather than its dimensions, which mattered, because it ended the exclusive acceptance of the Westminster Confession.

The mid-eighteenth century thus saw the development in different sections of society of two drastically opposed currents of thought. On one hand, aided in some cases by the revival meetings, a theology more inviting and individualist than traditional Calvinism was offering participation and support to the unpropertied part of society. On the other hand, educated men had the opportunity to

38 Arthur Fawcett, *The Cambuslang Revival* (London, 1971); T. C. Smout, 'Born again at Cambuslang: new evidence on popular religion and literacy in eighteenth century Scotland', *Past and Present* 97 (1982), pp. 114–27.

39 The figure is quoted in Bruce Lenman, *Integration, Enlightenment and Industrialisation: Scotland 1746–1832* (London, 1981), p. 146.

enter into the new exploration of the physical world and of the social influences of mankind which was the Enlightenment.

The Enlightenment was particularly the expression of ideas among the mixture of landed gentry and professional men who congregated in Edinburgh and Glasgow. Its main foci were the clubs in the cities – clubs for the discussion of specific intellectual matters and clubs concerned to promote the economy of Scotland. Two of these which still survive represent the range of interest: the Royal Society of Edinburgh and the Highland Society.

A striking illustration of the width of dispassionate intellectual interest expressed in these clubs, and the gulf between their concerns and what the seventeenth century Church would have considered acceptable, is shown in a recently published essay 'On Venery', written by the minister Robert Wallace. In this paper, for which no contemporary references survive, Wallace urged that it be recognized that the sexual urge was as strong in women as in men, and that there was an inevitable sexual element in all close relationships between people of different sex. He suggested that a system of trial marriage be set up for young people to avoid marital disharmony. His view of fornication was that it should be discouraged, but not regarded as a stigma. The most interesting aspect of this paper is that one of the more influential members of the clergy should feel free to discuss sexual matters without having to denounce deviancy.[40]

The club life was available to those ministers who could maintain contact with the dominant cities. A small group of such men in and around Edinburgh formed the core of the Moderate party in the Church, sharing in the culture of the Enlightenment and promoting the policy of co-operation between Church and civil society. Their existence polarized issues within the Church, and the Popular and Moderate parties took opposing sides on almost every significant issue. The Moderates were numerically in a minority, but for several decades following their emergence in 1752 they managed to dominate the decisions of the General Assembly by the votes of the gentry members.[41] Given the frequent occasions of hostility between 'Popular' ecclesiastics and landowners, this fact enhanced the bitterness between the parties. John Witherspoon, later to make his mark as first Principal of Princeton University, and less successfully as a land speculator

40 Norah Smith, 'Robert Wallace's "Of Venery"', *Texas Studies in Literature and Language* 15 (1973), pp. 429–44.
41 Richard B. Sher, *Church and University in the Scottish Enlightenment*, ch. 3.

in the new settlements in America, anonymously labelled his opponents as 'professed unbelievers, desiring to retain the name of Christian'. It is probably from the literal acceptance of abuse of this sort that the belief of many nineteenth-century ecclesiastical historians that the Moderates had abandoned Calvinism and were not concerned to maintain Church discipline stems. The evidence of kirk session registers does not support this view. Alexander Carlyle of Inveresk, a leading Moderate, for instance, can be seen in his parish's records to have been a conscientious minister particularly concerned with the welfare of the poor. His comments on his parish in the *OSA* also show a strong sympathy with the secular culture and aspirations of ordinary people.[42]

Carlyle's concerns, and the friendship network of the Moderates, reveal the real change occuring in people's minds, the acceptance of secular interests as permitted manifestations of individualism. Among the participants in the Enlightenment were men who accepted traditional Calvinism, but who were prepared to be friends with the acknowledged sceptic, David Hume, and Hume had made a very powerful attack on the claims of the Church to divine authority.

There was another current of influential thought not necessarily associated with the main figures of the Enlightenment, a new level of humanitarianism, particularly noticeable in some of the lawyers. These men had modified the severity of the criminal law on certain topics, most notably, as will be shown in chapter 3, on the definitions of incest. Statistical work on the use of the death penalty in eighteenth-century Scotland has not been carried out, and, indeed, all criminal statistics are of very dubious validity, but it is possible that the country experienced the changes in opinion which were reducing the penalty's use in England. There are other signs of humanitarian ethic, for instance the letters written to the *Scots Magazine* in 1757, arguing that it was fear of the process of Church discipline which led girls to infanticide, and urging that the procedures be made less intimidating.[43] In 1785, in a collection of criminal cases of the last two centuries, the distinguished lawyer, Hugh Arnot, made an attack on the presumption of guilt of infanticide which held in cases of concealment of pregnancy. That other lawyers were uneasy on this matter is shown by the drastic statutory modification of the law which took place in the early nineteenth century. In 1770, however, an Act of the General

42 *OSA* xvi (1795), Inveresk, pp. 1–52.
43 *Scots Magazine*, February 1757, pp. 80–2, and August 1757, pp. 401–2.

Assembly denouncing clandestine marriage stressed the dangerous social and moral effects which could follow carelessness or leniency in the examination by kirk sessions of claims to be married.[44] This Act shows that many in the Church wished to see discipline more systematically observed, and is a reminder that humanitarianism could be used to support severity as well as to oppose it.

The Church's capacity to repress had clearly become reduced in all classes of society. Signs of an overt and non-intellectual interest in sexuality, expressed in ways which at the beginning of the century the Church would certainly have denounced, can be seen. Surviving chapbooks, roughly dateable to this period, without being openly lewd show an independence of the views of the Church on fornication. In one of the most famous, *Jockey and Maggie's Courtship*,[45] the mother of the young man in trouble expresses a view that was to be very common in the high illegitimacy area of the north-east in the mid-nineteenth century: the man was praised as 'neither a thief nor a horse-dealer', and cheered by the reflection that 'ye're no the first that has done it, and ye'll no be the last'. His own statement was simply an unwillingness to do penance in public. The songs of Robert Burns give clear evidence of a rich tradition of bawdy, and since singing is a social affair, evidence also that there were places and times where the expression of undisguised sexuality was acceptable. Sexuality, not merely overt but ostentatious, in the upper class is revealed by the surviving documents of an erotic and voyeuristic club in Anstruther, Fife, confined, by the level of subscription required, to men of substance: lairds, merchants and the local officials of the customs service. This body held regular meetings from the 1720s until well on in the nineteenth century. Papers relating to it occur in four separate sets of aristocratic estate archives now lodged in the Scottish Record Office.[46] It is difficult to believe that a society

44 This Act, not surprisingly, was presented by the Reverend William Auld to the congregation of Mauchline parish, and is set out in the KSR of the parish.

45 The anonymous author was Dugald Graham.

46 *Records of the Most Ancient and Puissant Order of the Beggar's Benison and Merryland* (privately printed in Anstruther, 1892). This organization and the fashion for overt sexual references among the upper classes are discussed in Norah Smith, 'Sexual mores and attitudes in Enlightenment Scotland', in P. G. Boucé (ed.), *Sexuality in Eighteenth-Century Britain* (Manchester, 1982), pp. 47–73. The SRO collections in which the Beggar's Benison are mentioned are Leven and Melville (GD 26), Dalguise (GD 38), Airlie (GD 16) and Dalhousie (GD 45). These are all early deposits, represented in the first printed volume of catalogue for GD (Gifts and Deposits). There may well be more acquired later.

with such a high social profile in its membership, meeting regularly in a very small town with some score of people of local distinction attending, not to mention the services of some local girl hired for the occasion, could have been kept secret. But we have not found any denunciation of the organization in the records of either parish or presbytery. It is a point of minor contrast over time that one of the founder members had the surname Aikenhead. The activities of the club would not have led, in the 1720s, to the penalty imposed on Thomas Aikenhead in 1696, but they would, if pursued by men of the tenant and cotter class, at least have led to public denunciation.

Enlightenment thinkers had put forward the idea of the multiplicity of ends, that is the appreciation of the variety of human aspirations. Without necessarily sharing the philosophy that sustained this view, many sections of society by the later eighteenth century were prepared to accept that there were areas of life in which human participation was normal, even when these were in conflict with the views of organized religion. The expression of the Shorter Catechism, that the whole duty of man was to glorify God and enjoy Him for ever, simply did not fit their mental systems.

Several strands of development have been shown which unite to explain the cessation of effective discipline by the Church in the 1770s and 1780s. An important one was certainly the increasing humanitarianism in the upper and professional classes, and a respect for individualism. That this new attitude was not confined to Scotland is indicated by the changing response of the Roman Catholic clergy in the diocese of Montauban, southern France, to requests for dispensations for marriages within the prohibited degrees. After 1770 these clerics displayed a new readiness to admit the validity of affection as grounds for dispensation. A similar change is shown by the prison reform initiative of John Howard in England; and by the general failure in England to work the laws imposing the death penalty on relatively minor offences.[47] There was also the failure to apply penalties to the increasing number of people with Unitarian beliefs, a form of dissent not covered by the Toleration Act of 1690, and the new anti-slave trade movement. In Scotland this humanitarianism was particularly manifest in the judiciary. It may have owed something to the secular interest taken

---

47 Margaret H. Darrow, 'Popular concepts of marital choice in eighteenth century France', *Journal of Social History* 19 (1985–6), pp. 261–72; L. Radinowicz, *A History of English Criminal Law*, vol. 1 (London, 1948), chs 3, 4, 5.

by the Enlightenment in the variety of human activity. It may also have been a sign of the erosion of the acceptance of hard line and punitive Calvinism.

This blend of humanitarianism and respect for individuality is well shown in a letter of protest published in 1780 in the *Scots Magazine*. The writer objected to a parish attempting to exercise discipline by advertising in the press for information about a missing woman, thought to be pregnant. The letter called such an action a 'flagrant violation of decency' which would never have been made about a girl of higher social status.[48]

Relaxation of discipline was not universal, however. Some parish ministers continued to enforce, or attempt to enforce, the old severe discipline into the 1780s. An often quoted example of this, used because it involved the career of Robert Burns, was the incumbency of the Reverend William Auld, minister of Mauchline, Ayrshire, from 1742 to 1791. But, as is also well known, the attempt of his kirk session to penalize the minor landowner Gavin Hamilton for not attending Church, breaches of Sabbath behaviour and failure to hold family prayers, failed in the presbytery.[49]

The emphasis within Calvinism appears to have undergone alteration with the rise of the new tide of evangelicalism. Calvinism in Scotland had stressed the importance of the community, and its discipline was based on the claims of the local congregation as a social body to be part of the true Church. The new evangelism was individualist, and its emphasis does much to explain the religious ethos of the early nineteenth century with its distaste for communally based social activity, its insistence on the conversion, inspiration and commitment of the individual Christian and its relative indifference to the specific denominational group to which people belonged. In no sense did such ideas discourage traditional morality, but their exponents saw no particular merit in public penance, and indeed might view it as an encouragement to spiritual pride on the part of observers. Perhaps it was under this influence that early in the nineteenth century the Church of Scotland started to discourage the practice of public discipline.[50]

The increasing mobility of the population, as economic development provided new locations for activity, was transforming the

---

48 *Scots Magazine*, 1780, pp. 238–41.
49 Maurice Lindsay, *Robert Burns* (London, 1954), p. 77.
50 K. Boyd, *Scottish Church Attitudes to Sex, Marriage and the Family* (Edinburgh, 1980).

scene. All the signs point to a vastly enhanced mobility of people. Movement could involve minor journeying to markets, which now were much more frequent and busier, marriage at a greater distance than in the past, temporary or long-term movement for work or emigration overseas. It was most conspicuous culturally when Highlanders came to live and work in the Lowlands, but this was just one facet. The change is perhaps best, though fictionally, described in John Galt's novel, *Annals of the Parish*. Urban expansion, new centres of industry, the erection and successful management of turnpikes, all bear witness to the flow of people to new places and new opportunities and to a new scale of urban concentration.[51] There was bound to come a time when facilities for espionage, by the tapping of personal knowledge and by correspondence with distant ministers, simply could not maintain the level of information required for effective discipline. Presbytery records of individual cases show how important personal knowledge on the part of some ministers could be in the pursuit of wrongdoers. A situation in which a few ministers saw no advantage to morality in prosecuting offenders would restrict the sources of information for many other parishes. The striking feature of Scottish church discipline in the early eighteenth century, that it extended over the whole country and there was no refuge for the common people from it, could be destroyed by inertia on the part of only a few places. Work on English church discipline in the early seventeenth century shows that the main reason that it was not effective was that offenders could move away and not be traced.[52]

Mobility also made easier the spread of irregular marriage. Though this practice seems to have grown as a fashion on its own, it was available in fact only to those able to get to one of the few bigger towns; yet in the 1750s this had become possible for some couples in relatively remote places. The comment in the *OSA* for Whitburn, that nearly all the marriages were irregular, was typical of the hinterland of a city by the end of the eighteenth century.[53] (Irregular marriage is discussed in chapter 4). A high level of

51 Unpublished work by Ian Whyte, which has been generously communicated, shows that in Scotland the urban sector grew more rapidly in the eighteenth century than in any other European country, and that much of this growth was in the small towns.

52 M. Ingram, 'Church courts and neighbourhood: aspects of social control in Wiltshire, 1600–41' (unpublished D.Phil. thesis, Oxford University, 1976); E. H. Stenning, 'Manx Spiritual Laws', *Isle of Man Natural History and Antiquarian Society Proceedings* v (1942–56).

53 *OSA* xvii (1796), p. 300.

irregular marriage meant that until a couple entered such a marriage in the parish register, paying the fine due, an event which might wait on pregnancy, it would not be clear to the elders whether cohabitation was marital or not. The fashion for irregular marriage was not only a cause of weakened church discipline, but also a sign that the Church's concept of social order was no longer adhered to by many of the younger people, who were prepared to ignore its rulings.

The Church itself in Scotland had been abandoned by 1770 by many, perhaps 100,000 people, those adhering to dissenting presbyterian communions. The spread of dissent did not directly damage discipline: many of the local communities now outwith the establishment had a higher commitment to traditional morality than the average units of the Church of Scotland, and in any case that Church considered itself as still entitled and obliged to exercise discipline over those not of its communion. But it made a further dent in the capacity of the Church to trace individuals, since the normal bonds of communication were weakened.

The weakening of discipline was usually first shown in the readiness of a session to accept extra money, above the level of fine, often specifically labelled for the poor, instead of public appearances. This was not a totally new feature: in 1585 the Provost of Elgin, while confessing his fornication to the session, had argued that 'repentance consistit not in the external gestoir of the bodie . . . but in the hart', and had been let off external gestures in return for repairing the north window of the church.[54] But a provost was in an unusually strong position for persuasion. In 1673 in Dalkeith, Francis Scot, perhaps a man with powerful local kin, had been unable to persuade the session to let him buy himself off appearances, but was more effective at presbytery level, and there struck a bargain for one appearance only. In some places, for instance Ellon, Aberdeenshire, buying off penance had become regular in the 1750s, in Foveran in the 1760s. Dalrymple session (Ayrshire) in 1769 made a ruling that anyone could avoid appearances by paying half a guinea; the fact that most offenders did not, and still faced public penance, shows that this level of payment was beyond their means. The practice became more general in the 1770s. A good example of the type of appeal comes in Straiton, Ayrshire, from 1778:

---

54 W. Cramond and S. Ree (eds), *The Records of Elgin*, vol. 2 (New Spalding Club, Aberdeen, 1908), p. 4.

Revd. Sir,

This serves to inform you that Margaret Campbell my father's servant says she is with child and that it is mine. I think myself unlucky that I cannot deny the accusation and in order to give the church as little unnecessary trouble as in my power to do hereby acknowledge the charge. I am sorry for the offence given to God, I regret the injury done the poor Girl, and lament the breach of good order in society. I trust my future conduct will make it appear that my repentance is most sincere. I am ready to atone for the crime but am unwilling to make a public appearance which I hope your regulations will dispense with upon giving something to the poor.

(sic subscrivitur) James Mcharg.

The session, delighted, so it said, with the respectful language and the true spirit of penitence, readily agreed.

The ability to write a smooth letter, still more the ability to find an adequate sum of money, meant that such evasions of penance were more likely to be achieved by men than by women. Before the 1770s most sessions would not have responded, as did Straiton, to either, and indeed on occasions when some sort of special pleading was used, there was likely to be unease if it were effective. In the case quoted in chapter 7 from Spott (1697), the minister was not happy that the offending man obtained remission of penance while the girl still had to do it. By contrast in Grange, 1771, the presbytery advised the session to let an adulterer off penance on payment of 100 pounds Scots, while the woman made seven appearances. The intervention of the presbytery may have been based on some unrecorded recognition of political issues in the case, but it is evidence of a slackening of severity and a weakening of the pressure for equal treatment of the two sexes.

If the opinion of some of those who managed church affairs had changed, the level of adherence to the rules by individual parishioners does not yet appear to have weakened. As will be shown, not only is there no clear evidence of a general upward trend of illegitimacy ratios before 1780, but also the percentage of men admitting their responsibility within a month of being named by the women, though it varied from region to region, shows a downward trend only in southern Scotland, and even then not to a marked degree. The figure for Scotland as a whole stood at 72 per cent in the 1760s; in the next decade it had fallen to 58 per cent (see table 7 in chapter 7). Though this is a drop, it is not clear evidence of withdrawal of assent to the principle of discipline among the people under it. (For further discussion of this subject see chapter 7). Indeed, in many parishes by the 1770s fornication cases, or antenuptial pregnancy instances, were brought to the attention of the sessions by couples coming forward voluntarily to report themselves. The absolution of the Church was still valued by those who had broken its rules and the practice of couples accepting being fined for fornication went on in some parishes until the end of the nineteenth century.[55]

Other elements in church discipline faded before the sexual. Church discipline had been stated in the 1560 Confession of Faith as a sign of a true church, and had been reasserted in the Confession of 1690. By Calvinist dogma a congregation not prepared to censure breaches of rule was labelling itself as outside the true church; in other words, it was abandoning the claim of the status of the elect for its members. Yet, the decline in prosecutions for breach of sabbath observance from the 1740s suggests that this dangerous step was being tacitly taken.

The slackening of activity over the sabbath was followed by less concern over irregular marriage. There is some reason to think that Church activity over premarital pregnancy becomes less common in the 1760s. So the weakening of discipline over fornication was the final stage in the dismantling of church discipline. That action might still be taken after 1780 is shown by a case reported for Ayrshire in 1809 which records a recent case of a girl resistant to discipline (she stated that she would not know who was responsible for her pregnancy until she knew the date of birth) who was dealt within a way not usually found even when discipline was effective, for the session appealed to the local justice who sent his officers to break down her door and enable the session to interview her.[56] But the whole tenor of the description shows that this event was seen by all involved as exceptional. In the early nineteenth-century presbyteries are to be found advising parishes to confine discipline to private rebuke. A traveller writing in 1807 spoke of the abandonment of public repentance by most ministers, for fear of causing child murder.[57] The attitude of the Church to the role of the congregation had totally changed.

The decline of public discipline has to be seen in the context of

---

55 Cases can frequently be found in KSRs. See also Boyd, *Scottish Church Attitudes to Sex, Marriage and the Family*, chs 3 and 9.

56 W. Aiton, *General View of the Agriculture of the County of Ayr* . . . (Glasgow, 1811), p. 162.

57 Boyd, *Scottish Church Attitudes to Sex, Marriage and the Family*, ch. 2; James Hall, *Travels in Scotland* (London, 1807), vol. II, p. 351.

major changes in Church allegiance, and accompanying shifts in dogma. Printed sermons of the later eighteenth century, produced by the established clergy of either of the two important parties in the established Church, keep a low profile on the issue of determinism, in striking contrast to those of Ebenezer Erskine of the Original Secession which hardly concern themselves with anything else. Robert Walker, who appears to have occupied a middle position between the ecclesiastical parties, also shows hesitation on this topic. It is alleged by the historian of the Cambuslang revival that Robert Wallace, at one time Moderator of the Kirk and not one of the Moderate party, sympathized with those ministers who had difficulty in accepting the Westminster Confession but who were not prepared to leave the Church.[58]

Outside the clergy there is clear evidence, from 1750 onwards, of refusal by the landowning class and others of intellectual influence to accept the intellectual restrictions of Calvinism. Efforts by the Church to have the sceptical writings of David Hume suppressed produced numerous pamphlets and protests in the later 1750s, and the relative failure of this approach led to many intemperate sermons. Evidence of the gulf in opinion between the more orthodox clergy and the society of landed gentry can be seen in the type of topic considered suitable for discussion in the *Scots Magazine*. In 1752, for instance, there was a long article discussing anti-Trinitarian opinions.[59] Though the Church of Scotland never formally accepted the authority of the Councils of Nicaea and Chalcedon in which Trinitarianism was defined, it had always taken the dogma expressed by these Councils for granted and did not sympathize with any questioning of it.

The ecclesiastical and intellectual developments among the upper and professional classes meant that hard-line Calvinism, and with it traditional discipline, were under attack from more than one side. There was, by the mid-1760s, a dissenting church prepared to ignore earlier divisions, open its communion to independents and episcopalians and preach free grace. The Episcopal Church was also allowing room for Arminian opinions which would not have been acceptable in its early days, and becoming more attractive to those who did not adhere to Jacobitism. The dominant party in the Church of Scotland was

---

58 Robert Walker, *Sermons on Practical Subjects* (London, 1826); Arthur Fawcett, *The Cambuslang Revival*.

59 *Scots Magazine*, June 1752, pp. 302–3.

evading the preaching of Calvinism and was not alone in this. The traditional discipline, which had not, except in the mid-seventeenth century, been applied to the upper classes, now had a weakened intellectual base there, even before this group began to adhere to the more distinctive humanitarianism derived from the Enlightenment.

Public acceptance of Calvinist dogma had been the mainstay of discipline, and the continuation in most of Scotland of low levels of illegitimacy and the readiness of fathers of bastards to accept responsibility for them suggests that this general support continued. But discipline had also relied on the network of communications and the monitoring of movement from one parish to another. When those moving from one parish to another had had to present a 'testificat', and while the great bulk of the population in a parish was personally known to members of a kirk session, discipline was effective. But even a few areas of well-established dissent, or a group of ministers known to be unwilling to enquire closely into the behaviour of individuals, would cause the system to break down. With the increased mobility of the population in the last quarter of the eighteenth century, and the intellectual and doctrinal opinions in the upper class which were becoming manifest from the 1760s, it was no longer possible for the Church to keep up the old system of control. It was abandoned from the top while still acceptable to the bulk of the people.

3

Regular Marriage

Before we can discuss the bearing of children out of wedlock, it is essential first to establish what actually constituted wedlock, a question by no means as straightforward as it might appear. Scots law allowed for the legitimation of children by the subsequent marriage of their parents, but in this enquiry we are concerned only with the status of children at birth. In any case such legitimation was a legal feature of interest only to those owning property.

Post-Reformation Scotland adhered on marriage to what a modern historian has called a 'blindingly simple doctrine' and a nineteenth century English judge labelled 'monstrous' and 'barbarous', that is the definition that if two people capable of marriage freely declared that they married each other, this constituted a valid marriage.[1] Marriage was not a sacrament: in the wording of the *Westminster Directory*, the usual service book for Scotland, it was made clear that the minister declared a couple married because they had given their mutual consents.

The bars to marriage were few. The couple had to be free of any current marriage, they had to be capable of intercourse and of age (14 for boys and 12 for girls), and they must not be within the prohibited degrees of kindred or affinity. The prohibited degrees had been reduced after the Reformation to the list supplied in Leviticus XVIII, to which, by an Act of Parliament of 1649, a parallel list of similar relationships had been added. This Act would have become invalid on the passing of the Act Rescissory of 1661, but this did not result in any change of the accepted rules, and part of the 1649 Act was re-enacted in the Confession of Faith

---

1 T. C. Smout, 'Scottish Marriage, Regular and Irregular, 1500–1940' in R. B. Outhwaite (ed.), *Marriage and Society* (London, 1981), pp. 204–36; *Report of the Select Committee on the marriage law, Scotland* (PP 1849 xii), p. 15, Mr Baron Bayley, quoted by Lord Brougham.

of 1690 with the words 'a man may not marry any of his wife's kindred nearer in blood than he may of his own, nor the woman any of her husband's kindred nearer in blood than of her own.'[2]

Incest was not just a bar to marriage. Intercourse within the prohibited degrees, whether in marriage or not, was a capital offence. The legislation of 1690 was a definition of affinity solely in relationship to marriage. But the Church had added to this the concept of affinity established by sexual intercourse. There is evidence that, for a time, the State accepted this view. In 1669 Callum oig McGregor was tried in the Justiciary Court for incest, an accusation based on intercourse with two sisters, but one cannot be sure in any case dealing with a McGregor that breach of the law was the sole motivation of prosecution.[3] A later case, of a man who had intercourse with his deceased wife's sister (the case of William Drysdale and Barbara Tannahill, 1705) shows similar severity, but here the affinity link was established by marriage.[4] Tannahill confessed and was executed, Drysdale denied the charge and was banished. Some time after this legal opinion came to favour staying within the precise wording of Leviticus XVIII and acknowledging the implication of verse 18, which calls union with a wife's sister incestuous *while the wife is alive*. Baron Hume states that the Tannahill decision was held by Lord Royston to be very doubtful, since it went beyond biblical wording and the bible was the basis of the definition of incest. Royston's papers unfortunately do not survive. He was a judge of the Justiciary Court from 1711 to 1744, which gives us only a broad period of time in which to locate the change of legal opinion. Alison in his *Principles* goes further in modifying the range of the law. He holds that sexual intercourse alone did not create affinity, and that to prove incest the link by kin or affinity had to be clearly established and by a surviving link: a bastard, for instance, could commit incest only with his mother, since all other relationships were in doubt. The shortage of recorded cases dealing with affinity is not helped by misdirection by this authority. Alison quotes the case of Katherine Nairne and

2 For the Confession of Faith, see *APS* IX 128, 133 and Appendix 147b. The reduction of the scope of incest at the Reformation meant that first cousins could legally marry, and even David Hume's father and mother, whose widowed parents had made a second marriage with each other, were not held to be in an incestuous union. The Reformation also abolished the canon law definition of spiritual affinity, that is affinity created by sponsorship at baptism.

3 W. G. Scott-Moncrieff (ed.), *The Records and Proceedings of the Justiciary Court 1661–78* (Scottish History Society, Edinburgh, 1905), I, pp. 315–19.

4 Hugh Arnot, *A Collection and Abridgement of Celebrated Criminal Trials in Scotland from 1530 to 1784* (Edinburgh, 1785), pp. 307–11.

her husband's brother, Patrick Ogilvie, sentenced to death in 1764, and attributes the death penalty then imposed to 'morose times'. But since the couple had removed the affinity link by murder we do not need to regard the times as particularly morose. Indeed, in other matters legal severity by then was relaxed, and the absence of incest trials from the main collections is an indication that there was little legal enthusiasm for such matters. Recent published work shows that the civil law of incest in Scotland has contained inconsistencies into the later twentieth century.[5]

By contrast the Church continued to hold incest by affinity, which included affinity by intercourse, as prohibited, even where the link had been broken by death. We have no instances of the deceased wife's sister type, so it may be that the qualification of verse 18 was being respected. But in 1704 in Kilmory, Mary McMullen, a niece of a man's first wife, was accused of incestuous fornication with him. There are several similar cases in Caithness, for instance that of Wattin of 1757, when Margaret Sutherland was accused of incest with her deceased husband's brother's son. That these were not just a local survival in interpretation is shown by the 1742 case in Forgandenny of a widow, Margaret Anderson, accused of intercourse with her late husband's nephew. There are also eighteenth century Church cases where an affinity was alleged on intercourse alone. This was the case in Dailly, 1731, when a man was in trouble for sexual activity with two sisters. In 1768 in New Monkland the session refused marriage to Helen Wilkie and Duncan Shaw on evidence of what would now be called 'petting' between her and his brother some seven years earlier. The witness of these activities had been a girl of 12 at the time, but it was also alleged that 'it was the received opinion of the neighbourhood that they would marry.' The session stated that the evidence was not sufficient for a legal process. It also said that, if ordered by a superior court, it would allow the marriage. The Church's definitions went, by then, beyond those acceptable to the criminal lawyers, but though its attitude might force a couple to recognize that only by absconding could there be a marriage, it did not endanger lives.

The material that we collected from session registers did not contain any cases of incest by near kin, a fact probably resulting from the pattern of service by which young people of both sexes

---

5 David Hume, *Commentary on the Law of Scotland respecting Crimes* (Edinburgh, 1986), I, p. 446; David Sellar, 'Leviticus xviii, the forbidden degrees and the law of incest in Scotland', *Jewish Law Annual* I (Leiden, 1978), pp. 229–32.

left home before puberty. Even if a girl had been involved in an incestuous relationship with a father or a brother, it would be unlikely to lead to pregnancy, and it was on the appearance of pregnancy that the session took action. That incest of near kin certainly existed is shown by a very murky case of brother and sister incest in landowning society, which took up the time of the synod of Glenelg in the 1740s.[6]

Where a couple was free to marry the essential feature of marriage was consent. Consent, the 'one thing sufficient and indispensable' for marriage, in the eyes of both Church and State, had to be free, that is, not the result of force, fraud or frivolity. In the later years of James VI the Privy Council had been much involved with problems of abduction and rape, and had produced an Act of 1612 against ravishers of women, but in this matter its interest was not so much concern that the women should consent freely as to prevent seductions and marriages which went against the wishes of parents. In 1688 it annulled the marriage made between a young girl and her music teacher in which a witness had been in disguise, and put the teacher in the pillory.[7]

The Church, though clearly against forced marriage, seems to have been uncertain about fraud. In 1729 the Reverend Robert Wodrow wrote out a long debate with himself over a case in which a girl of 13 had been beguiled into marriage with the 23 year old son of her foster parents, under the impression that he would otherwise die. In spite of the fact that the girl had no idea of the significance of marriage promises, and that the Church at various times had stated that knowledge of the Christian religion and of the mutual duties of husband and wife should be ascertained before a marriage took place, Wodrow did not appear to consider that the marriage could be declared invalid.[8] Frivolous marriage was not a frequent event, but we have a case from Wemyss in November 1768 in which an allegation of an irregular marriage, made by an accuser with witnesses, was dismissed by the kirk session on the statement by the girl involved that she and others had 'made a sport one evening like a marriage ceremony', but had not proceeded to intercourse.

6 W. Ferguson, 'The problems of the Established Church in the Western Highlands and Islands in the Eighteenth Century', *Records of the Scottish Church History Society* XVII (1969–70), pp. 25–8.

7 *RPCS* XIII, p. 207 (1688); Sir John Lauder of Fountainhall, *Historical Notices* (Bannatyne Club, Edinburgh, 1848), II, p. 858.

8 Robert Wodrow, *Analecta* (Maitland Club, Edinburgh, 1843) IV, p. 33.

The issue of parental consent was one where Church and State diverged in the seventeenth century. The Directory of 1645 required children to request the consent of parents before a marriage was proclaimed. In 1644 the General Assembly had considered an overture which would have enabled the propertied parents of boys under full age to invalidate betrothals which followed fornication with women whose friends were stated to have 'seduced' the young boys into promises. The language of the overture was heavily slanted against the women. There is no information available on any decision reached in the Assembly, but the proposal ran counter to the views of the Church on the basis of marriage in free consent. In 1646, for instance, the Synod of Lothian and Tweeddale told the presbytery of Dunbar that it should attempt to obtain parental consent in cases where there had already been intercourse 'under promises'. The editor of the records of this synod holds that this shows that parental consent was 'virtually essential', but the evidence does not show that it was regarded as more than desirable.[9] This had been the stance taken by the Church in the First Book of Discipline, and continued to be asserted in cases in the early eighteenth century. Parental consent was desirable, and should not be withheld for worldly reasons. A couple with a recalcitrant parent would be urged to be considerate, but it is clear from instances given below that there was no real obstacle to marriage against the wishes of parents. The lack of parental legal power is shown by the fact that in 1758 a couple was led to advertize in an Edinburgh newspaper that their children, if marrying against parental wishes, would be disinherited.[10]

Parental consent came up in the lay courts or the Privy Council only when there was property involved. Cases in the later seventeenth century, all based on the Border region, show that in any disagreement between mother and father over a match, it was the father who counted as a parent. In the Ayton case of 1678, when one part of the Home kinship wished to secure a Home heiress, the girl was abducted as soon as she reached the age of 12 and married to the juvenile George Home in England. The Council had no hesitation in fining and imprisoning the couple, and fining the others involved, but it did not declare the marriage invalid. The penalties were for contempt of Council, to whom the control of the girl had been given, and for contempt of the Church by a

---

9 James Kirk (ed.), *The Records of the Synod of Lothian and Tweeddale* (Stair Society, Edinburgh, 1977), pp. xiv, 191.

10 *Edinburgh Evening Courant*, 28 October 1758.

marriage by an English minister. There are other cases of this period which show the Privy Council pursuing the same line, i.e. that the marriage was valid but that the participants should be penalized for having ignored parental wishes.[11]

Parental consent will be discussed further when we look at kirk session material, but it is clear that in the case of unpropertied couples the main obstacle which prevented sexual union being confirmed by formal marriage was, as elsewhere in Western Europe, the accepted need of a couple to be able to support a family. What scraps of information we have on the age of marriage in Scotland and the proportion not marrying imply that the Hajnal pattern of late and restricted marriage opportunities operated there.[12] For marriage to be feasible a man needed to be sure of a slot in the economy – the position of a tenant or a cottar in peasant society, or prospects of support as a craftsman. Besides the direct economic problems concerned with marriage there were also ones relating to the pattern of employment of young adults. Most young men and young women were working as servants or apprentices and living in the households of their masters. In this position it was not possible to marry. At the end of any term of service the question of further employment would come to the fore, and only for a small proportion was this likely to include the chance to make an independent household.

Church and State agreed on how marriage should be conducted. Regular marriage consisted of the proclamation of banns in the parish churches of the couple of three consecutive Sundays, followed by exchange of consents in the church 'in the face of the congregation'. The parish would extract a deposit, known as 'consignation money', at the time of proclamation as a guarantee of behaviour. It would eventually be returned to the couple, unless there had been an undue amount of merrymaking at the wedding or the first child was born too soon for conception to have taken place within marriage. Session material does not expand on the particular forms of popular ritual and joviality which it aimed at repressing. A phrase used to cover unseemly wedding celebrations was 'penny weddings': these were forbidden as boisterous and likely to involve scandalous carriage and drunkenness. Church and

11 *RCPS* v (1676–8) pp. 398–400.
12 J. Hajnal, 'European Marriage patterns in Perspective', in D. V. Glass and D. E. C. Eversley (eds), *Population in History* (London, 1965), pp. 101–43; M. W. Flinn (ed.), *Scottish Population History from the Seventeenth Century to the 1930s* (Cambridge, 1977), pp. 271–83.

State in the seventeenth century were united in disapproving of these affairs, though for different reasons. The State tried to prevent large assemblies of people where feuds might originate, and tried to limit the number of attenders at all rites of passage: weddings were particularly the subject of prohibitions by Parliament and the Privy Council in the 1680s. The Church's disapproval was made known by rulings of the lesser courts, sometimes in conjunction with burgh councils.[13]

There is some evidence that by the later eighteenth century the three proclamations might be made all on the same day. At various times the General Assembly or a presbytery had ruled on what days and parts of days the celebration of marriage should take place: the first Book of Discipline, for instance, required it to be on a Sunday and before noon, whereas later the Church tried to keep marriage off either Sunday or Saturday because the sabbath might be defaced by unsuitable merrymaking afterwards. Andrew Symson, for Galloway in the late seventeenth century, says that almost all marriages in his church had taken place on a Tuesday or a Thursday and while the moon was waxing,[14] but there seems to have been no ecclesiastical ruling on this.

Besides regular marriage both Church and State (as explained more fully in chapter 4) recognized as valid marriages which were not properly conducted but at which consent had been, or could be assumed to have been, given. The State recognized two forms of consent to marriage, *verba de praesenti*, a straightforward agreement, and *verba de futuro*, a promise to marry in the future which was followed by intercourse. The Church recognized only the former of these.

Marriage was considered to be for life; however, very soon after the Reformation the Church declared that divorce was legally available in cases of adultery. On the grounds that an adulterer should be considered legally dead (and the reformers would have liked to have had the death penalty applied in fact), the spouse was free to remarry.[15] This was stated in the First Book of Discipline. Eventually divorce became the concern of the consistory courts, but since these were not set up for some time, it was in practice

13 Henry Grey Graham, *Social Life in Scotland in the Eighteenth Century* (London, 1937), p. 186; J. R. Hardy, 'The Attitudes of Church and State in Scotland to Sex and Marriage, 1500–1707' (unpublished M.Phil. thesis, Edinburgh University, 1978), ch. 4; *RPCS* VIII, p. 496 (1684) and XIII, p. viii (1687); *APS* VIII 350 (1681).

14 Andrew Symson, *A Large Description of Galloway* (Edinburgh, 1823), p. 95.

15 Hardy, 'The Attitudes of Church and State in Scotland to Sex and Marriage, 1500–1707', ch. 6; J. R. Cameron (ed.), *The First Book of Discipline* (Edinburgh, 1972), pp. 196–8.

handled by kirk sessions at first. Parliament recognized such divorces in an Act of 1563. There remained the problem of whether the adulterer, if he were not to be executed, could remarry, and, in particular, whether he could marry his paramour. The Church's belief that marriage was necessary to prevent sin led to acceptance of the right to remarriage, but in 1601 an Act of Parliament forbade marriage to the paramour. The result of this was the development of the practice of not naming the paramour in the process of divorce, so that marriage was left open to the couple.[16] Women were treated more illiberally than men over property. The principle of legal death was used to prevent adulteresses regaining their tochers, whereas, because of the need to protect the interests of the heir, male adulterers retained their property. Women were accepted as witnesses in establishing adultery. Even if undefended, adultery had to be proved in the Commissary Court, and, even if it were proved, the case might fail on collusion, forgiveness and, at some periods, 'recrimination', in other words allegations that the divorcer was also guilty.

Divorce for adultery was a genuine possibility for anyone who could afford to go to court. But, at least in the seventeenth century, there hung the risk for the guilty party of criminal conviction for 'notour' or persistent adultery, for which the sentence had been capital since 1581. Nevertheless, the wording of the Act of 1581 appears designed to make conviction unlikely. 'Notour' adultery had to involve open and persistent cohabitation, continuing after warnings and excommunication. The few cases in which adulterers were sentenced to death were all ones where the offence could be regarded as aggravated by others, and seem to be examples of the seventeenth-century tendency to stretch the criminal law against offenders considered generally undesirable. By 1770 the legislation had, in practice, been modified. Mackenzie, writing in the 1670s, had commented that sentencing for the offence was an arbitrary choice between banishment, whipping, fine and prison. As late as 1699 a couple was banished, but clearly the Act of 1581 was not being fully used.[17] Still, there might be hesitation on the part of a wronged spouse in bringing an action on the grounds of adultery with such a law on the statute book.

16 Hardy, 'The Attitudes of Church and State in Scotland to Sex and Marriage, 1500–1707', ch. 8; Patrick Fraser, *Treatise on the Law of Scotland as applicable to personal and domestic relations* (Edinburgh, 1846), I, pp. 686–9.

17 Hardy, 'The Attitudes of Church and State in Scotland to Sex and Marriage, 1500–1707', ch. 8; Sir George Mackenzie, *Law and Customs of Scotland in matters Criminal* (Edinburgh, 1678), p. 174.

Divorce for desertion was more slowly established. An Act of Parliament of 1573 stated that after four years of desertion without reasonable cause, proved in front of a judge, a deserted spouse could sue for 'adherence', that is return of the deserter, in the Commissary Court. If this did not produce a return, the spouse could obtain letters 'of four Forms', later letters of horning, in the Court of Session.[18] The deserter could then be called on by the bishop to adhere, and be excommunicated if this failed. Divorce was then achieved. Attempts in the 1690s to get the procedure simplified failed, and the law stood thus, with removal of the action by the bishop, until the 1860s.

We have not found any cases in which divorce was being thought of as a possibility by a deserted spouse, though in one instance a minister enquired whether it had happened. It seems clear that the ordinary people whose affairs came under the scrutiny of the sessions could not have afforded to brief lawyers, still less to carry through the elaborate procedure in different courts on the grounds of desertion. The need to prove that the deserting offender had repeatedly been called on to return to the spouse was an absolute hindrance: men or women who deserted did not set up house somewhere they could be traced; they simply walked away from family responsibilities, sometimes to England, sometimes to become a soldier if male, or to cohabit with one if female. They left no trace. The sessions dealing with the wish of a deserted person to remarry would require the production of evidence of the death of the first spouse. The couple would be called upon to advertise for the missing spouse at the ports, or to trace witnesses to his or her death. To carry through these requirements was difficult, costing time and money, though not as difficult as the procedure for divorce. In June 1717 Helen Roberts in Torphichen, a deserted wife, admitted that she was pregnant by a man Thomson. 'Being asked if her Husband was dead she answered she knew not Only she was informed by One that was in the Ship with him that he dyed in the Ship going to Flanders And told she never heard from him since he went Away which was nine years since.' She was forbidden to have private converse with Thomson and the case, which would be one of adultery if her husband was still alive, was referred to the presbytery. A year later she and Thomson were ordered to be rebuked, so it appears that they got off lightly. Session would accept hearsay evidence of

18 J. Fergusson, *Treatise on the Present State of Consistorial Law in Scotland* (Edinburgh, 1829), ch. 4.

a death, and long silence after public enquiries at ports might count towards a presumption of death. In Stranraer in 1698 three years' disappearance and a search of seaports allowed the session to consider a husband's death morally certain. A woman in Pencaitland (October 1701), whose husband had disappeared in a nearby parish which was overwhelmed by deaths in the famine of the 1690s, was helped by the minister to advertize for him, and had her liaison treated as mere fornication.

These cases all show that the absence of divorce as an option could create considerable hardship. The Church was not insensitive to this. As these examples show, sessions could be lenient. In 1614 the Synod of Fife set up a system which, after public summonsing, would allow the death of a missing spouse to be presumed, but this does not appear to have become generally accepted. As always in the seventeenth century, it was the fact of a breach of law which the Church considered should be punished, not the intent.[19]

The absolute silence of sessions on divorce suggests not just that it was seen as impracticable, but that it was not thought to be an available procedure. This once again raises the question – already discussed in this chapter and in chapter 4 – of whether the Church held by one law for the rich and another for the poor.

Although the local courts constituted for disputed questions of marriage were the Commissary Courts, it was chiefly the propertied who would have recourse to such courts. At the level of small tenants, subtenants and cottars, it was the kirk session who would first be referred to on tricky marriage questions. Apart from its disciplinary function, the session was frequently called upon – especially in the seventeenth and early eighteenth century – to act as mediator in local disputes and disagreements, and therefore it is not surprising to find it intervening in matters concerning marriage. Thus, by means of kirk session records, we are enabled to move from legislation and broad theoretical views on marriage to specific local examples of how various aspects of marriage were regarded and treated at parish level.

The first stage was the promise of marriage. One difficulty was that promises of marriage were rarely witnessed and therefore difficult to prove. An unmarried woman who became pregnant might claim that this was under promise of marriage, but this

19 Hardy, 'The Attitudes of Church and State in Scotland to Sex and Marriage, 1500–1707', p. 180.

would not get her very far unless the man concurred. In Eskdalemuir (February 1753) Jean Linton claimed that the man responsible, who held a position in the church as precentor, had promised her marriage. His response was that he had made proposals of marriage but no solemn promise. He lost his church position because of the scandal but was not considered under an obligation to marry her. Even when a man admitted the promise he still might not fulfil it. In Troqueer (April 1759) Isabell McGarroch named John Ogilvie, who had recently admitted being responsible for another woman's pregnancy, as father of her unborn child. She claimed he had often promised to marry her, 'both before and after his guilt with her'. He 'acknowledged that he told the said Isabell that he intended to marry her and added that he continued in that intention till about a Month ago, when he received some Informations which made him alter his design of Marriage'. No further light is thrown on the nature of his objection, and he was exhorted to fulfil his intention of marriage with her 'as the best Reparation he could make her for seducing her to be guilty with him'. (Whether he actually did so is not known.)

The question of promise of marriage surfaces most frequently in cases where a woman attempted to stop a marriage proclamation on the grounds that a promise had previously been made to her. Kirk sessions took such allegations seriously. In Kilmarnock (June 1699) Isobel Robertson voluntarily confessed guilt of fornication in order to stop the man's marriage to someone else. The man denied promises of marriage to her, but the session stopped his marriage proclamations with the other woman until the alleged promise was either proven or disproven. In Kilbrandon (March 1759) Ann McDougald, on information that Alan Campbell was on terms of marriage with another woman, came to the session to stop the proclamations, presenting to them 'four letters from the said Alan containing the strongest protestations of Love & most solemn promises of Marriage within a month or six weeks time that possibly could be.' She also declared she was with child to him, which he did not deny. 'But he refused to adhere to his former promises of Marriage to her & declared that he would never marry her upon any account.' The session ordered his proclamations with the other woman to be stopped and 'desired Ann McDougald if she had a mind that she might pursue Alan as Law would direct'.

In some cases, the session realized that the woman was not really expecting to stop a marriage but was coming forward with a more mercenary motive. Two such cases appeared in the same year in

Drainie (April and November 1708), and a note of cynicism is very evident in the records. In the first one Ann Gordon attempted to stop the marriage of James Cuming to another woman. Cuming denied having given her any promise and said he could swear to this:

The Session alledging they had grounds enough to suspect he could not swear so, with a good conscience, as also supposing that if he gave the forsaid Ann a piece of money (which was all she was aiming at) she would pass from her compearance. They advised the said James that it would be every way his safest course to give so much to the said Ann, as would satisffie her, whither he had made any promises to her or not.

Cuming refused to pay her, and eventually the session agreed to give her 20 merks 'for paying her penalty & nursing his child', and allowed the proclamations to proceed.

In the second case, Christian Ritchie, who had had William Winster's child, wanted to stop his marriage proclamations. As far as the session were concerned, 'it was not so much marriage as a piece of money the Woman aimed at.' The man denied having promised marriage to her, 'and said if he gave her any money to silence her clamours, it would not be so much as she would demand.' Once again the proclamations were temporarily stopped, but a month later it was reported he had given her some money after all.

More unusually, in Kilmarnock (November 1742) a man complained against a woman. John Campbell said he had had repeated promises of marriage from Mary McKissag, as well as the consent of her mother and stepfather, but that she was now proclaimed with another man. He craved the session 'wou'd oblige her to adhere to her first Promises or see the Complainer have justice as to the Expence incurrd by him in his Courtship.' Mary McKissag admitted 'she was so foolish as to make & give several Promises to the said John to that Effect but they were only on Condition that all her Friends would be satisfyd with the Match and confessed she was once willing to marry the said John but found her friends against it.' Her mother was also cited and 'could not deny but she was witness to several Promises which passd between them & for her part was not against the Match but she found her Daughters friends were rather inclin'd she shou'd marry the Person to whom she is now contracted.' The session found Mary McKissag to blame 'for her rash Promises', but as she repented and had been contracted and proclaimed with the second man, her marriage was allowed to proceed. Campbell was told to apply to the civil magistrate 'in Regard the Session can do nothing as to his Expences.'

A most interesting case concerning promise of marriage arose in Kinglassie (April 1760). The church's precentor reported that after George Chrystie, foreman to the Earl of Rothes, had been proclaimed for the first time with Janet Storrar, a widow, Ann Robertson had put in his hands a formal Protest, on the grounds that Chrystie had given her promises of marriage both before and after the birth of their illegitimate child six years earlier. Subsequently she had put in his hands a Discharge, 'loosing the said George from any promise of marriage she had asserted he had given her for the sum of four pound sterling he had paid to her in order to be loosed from said Promises and allowing him to go on with the proclamation.' However, in the Discharge she still insisted there had been repeated promises of marriage, and because of this some doubt had arisen about the legality of Chrystie's proposed marriage with Janet Storrar. Ann Robertson was called before the session and reiterated the claim, declaring 'that she reckoned herself married to him till Death should part them tho' she was not to pursue him if he married another.' She had absolutely nothing to gain by making such a statement, and therefore one must accept the sincerity of her belief that, even if the man married someone else, his promise to her could not be denied and constituted in her mind a kind of marriage vow. The fact that this promise alone – even after she had released him from it – gave cause for doubt concerning the legality of another marriage (though, as Ann Robertson raised no further claims on him, he was eventually allowed to proceed) shows that the Church could at times take a promise of marriage as seriously as a contract. More seriously, even, for there are a number of breaches of marriage contracts in our records, and they rarely created as much consternation as the above case.[20]

The contract was, of course, the stage following promise of marriage and preceding proclamation of banns. In Dundee (February 1691), Andrew Jameson confessed fornication with Katharine Creightoune and did not deny it was under promise of marriage, 'but he sayes he was willing to Contract with hir befor

---

20 For English parallels, see John R. Gillis, *For Better, For Worse: British Marriages, 1600 to the Present* (Oxford, 1985), pp. 52–4. In spite of its title this work does not cover Scotland.

the scandall brok out but she would not therefor he is free of his promise.' The woman acknowledged that he had 'offered to contract with her befor the scandal brok out but she sayes she desyred him to delay it for a day till she payd off some small debts she was resting (owing) that he might not say he had maried ane woman drownd in debt and so render the rest of her lyff comfortless.' (It is worth remarking here that this is one of a number of cases we found where seventeenth and eighteenth century women demonstrated they had minds of their own.) The minister subsequently reported he had persuaded Jameson 'to perform his promise of marriage to hir'.

There is some indication in the material on fornication before marriage (see chapter 5) that some couples regarded the contract as equivalent to the later marriage ceremony and went to bed together on the strength of it.[21] Needless to say, the Church did not concur with this view. However, the evidence shows that 'resiling' from a marriage contract was not very difficult, although a hefty fine would normally be exacted.

Various reasons were given for resiling. When Canisbay session (January 1729) asked Isobell Rigg why she had stopped the proclamation of banns with Magnus McBeath she replied that

prior to her Contracting with him he gave himself out for more substance than he really had, & That he had no settled Residence, so that after their Marriage they would be oblig'd to go to service & that she chooses rather to keep in service while she is single than be oblig'd to serve when ty'd in Wedlock.

Mary Couper in Thurso (December 1727) said the man responsible for her pregnancy had contracted to marry her but now refused. He said this was because 'there were some things promised to him by her friends antecedent to the Marriage which were not performed.'

Kirk sessions were willing to take seriously any valid reason for not going on with a marriage; what they objected strongly to was 'flighty' behaviour. In Canisbay (January 1713) Jean Grott had broken marriage contracts with two men and laid the blame on them. One of the men was asked why he resiled and replied that it was the woman's doing; 'being interrogate if he was still willing to

---

21 By the State's definition, if the intercourse had been subsequent to the promise, Ann Robertson would have been able to claim that marriage had taken place. It is instructive that she did not so claim.

marry her, Answer'd he found her ane unsettl'd changable woman.' The session declared Jean Grott to be 'a foolish unsolid woman' who should be severely fined. Also in Canisbay (February 1730) Donald Banks, when asked why he stopped his proclamation of marriage with Barbara Mcferson, 'said his Heart did not lie to it Being asked if he had any further Objection said he had none Whereupon the Session taking his Inconstancy and Perfidiousness to Consideration appoint the Session Baillie to Decern him in a fine of ten pound Scots.'

One must assume in the above case that the session believed the man was taking the matter altogether too lightly; reasons of lack of inclination were generally taken seriously and listened to sympathetically. Two such cases appeared in Kilmory session records. In August 1707 Elizabeth NcGrigor's father brought a complaint against James Stuart for resiling from his contract with her. Asked the reasons for his action, Stuart

replyed that his mind & inclination did not at all from first to last sway that way although in a manner compelled to tender love to the said Elizabeth NcGrigor through the continuall importunity of his friends and relations who in some measure contrary to his own will contracted them together. Moreover he added that he never had true affection for her.

The session declared they 'truly think him under no obligation to marry the said person especially considering that . . . the said Elizabeth NcGrigor did freely quitt with him, allowing him his freedom of choice in his marriage with any other he pleased.'

The session's attitude on the subject was made even plainer in an earlier case (August 1704). John Fergusson, when asked why he designed to resile from his purpose of marrying Margaret NcMurchie, 'told that he had no other reason than this, that his Inclination did not tend that way & therefore could not marry her without the great reluctancy In regard he had no true love for her.' Being asked 'what moved him to proceed so farr on in a matter of this moment, Replyed, that it was the advice of his Friends, rather than his own Choice & Inclination.' After debating the matter, the session 'considering the Inconveniences that might follow upon the Restraint & Compulltion of the Session in a matter of free choice which ought to be carried on from a principal of Love and affection between parties Contracted in Order to a married state thought fit to leave him to his own minde, only forfeiting the Consignation money from him.'

As has been indicated, parents' consent was not a legal requirement for adults to marry, though, in the cases just discussed, *pressure* by parents and relatives was a definite factor when it came to choice of marriage partner. In Foveran (October 1736) a letter from Mary Young was laid before the session in which she stated that, although she had been proclaimed the previous Sunday with John Milne, 'it is evidently known to God & the world that I hade no design to marry him, only to satisfy my Parents.' She went on to ask to be proclaimed with the man of her own choice, Alexander Aberdeen. There was also a letter from John Milne entreating that the proclamations be continued. However, the session clerk advised that Mary Young's father had desired the proclamations be stopped, and the woman herself appearing before the session with Alexander Aberdeen, 'judicially declared their mutual adherence to one another and craved of the Session to be three times proclaimed this day in order to marriage. Upon all which the Session finding it was too Evident the said Mary hade been compelled to give consent to the said John Milne, did agree their proclamations should be intimate.'

The parental pressure in the above case was in favour of a particular partner; more usual was parental opposition to the partner chosen by their son or daughter. In Sorn (September 1723) Margaret White and James Wilson had three illegitimate children before they finally married, the delay being 'because of his fathers great aversion'. In Pencaitland (December 1711), when Christian Bennet gave birth to an illegitimate child in secret, it was said that the reason for this was that the man had uttered threats, 'he being affraid of his mother, who had hindered him to marry the said Christian Bennet.'

In Calder (July 1699), a girl's father objected to her chosen marriage partner. He was not able to give any grounds for his opposition but said to the minister, 'he might marrie them if he liked but he should leave his blood upon them and him that married these.' The couple were given permission to marry but admonished to deal calmly and tenderly with the parent. John Leckie and Janet Futt (Fossoway, February 1718) asked to be proclaimed, but the session, being informed that the girl's parents objected to the man, insisted on hearing the reasons first, which were given as follows:

1mo in regard he never countenanced her parents in the matter *2do* that he unsuitably inticed her out of her parents house both in the night and day time without their knowledge *3tio* that the match is altogether unequal in respect of parentage *4to & ultimo* that he never proposed any manner of way for her to live suitable to her fathers Daughter.

None of these reasons gave just grounds to stop the marriage going forward.

The two main reasons for parental opposition were economic circumstances and supposed inequalities of status. In Dysart (April 1671) the session allowed the marriage of David Anderson and Euphan Marton to go ahead in spite of her mother's opposition, 'the Session finding, after they had heard her, that shee asserts nothing against the young man, except as shee alledges, that his state is not so good as shee wold have it.' In Sorn (November 1707) James Brown's father objected to his son's proposed marriage to Margaret Smith 'because as he thinks of its inconveniency by reason of the mean poor circumstances of both parties'; the proclamations were allowed to proceed.

As parental opposition without genuine legal grounds was not sufficient to stop a marriage, it is not surprising to find the session experiencing little difficulty in coming to a decision in these cases. In the two instances where we found sessions having problems, it was not because more valid objections were made but because the parties involved were of higher social standing. In the Wigtown case (September 1719) Provost Gulline, a church elder, desired marriage with Jean McKie, daughter of a landowner, David McKie of Maidland. Maidland opposed the marriage, and as he was going to be away asked the session to decide nothing in his absence. The session asked the provost to do everything in his power to obtain Maidland's consent, but it seems he was not successful, for when they met again Maidland was still opposing the mariage. It is clear that the reasons he put forward were not sufficient, for the marriage was allowed, but the session deferred sufficiently to the landowner to impose special conditions, that the contract of marriage would be drawn up in the sight of someone whom Maidland would appoint and then be deposited with the minister or a member of the session. The provost expressed indignation at such treatment, 'whereupon the Session declare that they find it agreeable to the discipline of the Church of Scotland and the Word of God that all caution and deliberation be exercised by the judicatories of the Church, especially when parents refuse their consent upon reasons to the marriage of their children.' Such caution and deliberation did not appear so necessary to kirk sessions when members of the gentry class were not involved.

The other gentry case we found occurred in Belhelvie (March 1729). The minister informed the session that John Montfod, officer of excise, had applied to him for proclamation of banns to Susana Ker, daughter to Alexander Ker of Meny. The minister was 'straitned and difficulted in this matter on account of Meny and his Lady their refusal to give their Consent'. The session advised Montfod that they felt they could proceed no further at the time, 'upon which he represented to the Session that Parents their refusall to consent to the Mariage of their Children, is not sufficient to hinder the proclamation of their Matrimoniall banns, unless they give clear and convincing reasons, for their dissent, which he said, Meny and his Lady had not done in this case.' The session continued to procrastinate, and an angry Montfod appealed the case to presbytery. Legally the session did not have a leg to stand on, but it is clear it was thoroughly cowed by this local landowner.

We found only one case where the session acted to stop a marriage opposed by a parent, and the son concerned in that case was a minor (Kilmory, August 1704). Even then the session did not simply forbid the marriage, as legally it might have done. It called the couple before it and asked if they had promised to marry one another, to which they both replied that they had:

The Session therefor taking occasion from their Confessions to represent to them both, the folly, the rashness, hazard & inconveniences, together with the bad Consequences of suchlike irreligious & irrational promises how sinfull they are in the sight of God, and even the invalidity of their Promise in parlar is in the sight of man especially when done in their Minority and nonage, and how grievous it might prove to their parants, and other friends or well-wishers of their concerns, and especially when so Repugnant to the Doctrine of the Gospell, as incroaching upon the most holy & wise Providence of the soverraigne Disposer of all Creatures and in all their actions and that notwithstanding of their Proposing yet God would dispose as he thought fit and conveneint for them, thus the Vanity of their foolish promise being Represented to them.

Under the weight of such pressure, not surprisingly the couple capitulated and agreed to part.

The concern of kirk sessions with marriage did not end with the ceremony. There are cases throughout our period of sessions intervening in the guise of what might in modern parlance be termed marriage counsellors. In Dailly (April 1694) the session cited James Davisone and Janet McClure, his wife, for not living together. The man 'says it is not his fault for he is content to live with her, Janet McClure compeirs and says that she cannot have a heart to live with her husband at all, she is rebuked & commanded to live with her husband under the pain of being prosecuted for wilful desertion.' In other words, affection might be important in determining the marriage partner, but once married a woman had made her bed and must lie on it. Of course, men often deserted their wives by simply leaving the parish and enlisting in the army or finding casual work elsewhere, options which were not readily available to women, especially as most had children.

The attitude expressed in the above case towards a woman unhappy in her marriage is echoed constantly during our period. All the other cases we collected involved men actually ill-treating their wives, yet in not one of them did the session consider this to be justification for the wife to leave her husband. At least in the seventeenth century the session might impose financial constraints on the man to make him behave better. In Grange (May 1684) Alexander Gawin and his wife were cited before the session 'for their Unchristian & unconjugall way of living, he by oppressing & striking of her, especiallie on the Sabbath day, & she by deserting of him, & not cohabiting with him, he was enjoined to find surety that she should be harmless & skaithlesse of him (as also her children) in all tyme coming.' In another seventeenth-century case (Sorn, November 1697) the woman said she would only return to her husband if 'he find cautione for her life & fortune'. In this instance the session was not willing to take this on themselves but advised her, 'if she would have him obliedged so to do, she behoved to get him obliedged befor a judge.'

The frequency of session intervention in wife beating cases in the late seventeenth century, which was not confined to events that took place on the sabbath or could be held to have caused public scandal (for instance by the wife taking refuge in the house of another family) suggests that there was, for a period, a real attempt to reduce domestic violence. In the eighteenth century cases are less frequent, but it is not clear whether this is because the attempt had been abandoned, or because violence had lessened.

In the eighteenth century sessions appeared to consider a promise of good behaviour in cases of marital violence sufficient without legal obligations. In Canisbay (August 1729) it was reported that Andrew Groat and Katharine Lyell were living apart. He, being Interrogate why he put away his Wife said he did what in him lay to persuade her to stay with him but she would not. The said Katharine Lyell being Interrogate why she would not Cohabite with her Husband said she was afraid of her Life if she would stay with him Being asked if he did strick her at any time said he did not but threatened her oft times & he hounded out his sister-in-law to abuse & threaten her & she accordingly came to the House & did so. The said Andrew Groat being asked if he would accept of his Wife again said he would wherupon being Exhorted to be more loving & tender of her than formerly & set up the Worship of God in his Family & she being Exhorted to be more obedient.

The sting in the tail of those last words shows all too clearly how the Church viewed a woman's role in a marriage.

By the second half of the eighteenth century sessions would be unlikely to intervene even if they knew a married couple was not cohabiting. However, in Kenmore (June 1755) the woman involved brought her own case before the session. Florence McGrigor complained that her husband, Donald McGregor, 'us'd her barbarously for these four years past, and that she is not able to bear with the bad usage she meets from him and declares that if he does not treat her better she'll be obliged to part with him, therefore begg'd the session to do what they can to redress her grievances.' The husband, when cited, 'compear'd professing his sorrow for what differences had happened betwixt him and his wife, and promises that, God assisting, he shall so behave towards her as becomes a husband to his wife; And she promises that she shall be dutiful as becomes a wife.' The final exhortation comes as no surprise by now, and one can hardly avoid a certain cynicism concerning the promises of a man who had ill-treated his wife for four years, but at least in the changing climate of the time, the kirk session was less likely to interfere if she did in the end go off and leave him.

In its approach to marital disharmony the Kirk did not discriminate between couples married regularly and those with irregular marriages. The emphasis on consent meant that marriage was marriage however arrived at. The ramifications of irregular marriage form the subject of our next chapter.

4

Irregular Marriage

Besides regular marriage there was also irregular marriage. Both Church and State accepted as valid marriages which were conducted in violation of their regulations, though they appear to have differed in their definitions. The civil law of Scotland accepted what it defined as *verba de praesenti*, that is the statement of consent, but for proof of this event it required evidence. Witnesses would be accepted, if male, but other evidence could be used. For instance, letters from a man to a woman in which she was referred to as wife would be evidence of marriage. Evidence that other people called a woman a man's wife in his presence and without contradiction was not enough to establish a marriage.[1]

A further form of marriage accepted by the State was *verba de futuro*, a promise of marriage in the future, followed by sexual intercourse. Here again, some sort of evidence about the promise would be required. Our cases suggest strongly that this form of marriage was not accepted by the Church. There were two cases in 1759, one in Troqueer, the other in Kilbrandon, where evidence was advanced of a promise of marriage followed by intercourse, and where the man admitted that there had been promises of marriage, but the session accepted neither as marriages. In Troqueer the session exhorted the man 'to fulfil his Intentions of Marriage'; in Kilbrandon the session ordered the stop of proclamations of the man with another woman and reminded the girl to whom the promises had been made that she might pursue the man at law. Both cases would have been held to constitute valid

---

1 Ronald D. Ireland, 'Husband and Wife', in *Introduction to Scottish Legal History* (Stair Society, Edinburgh, 1958), pp. 82–9; J. R. Hardy, 'The Attitudes of Church and State in Scotland to Sex and Marriage' (unpublished M.Phil. thesis, Edinburgh University, 1978). Failure to recognize that Church and State used different law is responsible for some confusion in Patrick Fraser, *Treatise on the Law of Scotland as applicable to Personal and Domestic Relations* (Edinburgh, 1846), I, p. 334 on irregular marriage.

irregular marriages by the civil law, but neither was accepted by the Church. In cases where a couple wished such a marriage to be recognized by the Church the session would call on them to declare their contract in public, and then would hold them to be married.

It has been held that there was a third form of irregular marriage in Scotland, 'by habit and repute'. Lawyers prefer to consider this not as a separate form of marriage, but as a separate type of evidence by which marriage might be established. A couple living together and regarded as married could claim to be married by habit and repute, and the lawyers would hold that at some time a promise would have been exchanged. It was very rarely that a claim for acceptance of such a marriage came up in church material; except in times of civil disturbance it would be difficult for a couple to cohabit for any length of time without enquiry by the local session as to their marital status. Normally the couple would be asked to produce a certificate of marriage or a 'testificat' stating marriage from another parish. Correspondence would be initiated to enquire into the couple's background.

An exception to this occurred in Dumfries (August 1696). James Allan,

being brought before the session, with Janet Vetch whom he owned as his wife these eight years since they came from Ireland; And both of them judicially acknowledged that they were never married, tho they have cohabited together as married persons these foresaid eight years, and have four children, and were reputed married persons in the place where they lived in Ireland before they came hither. Whereupon the session committed them to the Magistrate to be secured in prison untill they gave Baill to amend and satisfie for their continued fornication.

The date of this case is doubtless significant; by the eighteenth century they would certainly have been considered irregularly married.

In Longside (December 1749) the minister called a meeting of the session because Alexander Miller, now resident in Forfar, had a matter to table before them. His story was that when he came over from France to fight in the 1745 rebellion he had met a woman, Helen Jordan, with whom he had cohabited in Longside parish, and that she had borne a child to him, but that they had never married. He claimed that his reason for telling them this was in order to satisfy discipline for their fornication, after which he would marry her. The woman insisted they were married, and suspicion arose that the man's real motive in attempting to prove he had never been married to her was his desire to marry another woman in Forfar; this was borne out by a letter from the minister of Forfar. After deliberating on this, the session did

unanimously agree that said Miller cannot be looked on as a free man but that he and said Helen Jordan are to be held married persons in regard they had of so long time been habit and repute such in this corner and had their child baptised upon the bona fide of said presumption – therefore they did and hereby do dismiss this process as invidious and unnatural on the man's part and as a design projected by him for obtaining marriage with another woman.

In Dalkeith (April 1770) Donald McDonald had been irregularly married to Helen Mckenzie; the session believed he was already married to another woman. The man declared he had cohabited with a woman called Christian Sword for some weeks in the spring of 1769, 'and that his neighbours considered them as man and wife'. They had gone their separate ways during harvest, then cohabited for a further three weeks, after which she had gone back to her parents in East Lothian, where he heard she had brought forth a child, but he had had no further correspondence with her since then. The session, after deliberation, decided that McDonald's cohabiting with Christian Sword 'amounted to a real Marriage' and forbade him to cohabit with Helen Mckenzie. The case was referred to presbytery, and the minister subsequently reported the presbytery's 'approval of what the session has don in that affair being of opinion that she said Donald Mcdonald and Christian Sword's cohabiting together so publicly amounted to a marriage and that his cohabiting with said Helen Mckenzie was notour Adultery'.

It is often alleged that at some period a further extremely irregular type of marriage existed, handfasting. This was said to be a system of temporary marriage generally recognized, for up to a year and a day, which could be dissolved on the decision of the parties. The allegations of this system relate either to the Highlands or to the border area. In an article of 1958 A. E. Anton has shown that the claim for this type of marriage probably arose from the practice of joining the hands of a couple at a public betrothal ceremony.[2] Marriage normally took place in two stages: mutual

2 A. E. Anton, 'Handfasting in Scotland', *Scottish Historical Review* xxxvii (1958), pp. 89–102; T. C. Smout, 'Scottish Marriage, Regular and Irregular, 1500–1940', in R. B. Outhwaite (ed.), *Marriage and Society* (London, 1981), p. 211.

promise of a later marriage, and the formal celebration. Sometimes a long interval could arise between the two. In 1562 the Aberdeen kirk session claimed that in some cases this was as much as seven years. In ordering a brisker outcome, and at the same time prohibiting intercourse in the interval, the session indicated that under civil law many offenders had probably completed a marriage by *verba de futuro*.

The references to handfasting as an accepted form of marriage place it well before current memory. Martin Martin says, for the Isles, that it was 'long time ago brought into disuse', and Pennant claimed that it had existed at Eskdale fair 'almost a century past'; elsewhere it has been claimed for Langholm but with no documentation.[3] These references, which are the nearest to contemporary, clearly place the custom in the realm of old wives' tales. All the same, David Sellar has shown that there is good reason to see the Western Highlands as having borrowed from Ireland a pattern of chiefly polygamy, which Irish historians have called 'Celtic secular marriage'.[4] By this system a chief could put away one wife and take another. It was forbidden in the first clause of the so-called Statutes of Iona of 1609 to which various Highland chiefs were forced to subscribe, but appears to have continued at least until the 1630s in the Outer Isles, for Randal MacDonald of Benbecula had ten sons by five wives, three of whom were 'put away' by this system. However, such forms of irregular marriage do not occur in kirk session registers, and it is the evidence of these records in which the reality of concepts of marriage is to be found.

In the cases of irregular marriage so far cited the existence of a marriage was deduced by the Church from details of circumstance and behaviour. But the bulk of the cases of irregular marriage was of a more formal type, in which a couple had gone through the exchange of promises in front of a celebrant and witnesses, to emerge with 'marriage lines', i.e. a certificate of the event. The difference between such a marriage and the regular form, in other words what made it irregular, was that the celebrant was not the parish minister of either participant, in fact often not in orders at all, and that the formality of proclamation was missing. Marriage could be 'bought' in this way on a trip to town, avoiding the delay

3 Martin Martin, *Description of the Western Isles of Scotland* (Glasgow, 1884), p. 124; T. Pennant, *Tour in Scotland* (London, 1790), II, pp. 91–7.

4 David Sellar, 'Marriage, Divorce and Concubinage in Gaelic Scotland', *Transactions of the Gaelic Society of Inverness* LI (1978–80), pp. 464–93.

involved in proclamation, with no opportunity for either family to give its opinion on the match and without the local publicity which could prevent bogus marrying by a man already possessed of a wife. The motives for irregular marriage are discussed below: here it is enough to say that, apart from some criminal intentions, they were a mixture of independence, convenience and fashion.

Irregular marriage carried statutory penalties. An Act of 1661, blending the penalties of Acts of the 1640s, ruled that the celebrator should be banished and those marrying were to be fined on a scale which ranged from 1,000 pounds Scots for a nobleman to 100 merks for a person of low status. The couple were liable also to three months in prison. A further Act of 1672 laid down that no one marrying to gain a dowry or an inheritance should receive them. This legislation may well have been aimed as much at those who dissented from the established Church as at the control of marriage. In 1690 the Acts against nonconformity were repealed, but in 1695 and 1698 further tariffs of fines were imposed on couples marrying irregularly, ranging from 2,000 pounds Scots to 200 merks. In 1698 a fine of 100 pounds was levied on witnesses, and the penalty on the celebrator of marriage could include corporal or pecuniary punishment at the will of the Privy Council.[5] The continuation of legislation against irregular marriage was probably infused with the recognition that the practice was a mechanism for evading parental wishes. Consent by parents to a marriage might have no formal place in the law, but clearly parental wishes played an important part in the marriages of those with expectations of property. In practice kirk sessions registered irregular marriage when it was reported and took a small fine from the couple. Whatever the law might have laid down, a fine greater than that demanded for fornication was not seen as practicable.

Legislation against irregular marriage thus bridged the change from an established episcopal Church to a presbyterian one in 1690. Those who wished to have the services of episcopalian clergy were forced into marrying irregularly. The position of some of these clerics became easier after the Toleration Act of 1712, which allowed services by such episcopalian clergy as would take the oaths of allegiance and pray for the intruded royal family. But many of this body of clergy remained Jacobite, and non-juring, and so liable to prosecution. In the absence of systematic work on sheriff court material, we cannot say how often episcopalian clergy

5 *APS* v 348 (1641), vi ii 184 (1649), vii 231 (1661), viii 71B (1672), ix 387 (1695) and x 149B (1698).

were punished for officiating, but there was one conspicuous case of such punishment in 1755 when John Connachar was arrested in the Highlands for officiating as a minister and conducting a marriage without having taken the oaths. In spite of a defence which pointed out that there had been no qualified minister available within 20 miles, he was sentenced to banishment.[6] It is unlikely that any non-juring episcopalian minister would have been in trouble in the Highlands before 1746, provided he kept out of areas where the dominant clans were of Whig sympathies. The Connachar case seems to be a manifestation of political nervousness on the part of government. The last Jacobite rebellion was not long past, and in the 1750s there are several signs of government unease over surviving Jacobitism in the Highlands, of which the conspicuous ones are the trial of James Stewart in the Appin murder case in 1752 and the arrest and execution of Dr Archibald Cameron in 1753. The Connachar case tells us more about the political fears of the establishment than of its views on irregular marriage.

Irregular marriage in the seventeenth century was taken to include marriages that took place between Scots in England or in Ireland. After 1690 some of these might be motivated by the desire for an episcopally ordained minister; others probably from a desire to escape the controls in the approved system. The Church's priority in our period was to have it clearly established that a marriage had taken place: punishing those who had broken its rules over the form or place of marriage took second place. Withholding baptism was not, as it had apparently been during the period of the Great Rebellion, an appropriate penalty.[7] We have found no similar severity in our period. Marriage of this kind in England became common only in the eighteenth century.

Though there are several seventeenth century instances of irregular marriage among the landed families of the Borders,[8] irregular marriage was otherwise almost non-existent before 1690, as table 1 shows.

The figures in table 1 are the numbers of irregular marriages registered by couples after the event, in their parish. The sample is

6 Hugh Arnot, *A Collection and Abridgement of Celebrated Criminal Trials in Scotland from A.D. 1536 to 1784* (Edinburgh, 1785), pp. 331–40; *Scots Magazine* 1755, pp. 307–9, 311–16.
7 James Kirk (ed.), *The Records of the Synod of Lothian and Tweeddale* (Stair Society, Edinburgh, 1977), pp. xiv, 154.
8 K. and H. Kelsall, *Scottish Lifestyle 300 Years ago* (Edinburgh, 1987).

Table 1 Numbers of irregular marriages subsequently registered, by decade

Decade	Lothians	Fife	Central Lowlands	Central and Eastern Highlands	Western Highlands	Aberdeenshire	North-east	Caithness	Ayrshire	South-west	Borders
1661–70	1	0	1	0	–	0	1	–	0	–	–
1671–80	0	0	4	0	0	0	0	0	0	8	–
1681–90	2	0	0	0	0	0	0	–	0	6	–
1691–1700	14	4	4	–	0	1	3	0	5	10	–
1701–10	15	9	8	–	1	0	3	0	3	19	24
1711–20	8	14	13	0	2	1	1	1	4	32	40
1721–30	48	18	20	0	2	1	1	1	5	30	41
1731–40	113	19	17	1	6	2	3	0	9	11	48
1741–50	78	21	16	2	6	2	1	0	1	25	–
1751–60	40	30	21	5	2	2	0	0	6	37	–
1761–70	83	67	25	1	15	2	0	0	4	49	77
1771–80	9	51	21	4	16	0	0	0	3	75	55

not related to the population of the region, but is based on the 78 parishes used for quantitative work. The parishes available for the period of the 1750s, when Webster's census gives a basis of population size, provide regional samples ranging upwards from three and a half thousand people. The parishes used for the Borders had a population altogether of 4,968 then.[9] Table 1 should not be used for comparisons between regions because of the disparities between base populations, but is set out to make possible a study of when irregular marriage became common in each region.

The exceptional pattern of irregular marriage is that of the south-west. Proximity to the English border made it easy to slip across and get married by a Church of England minister, which by Scots law constituted an irregular marriage. The curious thing is that although Dumfries kirk session (the only parish in this region for which records exist for the 1670s and 1680s) cited the couples for irregular marriage, the marriages were *not* regarded as valid: each couple had to be proclaimed and married 'de novo' before they would be allowed to cohabit. The words 'de novo' indicate that the session admitted a marriage had taken place, without accepting the validity of it. In all the records we examined this was the only parish and period where such an attitude and procedure were adopted.

As will be seen from table 1, in some areas numbers of irregular marriages increased after the presbyterian establishment replaced the episcopal. In some instances this was doubtless due to principle – the refusal to be married by a presbyterian minister because of adherence to the Episcopal Church. In Dundee there were no irregular marriages in this period, but two statutes were passed by the session (August 1700 and August 1702) in an attempt to stop the pattern by which many couples were legally proclaimed three times in the parish church and then went off and got married by an episcopal minister. However, the more potent reason for an increase in irregular marriages at this time was probably the availability of deposed episcopal ministers who were willing to perform the marriage ceremony with few questions asked.

The period of real growth in irregular marriages began in the 1720s and led to rapid acceleration from the 1730s onwards. As

9 The numbers within the regions by Webster's census, for those parishes used for the 1750s, are: Lothians 3,492; Fife 7,277; Central Lowlands 8,191; Central and Eastern Highlands 10,334; Western Highlands 6,724; Aberdeenshire 7,954; North-east 8,269; Caithness 3,780; Ayrshire 4,517; South-west 4,101; Borders 4,968. The parishes used for the Borders region are Longformacus, Sprouston, Yetholm and Kelso.

will be seen from table 1, however, this was a phenomenon which occurred only in certain regions, and there is no ready explanation to account for the existence of irregular marriage sellers, as one might term them, in certain areas but not in others. By the 1730s Edinburgh was the great irregular marriage centre of Scotland, and the overwhelming majority of couples residing in the Lothians, Fife and the Central Lowlands went to Edinburgh for their irregular marriages. Interestingly enough, although we know that there was a very high rate of irregular marriage in South Leith, only an infinitesimal number of couples came from other parishes to marry there. We do not think that records mentioning Edinburgh might actually have meant Leith, but the anxiety of some celebrators not to be traced may have led to false locations – e.g. Canongate, Pleasance, Potterrow – being put on certificates.[10] Even couples from as far away as the Eastern Highlands tended to come to Edinburgh for their irregular marriages.

On the theory that a port like Dundee might logically be a place where irregular marriages were performed, we examined the session records from the 1680s to 1750. Irregular marriage figures rose rapidly in the 1730s, and even more so in the 1740s, but virtually all those couples travelled to Edinburgh. Aberdeen had no irregular marriages to speak of, and Ayr parishioners travelled to Glasgow. The latter town was a minor centre for irregular marriages, and most West Highlanders seeking irregular marriage went there, or to Greenock.

Before the 1740s most of the irregular marriages in the south-west took place across the border in England, with the occasional one in Ireland or elsewhere in Scotland. However, from the 1740s onward Dumfries itself became a centre for irregular marriages, and thereafter couples had no need to go to England. As we stated in chapter 1, the Borders did not provide one of the regions for which we measured illegitimacy, because population changes in that region were too great for us to have had faith in any estimated birth figures we might have produced. However, in view of the propensity of parishioners in the south-west to slip across the border to get married, we decided to look at some parishes in the eastern borders to see if anything similar was occurring. Before the 1730s, virtually all of the irregular marriages were conducted by

10 James Scott Marshall, 'Irregular Marriages in Scotland as Reflected in Kirk Session Records', *Records of the Scottish Church History Society* 18 (1972–4), pp. 10–25, and also (ed.), *Calendar of Irregular Marriages in the South Leith Kirk Session Records 1697–1828* (Scottish Record Society, Edinburgh, 1968).

English vicars across the border. In the 1730s and 1740s, a large proportion were still performed in England, but a growing number of couples went to Edinburgh instead; from the 1750s onward most of the certificates were signed at Edinburgh.

Absolute numbers give us some idea of trends but no indication of the proportion of total marriages which those numbers represent. Counting regular marriages in OPRs is very time-consuming, and given the state of many Scottish registers is often not feasible. We therefore took a sample of parishes where numbers of irregular marriages appeared to be high, counted the regular marriages, and, after adding them to the irregular marriages, too the irregular marriage numbers as a percentage of the total. These percentages are shown in table 2.

Table 2 Irregular marriages as percentage of total marriages

	Dysart (Fife)	Dalkeith (Lothians)	Cramond (Lothians)	Muiravonside (Central Lowlands)	Troqueer (South-west)
1721–30	3.9	10			
1731–40	4.9	19.9	23.7		
1741–50	3.1	13.8	24	6.4	
1751–60	6.5		18.3	7.3	26.5
1761–70	13.2	29.2		10.3	25.9
1771–80	11.1			6.9	30.4

More striking than these figures is the proportion shown in South Leith. Between 1736 and 1766 an average 25 irregular marriages were registered each year in the parish. Yet in the 1730s and 1740s the regular marriages registered often numbered less than 20.[11]

Scottish irregular marriage ceased to be a purely internal matter when the similar activity in England was put to a stop by Lord Hardwicke's Marriage Act. This came into effect in March 1754, and its draconian penalties of transportation for the first offence and death for recidivists, imposed on clergy disobeying the regulations, effectively confined marriage in England to 'regular' procedures, which included the obtaining of parental consent for

---

11 Rosalind Mitchison, review of James Scott Marshall, *Calendar* in *Scottish Historical Review* LIX (1970), p. 116.

those under 21. There was a plan for a similar legal change for Scotland; a bill to this effect was read once on 1 April 1755, but was then dropped.[12] Legal gossip has not passed on the discussions behind the scenes, nor has the press, so we do not know the reasons for the abandonment of the bill. A possible one was the expectation of opposition from the Church. There had been a great deal of opposition to the English Act, which had included theological arguments. Politicians may have shirked the prospect of even stronger and more argumentative resistance from Scotland. At a lower level they may have not wished to add to the clerical exasperation already caused by the landowning defeat of the Augmentation Scheme (see chapter 2).

The creation of different marriage laws in the two countries created a pattern of runaway matches. Acquisitive men and wealthy heiresses from England could attempt to rush to the border, often pursued by indignant parents, and be married as soon as they were on Scottish soil, usually by a local innkeeper, who also benefited by other aspects of their custom. The favourite place for this came to be the most easily available parish of Gretna, but such matches also took place on other main road crossings, Coldstream Bridge and Lamberton Toll.[13] The practice may have enhanced the rising trend of irregular marriage by Scottish couples. These may have seen irregular marriage as a means of rejecting existing norms and regulations without incurring a reputation for criminality. The statutory penalties could be ignored, since there seems to have been no attempt to enforce them after the demise of the Scottish Privy Council in 1708; couples would be expected to pay the charges, as for regular marriage, to ensure the entry of the marriage in the parish register and would have already paid the irregular celebrant. By the 1760s, irregular marriage, as table 1 shows (see p. 105), was a common procedure in most regions.

The irregular celebration of marriage was made possible by the existence of individuals willing to perform such marriages. In the seventeenth century the only name which recurs (in Dumfries parish) is that of Christopher Knight, across the English border. In the early eighteenth century, however, when there was less risk of the imposition of the statutory penalties, there were several deposed episcopal ministers who performed such marriages; the

---

12 T. C. Smout, 'Scottish Marriage, Regular and Irregular, 1500–1940', pp. 204–36.
13 'Claverhouse', *Irregular Border Marriages* (Edinburgh, 1934), chs 1 and 2.

two who appear to have done so most frequently in Edinburgh were Samuel Mowat and John Barclay.

Samuel Mowat, who operated in Edinburgh, first appears in the records in 1701 as 'late Episcopal Minister at Crawfordjohn' (elsewhere he is described as 'sometime Curat in Crawfordjohn'). His signature continues to appear from time to time on marriage certificates until as late as 1716, though he cannot have been as notorious as some other celebrators, for even at that date Wemyss session had doubts about a marriage testificat because 'they knew not if the said Samuel Muat be a Minister or not'.

A name which can be found more often is that of John Barclay, 'late Episcopal minister at Cockburnspath', who operated in the Canongate. The first mention of his name was in 1704 and the last in September 1711, when Cramond kirk session recorded a paper received from the presbytery of Edinburgh about the many complaints made concerning Barclay; that he

does in ane Irregular and clandestin manner marry persons sometimes within the forbidden degrees, as also married men who had their wives alive at the time, and many are married by him without knowledge or consent of their parents, or proclamation of Bannes, as also that he gives false testimonialls, to cover the sin of uncleannesse, and being often cited to compeir and answer for the same, still refused, and never compeired.

Many of the points raised in this denunciation of Barclay will be discussed later in this chapter, but the point worth noting here is the difficulty which the presbytery had in taking effective action against him.

Further west, the most notorious person in this period was Gilbert Mushet, deposed episcopal minister of Cumbernauld, who was allegedly deposed 'for swearing cursing fighting, drinking and many Irregular marriages of unfree persons'.[14] He normally operated in Cumbernauld (though at least one Rothesay couple were married by him at Largs); and couples from as far afield as Torphichen in West Lothian, Muthill in Lowland Perthshire, St Ninians in Stirling, and Ayr town, were married by him, from the beginning of the eighteenth century until about 1716. Muthill session recorded an irregular marriage in 1712 by Mushet, 'alias cuple the beggars'.

In the south-west between 1711 and 1717 a number of couples were married by a Mr Hugh Clanny, and in March 1717 Dumfries

14 NLS Adv.MS 34-7-9. We are indebted to Tristram Clarke for this reference.

session recorded that he had been incarcerated for irregularly marrying persons in the town and would be prosecuted before the next Circuit Court. In the eastern borders, Kelso session recorded in November 1713 that one James Miller, minister at Lowick in Northumberland, frequently came to Kelso 'and marries severall persons most unwarrantablie & disorderly, which may prove of fatal consequence by encouraging many young women to disobey their parents, & altogether contemn their authority, by marrying to dragoons, & other idle persons, whereby they expose themselves to great misery to the grief & heavy affliction of their parents'; the town baillie was to be asked to apprehend the man and imprison him if he was found 'about such business'. Miller continued celebrating irregular marriages through the 1720s but did so on his own side of the border. By the 1730s, there were two well-established and conveniently placed English vicars – Thomas Ogle at Carham and Thomas Drake at Norham, who performed the overwhelming majority of over-the-border marriages.

Aside from the regulars, there were occasional cases of rogue individuals who performed marriages. In St Ninians (June 1723), Alexander Cleveland said he had been married by 'a Nottar who dwelt at the tron at the south end of the toun' by the name of Mackie. According to Cleveland's story, Mackie had gone off 'to sollicit the Curat to do it' and when he returned told him

that the Curat would not do it under a guiney and added moreover that he would do it much cheaper for he had done it to severals formerly whereupon the said Alexander returning with Mackie was married by him in his house at the Tron and another partie from Dunblane one after ane other that they might be witnesses to each other who haveing used a forme of prayer spoke of the duties and made them join hands and then declared them married persons and ther they stayed all night till each partie drank about a crown and then he did give them a testificat of their marriage in name of some other as if he had not done it.

In the 1730s nearly everyone who went to Edinburgh to get married went to David Strange (sometimes spelled Strang); he seems to have been a one-man marriage-performing industry. In 1739 Dysart session refused to baptize the child of a couple married by Strange without a sponsor 'in regard that Mr Strang is under the sentence of excommunication'. In 1738 Cramond session rebuked a couple who had been married by him 'for having recourse to an Infamous person for Marriage', and another in 1739 for 'being married by an abandoned & excommunicated person'.

Cramond session also recorded in September of that year that Strange had been banished from Scotland. His name disappears from the records for a year or two, but by 1742 he was back in business. By that time, however, a number of other 'marriage sellers' had set themselves up in the capital.

There are certain names which recur throughout the 1740s, 1750s, and 1760s: John Grierson, George Blaikie, William Jamieson, Patrick Douglas, and David Paterson. In 1743 Pencaitland session sharply rebuked a couple married by Paterson 'for being thus irregularly married by a person who never had been a Minister & who was justly Excommunicate for pretending to be one and acting as one & for other wicked & scandalous practices'. Irregular marriers in Leith in the 1770s and 1780s have been traced with the aid of the Edinburgh directories, and can be seen to have had other sources of income. John Stewart was a sheriff substitute, Thomas Murray and Charles Johnston were schoolmasters.[15] There was at least one advantage to the Church in having a known set of men conducting these marriages – having frequently seen their signatures, kirk sessions were instantly able to recognize when a certificate had been forged! And if an unfamiliar name appeared on a certificate a session was likely to doubt its veracity, as occurred in Forgandenny in March 1742. James Rintoul and Janet Marshal produced marriage lines here signed by David Williamson, Edinburgh. The session was of opinion that the lines were forged 'because of some very great Informalities in them and also because never any of them had ever heard of one under forsaid Name in or about Edinburgh that used to mary People in the Clandestine Way'; they refused to accept the marriage as valid without further proof. At the end of May the minister reported that when he was in Edinburgh for the General Assembly,

he was very certainly informed by Persons he could credit that there was a Man in or about Edinburgh that made a Practice of marrying People in a Clandestine way and subscribed the Marriage Lines he gave them David Williamson Minr tho' 'twas generally believed that was not his true name but that for his Security and the more Secrecy he had changed his name.

With additional attestations by churchmen known to the session, the marriage was duly accepted.

One explanation for acceptance of these irregular marriers may be provided by something which occurred in Muthill parish. In

---

15 Dorothy Leadbeater, 'Problems of Marriage Registration in Scotland, 1700–1855' (unpublished MA thesis, Edinburgh University, 1973, p. 8).

1743 two couples were irregularly married 'by one Douglas who never was Minister of any Denomination'. The session 'resolved to apply to som proper judges to cause that Douglas to be apprehended and punished according to Law'. What actually happened, as reported by the minister, was that after being apprehended and put in the roll book of Crieff, Douglas had been freed by the judge there who had refused to take the matter any further. As early as 1701, Dumfries session, fulminating against irregular marriages, noted that

albeit Civil Magistrates of the Bounds have been frequently addressed, & have sometimes promised to take Course with such persons Irregularly Married, Yet they have hitherto neglected to Execute the Laws against them; Yea some of these Magistrates, Instead of punishing, have by sham-fineing in some small fine (which was either never Exacted, or not bestowed as apointed by Law) endeavoured to protect the Delinquents.

If the civil authorities were refusing to back up church courts in prosecuting such men, then clearly the Church had to learn to live with them.

By the 1760s the lucrative practice of marrying couples irregularly had even led to corruption within the established Church. Kelso session recorded with horror more than one instance of an Edinburgh session clerk or depute clerk, on receipt of a sufficient sum, signing a 'testificat' which stated that a couple were resident in the parish and had been duly proclaimed – even when the couple themselves never claimed such a thing – so that the parish minister would, in ignorance, marry them in his church. A legal collection includes cases from the early nineteenth century where certificates of proclamation had been bought in Parliament Close – in one case for half a guinea. These could then be presented to a Mr Joseph Robertson (later described as a convict) in Leith Wynd Chapel, who would marry the couple. In one case in court in 1818, the acting session clerk stated that only one in 50 of those called 'proclaimed' would actually have been proclaimed.[16]

The irregular marriages of the numerous couples who produced certificates with known signatures did not cause problems for kirk sessions, but there were many claims to having been irregularly married which did not fit into this category, and it is interesting to see how kirk sessions decided which marriages they would accept as valid and which they would not.

16 James Fergusson, *Treatise on the Present State of Consistorial Law in Scotland* (Edinburgh, 1829), p. 61.

It was not at all unusual for a woman to produce a testificat of an irregular marriage to a soldier who had already left the parish. If it was a straightforward document, properly witnessed and signed, then the woman was usually accepted as married. But a pregnant woman whose soldier partner had gone off with his regiment might well have recourse to dubious means to claim a 'marriage'. In Kingsbarns in 1710 Janet Philp, craving baptism for her child, said she had been married to the father, Thomas Alexander, a soldier, when he was stationed at Leith. The minister refused baptism 'because of the insufficiency of her testificat'. The presbytery appointed two other ministers to meet with the session, and they found

several contradictions betwixt Janet Philps confession and the alledged testificat of her marriage . . . first, as to the date of her marriage . . . secondly as to the womans name she being called in the testificat Jean Philp whereas she calls herself Jannet Philp, thirdly as to the name of the Minister she calling him Mr Barklay and the testificat John Bartholomew besides other informalities in the testificat.

The woman eventually confessed she was not married but guilty of fornication. When asked 'how she had come to that forged testificate of marriage she answered it was sent to her enclosed in a letter from some of Thomas Alexanders Comerads whose name(s) she knew not'. Dundee saw two cases in 1748 and 1749 of women producing alleged marriage certificates which were ascertained to have been forged by soldiers; it was by no means an uncommon occurrence.

Forged certificates were treated differently if both the man and woman appeared before a session and claimed to be married. It is quite interesting to see the different lines taken by sessions and presbyteries in the period before irregular marriages became commonplace. Sessions demanded either watertight certificates or else the declaration of witnesses that they had seen the marriage performed. When neither of these criteria were met they usually referred the case to presbytery for advice; the presbytery virtually always told them that if the couple swore publicly to adhere to one another the marriage should be accepted. Examples could be produced from almost any part of the country, the earliest occurring in Cramond in 1698.

By the mid-eighteenth century most kirk sessions were taking the same line as presbyteries, that it was the couple's public declaration of adherence rather than the ceremony or documentation that mattered. Again, numerous examples can be found, of which we will cite two. When a couple appeared in Eskdalemuir parish in 1737, the session, deciding that their testimonial 'could not be depended on, it looking like a forged one the names of the Witnesses & pretended Celebrator appearing all to be writ by the same hand &c agreed that they should be rebuked publickly and declare their adherence to each other as husband & wife'. In Muthill in 1768 the couple concerned 'produc'd some confus'd Lines of Marriage altogether unintelligible – In presence of the Session they testified their mutual Willingness and Inclination as Man & Wife – The Minister exhorted and rebuk'd them, declared them married persons and dismiss'd them.'

The ease with which sessions were accepting irregular marriages by this time may be demonstrated by two cases in Troqueer parish. In the first, in 1753, a couple 'confessed that they were Irregullarly Maried . . . But produced no testimony thereof but their own assertion'. This marriage was accepted, as was that of 1760 when a couple confessed 'they were Irregularly Married Eight days ago, in the open fields near Bridgend of Dumfries, by one whom they did not know, & whose name they did not ask That they gave him a Guinea for Marrying them.'

In dubious cases there were two criteria, apart from a declaration made in front of the session, which could then be used to validate a marriage. The first was something in writing, particularly a letter, in which the man acknowledged the woman as his wife. In Inveraray (June 1748) Mary Walker compeared voluntarily before the session, asking for baptism. She said she was married to the father, an Irishman and a soldier, and produced two letters from him. The session was at first hesitant, 'not knowing whither they were genuine', but after she made further appearances, including one before presbytery, it accepted her as married.

In a case in Banff (December 1758), recorded in great detail, Isabel Murray claimed she was married to David Frigge, merchant, but that he refused to acknowledge her as his wife. According to her testimony, he had forced her to sign a paper renouncing her claim to him as her husbnd; she produced witnesses to the duress she had been put under to make her sign that paper. Her proof of the marriage was a series of letters signed 'Your Affectionate Husband'. The case was referred to presbytery, and in February 1759 the session transcribed the presbytery's decision, as follows:

That, as the Law of the Land with respect to Marriage is extremely plain, and as it as plainly appears to us, that there is a full and explicit consent of marriage and marriage plainly implied between the said Parties in the Letters laid before us, and as the said David Frigge did not refuse these Letters before the Kirk Session of Banff, and has not chosen to attend the Presbytery to advance any thing against the authority and effect of these letters, the Presbytery judged that they had all Reason to hold the Letters as good and to have been really wrote and signed by the said David Frigge, They therefore thought themselves fully warranted to assoilzie . . . the said Isabel Murray from the Scandal of Fornication as laid in the Reference. But at the same time from the Confession of the said Isabel Murray, and as none of the Parties adduce any Proof of a regular Marriage, they find their Marriage must have been clandestine, for which they are as yet censurable.

The Church was, of course, following civil law in this case.

The other criterion, rarely used, was the one already mentioned, 'habit and repute'. In Lochgoilhead (November 1752) Colin McEwen and Catharine McKellar declared they were irregularly married in Glasgow and produced lines. 'The lines did not appear at all likely or sufficient but as they had Cohabite so long together and Publickly acknowledged themselves Married Persons the Session Determined to look on them henceforward as Such.' A similar judgment was made in Spott in 1767, and in Dalkeith (December 1769) the actual wording was used. Margaret Innis, demanding baptism, said she had been irregularly married to John Scott but that he had left her. Apart from a certificate, she was able to produce neighbours who declared 'That they knew that they lived in the same house and were in habit and repute in the Neighbourhood to be man and wife.'

In Dysart (April 1780) Charles Arrot, a soldier, asked for baptism 'for his child brought forth by Elizabeth Patoun whom he calls his wife'. The minister informed the session that Arrot's officer

had signified by a Line that he had lived with the said woman as his wife since June last – The man owned he had not been married because his officer would not give him a Line because he did not desire the men to have wives, – and that without such line none would proclaim him – He was rebuked for the irregularity of his marriage & allowed Baptism for his Child.

The phraseology of this case is interesting because it is clear that no marriage ceremony of *any* kind took place, and the session was therefore considering habit and repute alone to make an irregular marriage.

The parish and period where habit and repute were regularly used to validate irregular marriages was Kelso in the 1770s. In July 1771 George Wood and Christian Bold produced a certificate of their marriage dated at Edinburgh in April of that year,

tho' by their own acknowledgement they received it at Coldstream, so stupidly written that no regard could be paid to it. But as it was known to the members of the Session, and inhabitants of this place, that they have lived as married persons since that Date they were rebuked for their irregularity severely, and exhorted as Christians to live in the married State.

The certificate of John Fox and Margaret Turnbull, dated 6 February 1744, was 'so strangely written that no regard could be paid to it; but it having been known & attested that they had lived in this place habit & repute as man & wife since about the beginning of Febr last' the marriage was accepted. Many more examples could be produced, and by the end of the decade the acceptability of virtually all the irregular marriages in Kelso was based on cohabiting, not on documentary evidence. It must be emphasized, however, that this was the only one of the parishes we examined in which such a pattern was established. And – to point up regional differences again – in Troqueer, in the south-west, as late as the 1760s and 1770s more than one couple appearing before the session insisted they had not yet cohabited 'because they wanted to satisfy the session for their Irregular Marriage previous to any Cohabitation'.

The question of why kirk sessions spent so much time endeavouring to establish the *bona fides* of irregular marriages has two basic answers. The first was the desire of the Church to maintain its own authority. As discussed elsewhere in this book, this became increasingly hard to do as the eighteenth century wore on, and the very fact that a couple did not require proclamation of banns in the parish kirk in order to get married represented one way in which the Church's authority was being undermined. By insisting that irregularly married couples appear before them, sessions did at least assert a measure of control. Baptism was, of course, the Church's greatest weapon, for baptism continued to be very important to parents, and their child would not be baptized until they had satisfied the session. Baptism was a sign of membership of the Church, but it also had other elements of significance. In secular terms it meant respectability. In non-material terms it calmed certain superstitious fears. Unbaptized children were regarded as unlucky, and in north-east Scotland and the Borders they were seen as likely to haunt their parents.[17]

However, the Church's concern was by no means only with holding on to its own authority; there was also a very genuine desire to protect innocent victims. There was no ambiguity about a couple who had been publicly proclaimed and married, but irregular marriages were not so straightforward, and doubts often arose. Either member of the alleged partnership could have dubious intent. In Stranraer (March 1774) Janet Campbell declared she had been married a fortnight earlier to John Mean, skipper of the Pelikan Sloop, in the house of Alexander McWhinnie, ships carpenter, and that they had lain together as man and wife. She further declared that on a subsequent date, in the presence of witnesses, he had asked her to deny the marriage, which she refused to do. Mean compeared and admitted being in McWhinnie's house that night, but said he had been so drunk he remembered nothing of what had happened. He had

since been told that Janet Campbell came into the Company while he was there, upon which as he imagines his Commerades wanting to divert themselves with him carried him upstairs and threw him into a Bed along with the said Janet Campbell; but that he knew not whether she is Man, or Woman, for he had no Commerce with her as a Woman and that he knows Nothing of a Marriage and that he had no Intention to be married that Day to any Woman, much less to her whom he had never seen before.

As for the subsequent meeting, he declared 'he had no such conversation with her as she alledges, only he offered her a Dram if she would tell him who helped to carry off his two Barrels of Herrings she had taken from the Shore.' Finally he declared he was very sorry 'for having been drunk, and for any Indecencies he may have been guilty of in Consequence of his Drunkenness'. It seems clear that the session did not consider this to be a marriage, and accepted that his concern at the later meeting was solely for the herring.

17 J. M. McPherson, *Primitive Beliefs in the North East of Scotland* (London, 1929), pp. 113–14. Pennant is said to have made a similar observation for Banffshire.

In Kinglassie (April 1759), Helen Smith showed the session a certificate of marriage to John Lauchlan, but there was a query about a supposed previous irregular marriage: in 1753 she had gone off with a common soldier, George Murray, and when she returned she had told the session she had been irregularly married to a Robert Roberts, though she had never produced any evidence. Her story now was that 'a certain Friend of hers had feign'd the whole story of a marriage with Robert Roberts and had prevailed with her to narrate it to the Session for fear of Censure upon the report of her having gone away to Leeth in company with George Murray . . . & she pled that she was then so young as to be easily prevaild with to tell any Thing to save her from the Censure of the Kirk'. The session believed her story,

that from the mere fear of Censure she had been imposed on to narrate of the story of a marriage with Roberts & that it was entirely groundless and they agreed she should be rebuked for her indecency in following George Murray, her falsehood in narrating the story of her marriage with Roberts & her irregularity in her clandestine marriage with Lauchlan.

In the above cases the ambiguities connected with irregular marriage did not have any serious consequences, but there was a number of cases where a man attempted to repudiate an irregular marriage. In Troqueer (July 1748) Margaret Reid admitted there had been no witnesses to her marriage with Robert Rogerson, but she had marriage lines and said she had cohabited with him since the marriage. Rogerson 'absolutely denied that ever he was Married regularly or Irregularly to the said Margaret Reid he likeways Refused that he had ever cohabited with hir and that what she had said about the Marriage lines was altogether false & groundless'. The woman in whose house they had spent their wedding night testified that she had been unwilling to allow them to share a bed until Rogerson had declared he had married Margaret Reid that same evening. He continued to deny the marriage in spite of other witnesses' declarations that he had slept in one bed with her and referred to her as his wife. In January 1750 he was publicly rebuked 'for his gross prevarication Dissimulation and Equivocation upon oath'. It seems apparent that the session considered them married, although it is not clear if it ever got the man to acknowledge the woman as his wife.

In St Ninians (September 1726) it was reported that James Gibson, who some years earlier had produced a certificate of his irregular marriage with Isobell Hendry, and had in due course presented their children for baptism, was now insisting that the certificate had been forged and he had never been married to her. The woman affirmed they had been married, and the case was referred to presbytery which 'sustained them as married persons'. In two of the other cases we found of a man attempting to repudiate the woman he had married irregularly (Troqueer, March 1753 and April 1776) there was a further complication in the shape of another woman to whom the man now claimed to be married. The ease with which irregular marriage made bigamy possible was one of the strongest objections of the Church to it and was why, if the man was not a parishioner, a session would normally demand not just a marriage certificate but also a testimonial from his last parish attesting to his single state. Soldiers constituted a very real problem in this respect.

If we turn to the question of why couples chose to marry irregularly, not surprisingly we find bigamy looming very large as a motive. Admittedly, we did find a case where a man acted 'honourably': in one of the instances noted earlier (see p. 114) of a woman producing a certificate forged by comrades of her soldier lover, she confessed that 'when she was seeking lawfull marriage of him he said that he was married to another woman' (Dundee 1749).

Much more typical is the case of Mary Black (Troqueer, September 1767), who confessed she had been irregularly married to William Pitchfurth, a solider,

and that she did cohabit with him as his wife for some time, but that afterwards he destroyed their Marriage-lines & left her. And . . . sometime after they were married that she heard some of his fellow-soldiers say, that he had a wife in England, tho the said William denyed to her that he was married to any other woman.

As those fellow soldiers had also declared to some members of the session that Pitchfurth had a wife in England, Mary Black was not held to be a married woman.

In a similar case (Kilmartin January 1761), Christian Smith had been irregularly married to Duncan McUrachadair, a soldier, who 'was married to another woman who was in life at the time of his marriage with her'. She was asked

how she came to marry a man whom for ought she knew might be married to another woman, answer'd that she was imposed upon for that he produced a Letter testifying that his former wife died sometime before and was decently interr'd and hoped this would alleviate her fault. The session taking the Premises under their Consideration they found her too credulous and rash in a matter of such weight yet made some allowance for her being impos'd upon.

However, it treated her as an adulteress. The starkness of yet another such tale does not disguise its sadness. In Dalkeith (November 1742), Janet Mortoun acknowledged she had been irregularly married to Arthur Wier, 'and that she went with her Child to him at Glasgow, and stayed, untill such time as another woman to whom he was married in Ireland, came to him, and they both went off together to Ireland, and she and her child were left to return home.'

An even sadder case – because it reveals the disadvantages which women, with their low literacy rates, laboured under – was that of Katharine Sooty in Wemyss (January 1737). She returned from harvest stating that she had been married to James Ogilvie, a soldier, 'who made her believe his wife he had last was dead, and he a widower, that she had cohabit with him as his lawful wife, till his wife, who he said was dead, came seeking him, which made him flee and leave them both.' When asked, 'If she had any marriage lines to show? Yes replied she, and gave in a paper, which she said, she got from him, and which he called marriage lines: Which being read, it was a summonds he had got for a certain debt.'

One must not, however, seek to portray all women as credulous innocents. In Wemyss (February 1759), Elspet Wemyss, cited for having been found in bed with John Taylor (who had been apprehended and carried off by the press gang at the time), said she was married to him, 'that at the time of their marriage she knew that he had other two wives then alive, & that she intended her marriage should have been kept secret till after the death of the other wife he has in this Country, had it not been accidentally discovered by as Letter of his to her being intercepted.' Although it was the man, not the woman, who had contracted the three marriages, presbytery considered her guilty of polygamy, though she fled before discipline could be imposed.

In Troqueer (December 1763), James Thomson claimed that his former wife, Ann Crosbie, was dead and that he had been irregularly married nine months earlier to Jain Chalmers, with whom he cohabited. The session were informed 'that the relations of Ann Crosbie Declare that she was alive last summer and that they have never heard of hir death.' In this case it seems clear that the fraud was intentional, but in other cases there was genuine doubt. For example, in Moulin (August 1761), Donald Drummond and Girzel Cunison were clandestinely married, and the case was considered 'of a singular nature'. Drummond had been married before, and some years earlier his wife

became greatly Disordered in her Judgment, travelled, Distracted thro' the world; left this country (i.e. region) entirely, & has not been seen in it, for near five years past; but still there is no Evidence of her being Dead; & it is said, & believed in the Country, that she was seen in Life by Persons that knew her in Argyleshire within two years past.

In Muiravonside (July 1769), John Dick, who married Janet Cochran irregularly, declared his former wife had been 'a bad woman with other Men' and had gone off with a soldier eight years earlier. Since then he declared he had 'heard by transient Report that she was dead and that he had caused call her at several Mercat Towns but could not hear any account of her and thereupon thought that he was in safety to Marry a second time.' In Kelso (May 1766), James Wilson married Elizabeth Hutchison irregularly. When asked if he had any evidence concerning his first wife's death he 'answered no But that he had lived ten years in Kelso without hearing from her & that he left her on account of her lewd and wicked life – and had reason to believe she was dead.' In all three of the above cases the sessions involved did not sustain the second marriages, and the parties were all referred to the relevant presbyteries. Unfortunately we were not able to discover the eventual outcomes.

Women did not often desert their husbands; it was much more frequent for the man to go. Cases of women whose husbands had left them years earlier and who now wished to remarry occur throughout our period, and the woman was always required to produce evidence of her first husband's death before the second marriage would be accepted. The earliest we found was in Dysart in 1669 (March–August), where George Dole and Isoball Weems had married irregularly in England. There was doubt about her former husband's death, and the case went as far as synod, but synod could only advise, as presbytery had done, that they be prohibited to cohabit until the requisite evidence was forthcoming. Eventually, at the woman's request, the minister wrote to the captain of the company in which her former husband, Andrew Tyrie, had been a soldier, and

received a returne from him which was read in the session and did bear that Andrew Tyrie was indeed one of the souldiours of his company and that having killed his neighbour he had fled and after that tyme he never heard more of him The Session judge that ther is a probability he is alive because it wold appear the only barre that keeps him from returning is the conviction he hes of murther and the fear of his lyfe therfor.

George Dole and Isoball Weems were treated as adulterers.

In Ayr (August 1692), Nance Cunningham, when asked how she could remarry when it was reported her 'latter husband' was still alive, 'Answered she knew very well that he was dead, because she had spoken with severall persons who had come from that Isle where he died and was at his buriall.' It is worth emphasizing here, as discussed in chapter 3, that divorce was not an option for a woman at this level of society, and proving the death of a husband who had disappeared was difficult.

The incentive this gave to marry irregularly was well expressed in a case in Banff (January 1705). Norman Denoon was asked how he could marry a woman

of whose husband's death there was no legal document, to all which the said Norman made answer, that he had made all possible search for a Testificate of her first husband's death & went to Edinburgh for that effect did (as it seems) gett some persons who did give some declaratione that way before an Episcopall incumbent there, who did marry the said Norman & Isabell, & being again interrogate why he did not proceed regularly in his marriage with an established Minister of the Government, made answer that he doubted they would accept so frankly of the declaration given anent the death of her Husband.

However, as an irregular marriage still had to be ratified by the kirk session, which would not do so without proof of a former spouse's death, a couple were likely to be separated and treated as adulterers unless they produced such proof.

One question which occurred to us was whether this particular motive for irregular marriage became more prevalent or less prevalent over time. Of the 27 cases we collected of what we might term possibe bigamy (the Church would not so term them because, if a death could not be proven, then the irregular marriage was not accepted as a legal marriage at all), only eight took place before

1740, the remaining 19 occurring between 1741 and 1780. The loading of cases into the later period might be the result of increased opportunities for travel, and hence for desertion, but it might also indicate a greater readiness to evade the rules of society and of the Church.

The other great fear of the Church beside possibe bigamy was that a couple irregularly married might be within the prohibited degrees of kinship and affinity, in other words the relationship might be incestuous. However, judging by the kirk session registers we looked at, this was not a common occurrence; indeed we came across only two such cases. The first occurred in Stranraer, in December 1744. The woman was her husband's 'grand niece from the same father but not from the same mother, but from a second marriage, so that her grand mother was his own half sister'. The case was referred to presbytery who declared this to be incest and forbade them to cohabit. In Muiravonside (July 1771), the woman concerned was 'full niece' to the man's former wife. Presbytery ordered them to separate, but the man declared, 'whom God had put together, no man should put asunder' and refused to do so. Eventually a sentence of lesser excommunication was pronounced on the couple.

Another motive for irregularly marrying concerned not the person being married but the timing. As will be discussed further in chapter 5, married couples whose first child was born less than nine calendar months after the wedding day would probably have had to satisfy publicly as antenuptial fornicators. In January 1779 the kirk session of Mauchline, inveighing against celebrators of irregular marriages, specifically condemned the fact that 'such persons do frequently if not always impose on the publick, particularly the Church Judicatories by forging or antedating marriage Lines in Order to conceal Antinuptial fornication.' There is no denying the fact that such antedated certificates do surface at various times. The wish to avoid public appearances obviously ranked as one motive for getting married by someone willing to forge the date on a certificate.

In our period, it seems that kirk sessions tended to know enough about the lives of their parishioners to make this attempted evasion more often than not unsuccessful. In July 1716, in Kelso, John Lorrain and Marion Nisbet produced a testificat of marriage dated 3 May. The session was 'jealous that it is antedated and that they went away only yesterday to be married'; two months later the couple confessed the truth of this. In Wemyss, in February 1721, the minister refused to baptize the child of James Watson and Margaret Youel 'in regard he suspected the Testimonial of their marriage antedated'. The man declared he had been married on 3 April 1720. He was grilled by the minister about where he had lodged on his wedding night and why he did not own his marriage at that time, to which he replied, 'he knew no reason for that, seeing he was immediately going to sea, and had not a house and other things provided, his wife therefore went to service; and as soon as he came home in November last, he owned his marriage'. The session ordered him to produce the witnesses to his marriage; when next cited he declared he could not do so because one was dead and the other out of town. Nothing daunted, the session then told him to produce an attestation by the minister at South Leith that the witnesses had declared the marriage took place on 3 April, otherwise the testimonial would not be accepted and they would be referred to the Justices of Peace. Two months later the woman compeared and confessed they had not married until 25 November and had been guilty of antenuptial fornication. This shows a session displaying an unusual level of assiduousness in pursuing such a case, but kirk sessions did not like being hoodwinked.

In another Fife case (Dysart 1722), the couple involved, William Stewart and Helen Cout, clearly had not been able to obtain an antedated marriage certificate. On 7 October the man craved baptism for a newborn child, saying he had been married a year ago 'but knew not who it was that married them and that the brieff of his marriage was lost'. The minister insisted he must prove his marriage or else be considered a fornicator. A month later the certificate was produced, dated 28 May, 'by which the session find them guilty of antenuptial fornication and lying and dissembling with the session'.

In Dundee (November 1733) John Simons and Margaret Brown produced a certificate signed by David Strange and dated 15 May. The session was convinced that this was antedated, and the couple confessed that in fact they had been married the previous Wednesday, 21 November. This was not enough for the session, which refused to accept a certificate with a fake date on it; the marriage was not accepted until many months later when the couple produced another line signed by Strange. In Pencaitland in 1753, a couple cited on 28 October produced a marriage certificate dated 20 June but admitted they had actually been married on 6 October. Recorded in the session register was the comment, it was 'pretty evident that Agnes Sanderson was far gone with child'.

Concealment of antenuptial pregnancy, all the same, was not a frequent motive for irregular marriage. As shown in chapter 5, levels of antenuptial pregnancy were generally low. The truth usually emerged in any case. More significantly, we found a large number of cases where couples admitted at the same time (or within a short space of time) both to irregular marriage and to antenuptial fornication, which they would not have done if they had married irregularly in the expectation or hope of concealing their prenuptial sexual activities.

It is not difficult to discover other motives for marrying irregularly, for example differences of religious persuasion. In Wigtown (August 1740) it was reported that William Man 'declared he was of the principles of the Church of England, and that he was married according to the order and custom of that Church'. When the woman, Mary McKie, produced the testificat, 'the Session rebuked her, being a member of this Church, for asking marriage of the Church of England.' Far more common was for the man involved to be Roman Catholic. We found Roman Catholic men marrying irregularly in the north-east, the south-west, the Lothians and the Central Lowlands.

In Cramond (January 1732), John Clerk 'confest he was married by one of his own way of thinking, that he had no lines of Marriage because their Minister uses to give none, but that he could produce witnesses to their Marriage if need shou'd require it'. The session, 'considering this to be a singular case and how contrary to the Laws of this Kingdom for a popish priest to marrie persons', referred the case to presbytery. Presbytery advised the session to examine the witnesses and if satisfied to rebuke the couple for their irregular marriage. The couple proved unable to produce the witnesses, so the case was referred back to presbytery, who advised that if the couple adhered to their marriage the session should accept it.

Most irregular marriages with a Roman Catholic were celebrated not by a priest but by those Edinburgh 'ministers' or lay marriers who celebrated most irregular marriages. It is possible, of course, that there was also a private religious ceremony, but it was the certificate supplied by the irregular minister which enabled the marriage to be accepted by the session. Two instances in particular demonstrate very clearly why irregular marriage was a logical step if a woman wanted to marry a Roman Catholic man. In Muthil (July 1760) Margaret Key was rebuked 'for marrying a Papist', and the session clerk recorded that 'They had been refused Proclamation of Banns as is usual in such cases conform to act of Session.' In New Abbey (Jan 1770) Stewart McPherson, a Roman Catholic, had asked to be proclaimed for marriage with Agnes McKie, a Protestant; when the minister refused, they went off and married irregularly. In both these cases, although the minister had refused to marry the couples regularly, the irregular marriage was accepted as perfectly valid.

An important motive for irregular marriage was parental opposition. As was noted in chapter 3, although parental consent was not a legal requirement, parental pressure could be difficult to withstand. Parents had various mechanisms of influence: scolding and bad temper, more seriously a refusal to help with material goods or a portion,[18] and in some cases a refusal to admit an errant child to share in a tenancy or craft position. It might be wiser to present them with a *fait accompli*.

In a seventeenth-century case – long before irregular marrige became commonplace – we found that although the couple involved did not give parental opposition as the reason for their action, the session clearly considered such a motive would have been the only one to excuse their behaviour. This was in Dalkeith (October 1670), where Andrew Fleming and Janat Mitchelson were 'charged with the scandalous and unorderlie way which they had taken to accomplish theire marriage which they might have done with far more credit at home and lesse offence to the people of God Especially theire being no such disparitie between them or theire fortunes but they might have easilie procured the consent of all parties enterested'.

In the 1690s we found two cases where parental opposition was specifically given. In Dysart (July 1695), when John Brown was asked why he had gone from the parish to marry Jean Gairdner 'seeing they might had the benefit of mariag hear answered that her parrents wold not allow her to marrie him'. In Dumfries (April 1698), John Irving and Agnes Duff were married 'beyond the border'; they acknowledged their fault, 'pretending withall, that they were forced to that course by her Mother who was against their marriage'. In Dumfries, in 1722, two of the couples who married irregularly not only did not have their parents' consent, but were also under age. Both cases were referred to presbytery; both marriages were subsequently accepted as valid.

18 See the examples quoted in chapter 3, at p. 83, *Edinburgh Evening Courant*, 28 October 1758.

Cases of parental opposition did not disappear over time. In Troqueer (September 1763) David Fergusson and Agnes Stott 'declared that the Reluctance of Agnes Stotts Mother & that of hir other friends to this Marriage was the Rasone why they married Irregularly'. Also in Troqueer (February 1764), James Ewing and Grizel Alexander added after their confession 'that they would have published their Irregular Marriage long ago had it not been that the said Grizels Relations were very averse to hir Marriage with the Said James Ewing.' A statement by a Dundee couple (March 1733), who had been married by David Strange in Edinburgh, suggests that parental opposition was so obviously the reason it hardly needed spelling out: 'being Interrogate if they hade consent of Parents answered they hade not for hade they hade that they would not have troubled Mr. Strange.'

Couples choosing irregular marriage may have opted for privacy. By this course they not only avoided exchanging promises in the face of the congregation, where there might be embarrassment from some earlier courtship, but also exempted themselves from the local popular customs associated with marriage, 'penny weddings' for instance, or the procession outside the church at East Linton described in 1725 where a cake was broken over the head of the bride. We did not find any instances of a couple giving this as a reason for marrying irregularly, but we did discover in Dunbarney (November 1698) a representation by the beadle 'that the Collections att Mariages being his due he sustains losse by severall persones, who tho they should be married in this place yet for privacie chose rather to goe in to the toun of Perth and therefore desireing that the Session would condescend upon for preventing his losse'.

An interesting article on civil marriage in Victorian England may have a bearing on the increase of irregular marriage in the later eighteenth century in Scotland.[19] The author states that two groups of people after 1837 sought civil marriage: young people who had recently come to an area with expanding employment prospects, and who had not yet been assimilated to the local community, and those on the border where there had been a longstanding habit of marrying by the simple exchange of promises, and where this could be done on either side. Though there is some evidence of a high level of irregular marriage among landed society in the border area at the end of the seventeenth century, our general parish

19 Olive Anderson, 'Civil Marriage in Victorian England and Wales', *Past and Present* 69 (1975), pp. 50–87.

figures, which certainly reach a high level at their peak, follow a similar trend to those in other lowland areas, and do not suggest any particular difference in custom, but merely that on both sides of the border the nearness of a ministry of another discipline made irregular marriage very simple. The movement of people to new ares of work certainly increased in Scotland in the later eighteenth century, but the development of it does not fit, in time or suddenness, with the apparent upsurge in irregular marriage. It is also clear that many of the couples using this method of marriage were not new to the district. We therefore do not find support for these arguments. It seems more probable that this development was partly a matter of fashion, but also of economy and suited to those who valued privacy.

In the case of a last minute change of mind, the need to be married privately must have seemed even more pressing. Two such cases surfaced in Kelso. In December 1728 James Ker had married irregularly a woman who was betrothed to his own brother. In February 1740 Jean Ker married William Lockie in England, though she had already been proclaimed twice with another man.

Other miscellaneous reasons for marrying irregularly appear from time to time in the records. It has already been noted that women often married soldiers irregularly. Ann Seaton and Peter Mckenzie appeared before Troqueer session (November 1764) to confess their irregular marriage, and remarked that 'as the said Peter was oblidged to go to Glasgow tomorrow to joyn the Regement there they had not time to be Regularly proclamed and Married.' Seamen likewise had constraints of time on them, and another Troqueer couple, Robert Stot and Isabell Carlyle (November 1764) 'said they would have Married Regularly had the said Robert not been oblidged to sail to Whitehaven upon Monday or Tuesday night'. In an unusual Highland case (Kilmartin, November 1734), Donald Campbell of Barmaddy abducted Margaret Campbell, daughter of Dugald Campbell of Kilmartin, and took her to the Lowlands where they were clandestinely married. He admitted 'that he carried away the Forementioned Margaret Campbell, sore against her will though afterwards he obtained her consent'. In Rothesay in 1772 Mary McDonald married Samuel Saunders, 'a negroe man late the property of Mr Campbell'.

The question which inevitably arises, however, is whether, given the sheer volume of irregular marriages in the later period, it is possible to believe that all of the couples had a good reason for marrying in such a way. Perhaps the case of David McKie and Agnes Hannay (Wigtown, December 1722) was actually more representative than many of the cases looked at in this chapter. The session clerk recorded that the couple 'could give no rational account why they married irregularly after two proclamations in this Church'. It should be emphasized that the cases where a session attempted to ascertain the reason for a couple's marrying irregularly were a very small percentage of the whole. In the high-volume areas, particularly, such marriages became so routine that the session merely took a fine and recorded the couples' names and other relevant details without further comment. The fine would be greater than the fee for regular marriage but the avoidance of celebrations after the event might make irregular marriage a cheap option. Without detailed personal accounts of such events we cannot say whether financial grounds were of significance.

One can only speculate as to why so many couples who could as easily – perhaps even more easily – have got married in their own parish church chose to marry irregularly, and it does not seem too far-fetched to posit a *fashion* in irregular marrying. If the majority of one's friends and acquaintances were getting married in this way, then perhaps one simply followed suit. It is noteworthy that the figures for irregular marriages did not continue to go up in the course of the nineteenth century. This serves to support the theory of fashion, for once irregular marriage was no longer *de rigueur*, then only couples who really did have a genuine reason for marrying irregularly rather than regularly would do so.

The general impression arising from the cases of irregular marriage coming before kirk sessions in the eighteenth century is that the policy of the Church was based more on a desire for social order than on a wish to punish deviancy. The social order to be protected thus was conceived of within an assumption that monogamy was the law of God.

In 1670 the Archbishop of St Andrews and the Synod of Fife had threatened to delate (report) to the civil magistrate for fining and for suspension from the sacraments all those going across the border for irregular marriage.[20] There is the drastic decision of the Synod of Lothian and Tweeddale already referred to (see p. 104). But these examples of severity or attempted severity were not sustained in the parishes and, in any case, similar decisions do not survive for the eighteenth century. What a session wished to

20 C. Baxter (ed.), *The Synod of Fife, 1611–1687* (Abbotsford Club, Edinburgh, 1837), p. 187.

ascertain, when it looked into a claimed irregular marriage, was whether what it considered a marriage had taken place. When there was doubt about the exchange of consent, and no subsequent marriage by either partner had occurred, it would establish the fact of marriage by calling on the couple to declare that they married each other.

Cases of claims of irregular marriage heard in the lay courts show more uncertainty in policy, amounting at times to confusion. This may be partly due to the fact that the procedures were adversarial: one party or the other had to win, and there was a tendency on the part of the consistorial court to wish to award the decision on the grounds of good behaviour. A good example of the confused standards of the judges is shown in *Campbell against Cochrane* in 1752.[21] In this case there was evidence, written by the husband, Captain John Campbell, that he had married Margaret Cochrane irregularly in 1724. The episcopalian minister used as celebrant was among those excluded from the Toleration Act and consequently refused himself to sign a certificate. Twenty two months later the captain 'married' a Miss Jean Campbell, a relative of the heir presumptive to the Duke of Argyll. The captain persuaded Margaret Cochrane to conceal the original marriage and maintain the subterfuge of the validity of the later one by treating Jean Campbell as married to him. After his death, when the first marriage was claimed, the court disallowed it because Margaret Cochrane had publicly acquiesced in the claim to the other one. It is possible that the court may have been influenced in its decision by the fact that this case might go to the House of Lords, as indeed it did. On no occasion have we found a session allowing subsequent behaviour to be regarded as relevant to the existence of a marriage. Sessions might comment on the behaviour or reputation of a claimant, but not with the intention of considering it material to a claim.

The other impression of the lay cases is that they tended to be resolved in favour of the male claimant. In *Pennycook against Grinton and Graite*[22] in 1751, for instance, where the man John Grinton admitted having frequently promised marriage to Alison Pennycook, but only when drunk, the court could not ignore the fact that he had also talked about it in the company of her family, and so had to allow a marriage by *verba de futuro*, but the comments made by the judges, and by later commentary, show

21 Fergusson, *Treatise on the Present State of Consistorial Law in Scotland*, pp. 84–95.
22 Ibid, pp. 95–115.

that lawyers felt that no man should be held to what he had said in liquor. The male preference may have resulted from the fact that the cases were all seen in a world dominated by the issues of property, and as the property of a wife all went to the husband on marriage it was natural for the judges to see it as a male accoutrement. By contrast, the Church refused to be influenced by the issue of property. Property was not, in its eyes, an adequate reason for parental opposition to a match.

As indicated, the rise in irregular marriage is likely to have contained some element of fashion: couples would choose this method because others in their parish had done so with only slight penalties. In this way today in many societies there are aspects of fashion in the accoutrements of marriage. But there are other influences. Irregular marriage became a possible procedure for many with the great increase in mobility which occurred after 1750 and meant that now people had access to urban centres. It was also an assertion of independence and individuality: couples wished to show that they did not give obedience to the regulations of the Church or the practices of traditional society. The more tolerant ethos of the late eighteenth century made the imposition of penalties on the celebrators of marriage unlikely. But there does not seem to be good evidence that the rise of irregular marriage was a sign of the sexual revolution asserted by Edward Shorter. We do not know enough about the motivation of most of the women so married to assert that this procedure was the result of a desire for sexual freedom, and indeed this is unlikely since these women were legally free to marry within the rulings of regular marriage, even if not at short notice. But in choosing irregular marriage women were abandoning an element of protection. The scrutiny the Church gave to regular marriage could prevent men already married seducing girls under cover of marriage. This may not have been an aspect considered by the women, but certainly the position of those irregularly married, if to spouses not well known to them, could be insecure.

Irregular marriage should be seen as one among the reasons for the abandonment of discipline in the late eighteenth century. It produced a situation in which there might be legally married couples living together whose status had not been declared to the Church, and the knowledge that such couples existed may well have discouraged the taking up of cases of apparent unmarried pregnancy.

What our cases bring out is the extreme ease of marrying in

Scotland. If two people without impediment were prepared to state in front of their kirk session that they married each other, then married they were. It is against this great facility of marriage that illegitimacy has to be seen.

5

Patterns in Illegitimacy and Pre-marital Conceptions

The previous chapters have set out the structure of the Church and the major changes in Scottish society in our period. They have also laid down the definitions of marriage. We now turn to our original concern with the varying levels of illegitimacy over time in our regions, to see what conclusions can be drawn. We follow this examination with an investigation of other aspects of sexual behaviour which can be measured: the levels of repeated bastard bearing, the readiness of fathers of illegitimate children to admit responsibility and provide support, the role of the upper class and employers, and the levels of pre-marital pregnancy.[1]

One of the questions we had set out to try and answer was whether the high levels of illegitimacy found in the north-east and the south-west in 1855 when Civil Registration had been set up, and which persisted for many decades, had obtained before the industrial and agrarian changes of the late eighteenth and early nineteenth centuries. For instance, the Registrar General in the annual report for 1858, by which time Civil Registration was well established, gave an illegitimacy ratio for Scotland as a whole of 8.9, but some counties attracted attention with very much higher figures: for instance Banffshire gave 16.0, Wigtownshire 12.1 and the Stewarty of Kirkcudbright 13.8. These contrast with the ratios of some other counties, Ross and Cromarty 8.8, Stirlingshire 7.8, Caithness 7.8, Fife 7.6, East Lothian 7.7. Individual parishes might have more startling ratios: Marnock (Banffshire) 21.2, Torthorwald (Dumfriesshire) 25.6, Knockando (Moray) 28.3.

Though levels of illegitimacy varied over the next 70 years, relatively high illegitimacy persisted in the north-east and south-west well into the twentieth century. So we set out to examine

---

1 Part of the quantitative results shown in this chapter have already been published in our article 'Scottish illegitimacy ratios in the early modern period', *Economic History Review* 2nd series XL (1987), pp. 45–63.

illegitimacy in these two regions over as long a time as our sources made possible and evaluate the changing pattern. But we needed to look not just at these regions and a notional 'national' sample, for in the late nineteenth century the regional variations in legitimate fertility were considerable in Scotland and implied a high level of cultural diversity.[2] Our desire, therefore, was to take figures from a fair-sized sample of parishes in a large number of identifiable regions and over as long a period as could be trusted to give reliable and comparable results. As explained in chapters 1 and 2, we found it necessary to confine our study to the period from 1660–1780.

Initially it was necessary to locate parishes which could supply long runs of kirk session registers. From survey by region, groups of parishes were selected which would give a substantial base population and then, decade by decade, the cases of unmarried pregnancy dealt with in the registers were collected, using only registers for which the internal consistency and quality was such as to give confidence of completeness.

We are sure that even at the end of our period the figures are sound, and that the lack of any rise in illegitimacy in most areas is not a reflection of lack of zeal on the part of the kirk sessions used. In parishes which had become remiss by the 1770s this is clear in the tone and content of the record. We abandoned a number of registers where discipline had slackened; as a result the sample for the 1770s is markedly smaller than for most other eighteenth-century periods.

A session operated as a court. Sometimes the evidence of the guilt of fornication was direct. In Wemyss, May 1754, 'the elder of Methill reported that one George Morrice and Anne Fairsoul had been caught in the Act of Uncleanness, at the back of Andrew Wilson's house.' This was, however, a rare occurrence: most couples were careful about where they fornicated. 'Scandalous carriage', i.e. improper behaviour, was in itself an offence to be disciplined, but it was not sufficient to establish fornication. In the *Form of Process* (1707) the first paragraph of chapter 4 stated that 'It falls frequently out that . . . all that can be proven is but the presumption of guilt of scandalous behaviour . . . this should oblige the kirk session to be very cautious . . . entering a process without a good warrant, where there is not a child in the case,

2 For the persistence of high illegitimacy see T. C. Smout, 'Sexual behaviour in nineteenth century Scotland', in Peter Laslett, Karla Oosterveen and Richard M. Smith (eds), *Bastardy and its Comparative History* (London, 1980), p. 200. For the fluctuations in general fertility, see M. Teitelbaum, *The British Fertility Decline* (Princeton, 1984), ch. 7.

unless the scandal be very flagrant.' Eventually pregnancy became the *sine qua non* in accusations of this nature.

The pregnancy of an unmarried woman would normally be noticed by the community in which she lived. The resident elder, when he saw the visible change, or heard the local gossip about it, would 'delate', that is report, the woman to the kirk session. The session would summon her to attend, enquire into the allegation, and also demand the name of the man responsible. Subsequently he also would be summoned and questioned. Admission of guilt or, in the case of the woman, the birth of the child, was the proof, and the session would then impose the penalties of fine and 'appearances'.

All investigations which aim at establishing quantitative features must make rules and definitions by which to work. In our case, since we wished to ascertain the numbers of cases of illegitimacy, we based our approach on the methodology of our basic source, the kirk sessions.

1 We have counted as illegitimate births in a particular parish those cases where the couples made their penitential appearances in the parish church, regardless of where the child was born. Normally kirk sessions confined their disciplinary activity to cases for which the intercourse was thought to have taken place in the parish.

2 We have not counted as illegitimate any case where the couple was already proclaimed for marriage or where the session accepted that it was contracted, as there was every likelihood the child would have been born after the marriage.

3 We have not counted any case where the mother was a married woman, even when the father was definitely not her husband, since the child would not be legally defined as a bastard.

4 We have assumed that when a case led to public appearances in church for fornication (as opposed to scandalous carriage) it definitely resulted in an illegitimate birth. In some parishes in the seventeenth century pregnancy was not explicitly referred to, but it appears a very constant pattern in the eighteenth century that the allegation of fornication was not made until a woman was visibly pregnant, usually in the sixth or seventh month.[3] In some cases there was reference to the child as already

3 Of 1,981 cases of fornication found by Stephen J. Davies in Stirlingshire between 1637–1747, only 26 of the women were not pregnant: 'Law and Order in Stirlingshire 1637–

born before the first citation, in many to its birth during the enquiry, which could often be lengthy. It was quite common for 'appearances' to be delayed or interrupted by the birth.

5 We have recorded twins only where the register makes explicit reference to a double birth. Since details of this kind are sometimes omitted, and since not all births occurred during the period of investigation, some multiple ones will have been accepted as single.

6 We have made no allowance for stillbirths, and we have counted as an illegitimate birth any case where the mother claimed that the child had been born dead. In this our suspicion of the possibility of infanticide is merely a reflection of that of the sessions, but even without infant killing the lack of skilled care will have meant that some weak children died immediately after birth. However, when it was reported that a mother had 'parted with the child', the phrase used for miscarriage, we have not counted a birth. These decisions were forced on us by the erratic timing of action by the kirk session, for though most sessions handled cases briskly, some met only monthly and some couples were difficult to get hold of, through illness, absence or recalcitrance.[4] There were also cases which, through successful concealment of pregnancy, came to light only after the birth of a child. We had no acceptable figure for the likely level of stillbirths, and so no basis on which to draw a line between the probable natural death of a foetus and infanticide.

We collected our figures by decades to smooth out annual fluctuations. A decade began in January (Scotland's calendar did not suffer from the English uncertainty about the start of the year). Where registers gave information for only part of the year, that year was not included. The most common reason for a lapse in recording by a session was the death or translation of an incumbent. During the ensuing vacancy not only did records sometimes become confused, but it was common for a session to leave discipline cases to be dealt with on the appointment of a new minister. This procedure means that the record during gaps, and

1747' (unpublished Ph.D. thesis, St Andrews University, 1984), p. 83; Walter Steuart, *Collections and Observations Concerning the Worship, Discipline and Government of the Church of Scotland* (Edinburgh, 1773) contains the *Form of Process in the Judicatories of the Church of Scotland*, 1707.

   4 For a description of kirk session methods of enforcing discipline, and the penalties imposed, see ch. 1.

immediately after them, may not give the real number of cases arising at that time.

It was not always possible to get the full decade from an individual parish: we set the minimum number of years in a decade which made a parish acceptable at six. Cases were taken as belonging in the year in which they first appeared, so cases initiated at the end of a previous decade were not included in the new decade; cases instigated at the end of December in the decade being surveyed were included.

Our figures for the average annual number of illegitimate births by decade had to be set against figures for total births to give illegitimacy ratios, which meant that estimates of parish population and regional birth rates had to be made. The only available figures of parish population for any time within our period are those for Webster's census of 1755, and these we have accepted. It was the opinion of the Flinn team that Webster's census was honestly and carefully made at the date that he stated, and that his parish figures should be taken seriously. It was also the team's opinion that population growth had been slow between 1660 and 1690, and very slow between 1700 and 1740: however, there intervened between these two periods the famine years of 1696–9 in which somewhere between 5 and 15 per cent of the population died, perhaps even more in the north-east.[5] All statements at present on Scotland's population in the seventeenth century are guesswork, but the evidence being gathered in current research on the number of households in various rural parishes in the early eighteenth century supports the idea of a fairly static number of families in any parish. Clearly there will be distortions produced by using Webster's parish figures for the period before 1755. However, except for the 1690s, there are unlikely to be discontinuities in the amount of distortion.

For regional birth rates we have abandoned the figure of 41.8 derived from Webster's age distribution by T. B. Hollingsworth for the Flinn team. Hollingsworth rationalized Webster's age distribution and compared it to parts of the Region North tables in the Princeton Model Life Tables, from this deriving this relatively high birth rate.[6] However, some doubt must attach to this age

5 M. W. Flinn (ed.), *Scottish Population History from the Seventeenth Century to the 1930s* (Cambridge, 1977), pp. 181, 200, 58–64; R. E. Tyson, 'The population of Aberdeenshire, 1695–1755: a new approach', *Northern Scotland* 6 (1985), pp. 113–31.

6 Flinn, ibid., pp. 258–60; Ansley Coale and Paul Demeny, *Regional Model Life Tables and Stable Populations* (Princeton, NJ, 1966).

distribution, for Webster both discounted as valid for Scotland, and then relied on, Halley's Breslau Life Table for calculating his total population, and in addition abandoned the basis of these calculations in his year-by-year age distribution. The ambiguity with which he expressed his age distribution has deflected criticism from its inherent inconsistencies.

In any case, the calculation made by Hollingsworth depended on the assumption that Webster's age group 0–10 really meant 0–9: however, Webster's figures for each year when added together show that he meant what he said.[7] If he is taken at his word, the age structure of his population has a smaller percentage in the juvenile groups, and this implies a lower fertility. The same conclusion comes from the information on the age of marriage of the rural population in Flinn, and the intervals between successive births for the population of Kilmarnock. It is difficult to accept a birth rate of nearly 42 in an early modern population with fairly high mortality, a median age of wives at first marriage of approximately 27 and birth intervals mostly over two years. Hollingsworth's figure also conflicts with the occasional information in the *OSA* when ministers give retrospective summaries of decadal births, using the evidence of the old parish registers in their keeping.[8]

We were therefore forced to use the only other major eighteenth century demographic compilation, the *OSA*, for the likely level of total births in a parish.[9] From the remarks of ministers in the *OSA* of the level of births at earlier periods in the eighteenth century, we calculated birth rates, ranging from 25 to 33, for each region based on all the material available in the *OSA* for all the parishes lying within the region.

The appearance of a major study on English population history since the publication of Flinn's book, which covers the eighteenth century, reinforces the need for revaluation of some of the conclusions about Scotland. England has now been shown to have had a 'low pressure' demographic system. The birth rates there range from 29.7 in 1676–80 to 36.3 in 1776–80. A similar system,

---

7 For Webster's age distribution see J. G. Kyd (ed.), *Scottish Population Statistics* (Scottish History Society, Edinburgh, 1952), pp. 80–1. A new calculation of birth and death rates from this distribution is forthcoming in Rosalind Mitchison, 'Webster revisited: a re-examination of the "census" of Scotland', in T. M. Devine (ed.), *Themes in Scottish Social History*.

8 Flinn, *Scottish Population History from the Seventeenth Century to the 1930s*, pp. 275–9, 287; Sir John Sinclair (ed.), *The Statistical Account of Scotland* (usually known as the *OSA*), 21 vols (Edinburgh, 1791–7).

9 Flinn, *Scottish Population History from the Seventeenth Century to the 1930s*, p. 285.

or at any rate a less 'high pressure' one, may have existed for Scotland. It would be surprising if Scotland, with a rural structure of society very similar to that of England, and in particular with a pattern of relatively late marriage, should have had a birth rate so much higher than the English, as appears from the contrast between Flinn's book and the English work.[10]

The main problem involved in using our regional base figures could be the absence in the *OSA* of information on the numbers of births to members of dissenting congregations. But these congregations within our period mostly used the registers of the established Church. The *OSA* reports indicate where there was any sizeable presence of dissent in the parish. It seems to us that the *OSA* material can be taken as giving the total number of registered births in the parishes, though an increase in the delay between birth and baptism in the 1770s will have increased slightly the shortfall due to early infant death.

It is unlikely that the ministers who gave information about the number of births in the *OSA* made adequate allowance for neonatal mortality in the gap between birth and baptism. This gap was small until the 1770s because baptism was usually very early, except for illegitimate children who would not be allowed baptism until their parents had completed church discipline. This is likely to make the *OSA* figures of birth rates too low by a few per cent. This adds to the other features of our calculations, almost all of which tend to overestimate the share of illegitimacy in total births. For the 1760s and 1770s we are more confident of our figures of total births, for the *OSA* ministers would be using for their reports registers often kept in their own ministry.

The patterns of regional illegitimacy ratios (percentage of total births) by decades, are set out in figures 1–4. Figure 1 shows that illegitimacy was consistently low in the south-east, except for the Lothians in the 1770s. This final upturn may be a significant change, but we cannot be sure of this since the study could not be continued into the 1780s. Figure 2, for the two highland regions, has gaps where source material was lacking: it shows a generally higher level. In the Western Highlands illegitimacy stood under 3 per cent of births only for the last decade. In both regions the trend over time is downward, and a similar downward trend is to be seen in figure 3 for the various regions in the north, Aberdeenshire, Caithness and the north-east (Moray and

10 E. A. Wrigley and R. S. Schofield, *The Population History of England 1541–1871* (1981); Rosalind Mitchison, 'Webster revisited'.

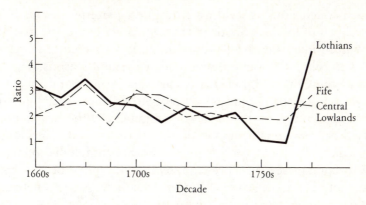

Figure 1 *Illegitimacy ratios, Lothians, Fife and Central Lowlands, by decade*

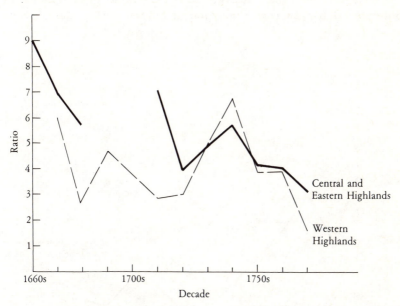

Figure 2 *Illegitimacy ratios, Western Highlands, and Central and Eastern Highlands, by decade*

Banffshire). The fall is from over 8 per cent to between 3 and 5 per cent. Clearly illegitimate births were more common in this area than in the south. The remaining regions, in figure 4, the south-west (Dumfriesshire and Galloway) and Ayrshire show by contrast no clear early downward trend, and a marked movement upward after 1750. Even so, illegitimacy stood at the moderate level of 4 per cent in the early decades of the eighteenth century.

Such conclusions as we draw from these patterns are that in the central belt of lowland Scotland the population contained its sexual life within marriage throughout the period covered, either from assent to religious opinion or for other cultural reasons. The low level of the Central Lowlands is particularly interesting since for several decades the populous parish of St Ninians, which figured in our sample, received the impact of a regiment of the British army, and a disproportionate number of cases was then laid at the door of the soldiers. In the Highlands it appears that church discipline was able to contain sexual expression, as this discipline became more surely founded in the later seventeenth century. A late nineteenth-century commentator noted about the kirk session:

Of all judicatories it was the most respected and best obeyed; for the Highlanders, remiss and careless in other matters, set great store by the ordinances of baptism and communion; and the cutty-stool and sackcloth

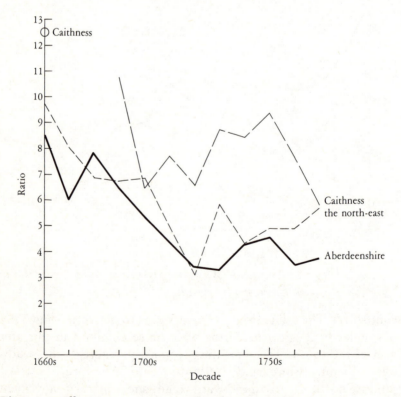

Figure 3 *Illegitimacy ratios, Aberdeenshire, the north-east and Caithness, by decade*

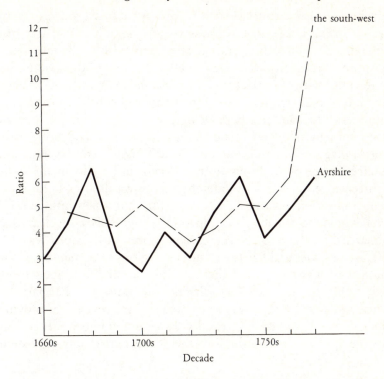

Figure 4 *Illegitimacy ratios, Ayrshire and the south-west, by decade*

gown were much more dreaded in 1700 than the threats of law and 'tout' of the royal horn. Seeing there were few restrictions on the intercourse of the sexes, and considering the oblique idea they had of some other moral duties, it is astonishing to find how little the evil of illegitimacy prevailed.[11]

In the whole north-eastern and northern areas the picture is different. Northern Scotland had, on the whole, taken a different political line from the south in the disturbances of the seventeenth century: in particular, the north-east and Aberdeenshire had a tradition of commitment to episcopacy, and consequently suffered severe dislocation after the Revolution of 1689, when the General Assembly concentrated on expelling ministers who had accepted episcopacy, often on trumped up charges, and intruding presbyterians in their place. It would be surprising if the

11 D. Campbell, *The Lairds of Glenlyon* (Perth, 1886), p. 113.

attachment to the court system of presbyterianism was as strong here as in the south. In Caithness we are looking at a society of a different ethnic mixture, and an area islanded by hills into semi-isolation. Such an area may well see no good reasons for conformity with the social rules of the country as a whole. There is no doubt that church discipline was vigorously enforced in Caithness, the sanction here being physical punishment, yet the ratio, though falling, can never be called low. The north-east, where illegitimacy had attained a strikingly high level in the nineteenth century, shows both a downward trend in the early eighteenth century and a moderate shift upwards after 1720: there is no indication on our graphs that the mid-nineteenth-century level would be a natural extrapolation, but it is also clear that unmarried mothers can never have been rare in the north-east.

The rise in decadal levels for the two regions of Ayrshire and the south-west was so marked that it seemed desirable to look more closely at the trends. The illegitimacy ratio of the parishes concerned year by year was calculated and the seven year moving averages were graphed. The results are set out in figure 5. It is clear that the upward trend in the south-west was remarkably consistent

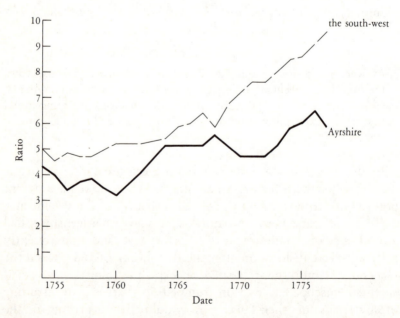

Figure 5 *Illegitimacy ratios, Ayrshire and the south-west, 1754–1777, by seven year moving average*

and that in both areas the decadal averages were not influenced by the exact divisions between decades but show a genuine trend.

The upward trend in the south-west from the 1750s can be seen as suggesting a movement toward the high levels of the mid-nineteenth century. Work in England has suggested links between 'proto-industrialization' and earlier marriage, and between earlier marriage and a rising illegitimacy ratio.[12] In Scotland the linen industry from the 1740s was sustaining an increasing number of family incomes all over the country, but probably less so in Galloway than anywhere else, for the expansion of coarse linen manufacture is a development associated particularly with eastern Scotland. Linen was probably the most significant industrial product of late seventeenth- and early eighteenth-century Scotland; it would be unwise, therefore, to postulate the expansion of industry as a major contributor to illegitimacy in the south-west, since neither the timing nor the geographic concentration fit such a theory.

Another possible reason for rising illegitimacy is that proposed by Edward Shorter (for the whole of Europe), that a change of mentality, causing a 'sexual revolution', took place amongst the labouring classes when the family ceased to be for them an agency of social control.[13] (This is discussed in the introduction.) However, this supposed change in mentality still rests on an assumption of a radical change in work patterns, which, as we have noted, did not take place in Galloway in this period. The longstanding resistance of Galloway to all forms of authority is an element which might be expected to contribute to high illegitimacy, but there is no reason to see this resistance as increasing in the mid-eighteenth century.

The unusual pattern of illegitimacy in this area should also be seen in relationship to an unusual level of resistance to church discipline all through our period. In the south-west the percentage of men rapidly admitting responsibility was markedly lower than in most parts of Scotland, and if Ayrshire is taken as linked to the south-west these areas are conspicuous in that usually less than half the cases made this rapid submission, whereas elsewhere the

12 Peter Laslett and Karla Oosterveen, 'Long term trends in bastardy in England', *Population Studies* xxvii (1973); David Levine, *Family Formation in an Age of Nascent Capitalism* (1977), ch. 5.
13 Edward Shorter, 'Illegitimacy, Sexual Revolution and Social Change in Modern Europe', in Robert I. Rotberg and Theodore K. Rabb (eds), *Marriage and Fertility* (Princeton, NJ, 1980).

'admission rate' was usually over two-thirds (see chapter 7 and table 7). We have even found a man in the south-west who refused to take the oath disclaiming adultery, and who therefore presumably could not have done so with a clear conscience, protesting about the discipline system to the highest court in the Church, the Commission of the General Assembly. His particular ground for resistance was the low social standing of the woman who had named him. The synod, to which the affair had also gone, did not share his sense of social superiority and considered that he was an undesirable example of the men who got girls into trouble and then deserted them: 'Poor women are decoyed by Men into Uncleanness', stated the synod and added, 'Men accused do usually deny and refuse to give Oath' but 'are prepared everywhere to acknowledge guilt except before a Church judicatory'.[14] In recalcitrance men of the south-west were often aided by the women, who would determinedly refuse to give names. There was also in these two regions a high proportion of cases where the women ran away rather than face discipline. It is of particular interest that Galloway, the base area of irreconcilable Covenanting sentiment and the only area of militant Lowland resistance to agricultural improvement, should all through have shown resistance to the sexual discipline of the Church.

The figures for Scotland as a whole (figure 6) show a downward trend to the 1720s, and after that they fluctuate. Since the study has to stop in 1780 we cannot be sure whether the apparent lift then showing was the start of an upward trend or merely a fluctuation.

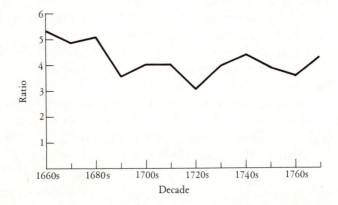

Figure 6 *Scottish illegitimacy ratios, national sample, by decade*

14 SRO, CH1/2/85.

In any case it is a movement strongly influenced by the upward trend in Ayrshire and the south-west. When set against the English quinquennial figures[15] what stands out is the markedly higher level of the Scottish ratios until the 1750s, in which decade the graphs cross. The English graph at this point is at an early stage in a marked upward acceleration. Though by the 1850s the Scottish level[16] at 9.5 per cent is much higher than the English level of 6.5 per cent, our research does not give a clear indication from when the upward trend in Scotland can be dated. A recent study based on the parish of Rothiemay in Banffshire shows that there illegitimacy began to rise towards its remarkably high level of the later nineteenth century only after 1811, though pre-marital pregnancy had begun its upward movement in the 1770s.[17] However, there is no reason to locate such a trend in the period of the expansion of the linen industry in the 1740s and 1750s.

The picture of the English ratios can be matched to some degree in the early decades with the levels of illegitimacy in the Lothians, Central Lowlands and Fife in figure 1, though in these regions it rarely fell below 2 per cent. What is striking in the national picture is that Scotland, with its clearly defined machinery for the forcing of sexual activity into marriage, and its uniform application by means of the supervision of presbyteries, did not manage to achieve the low ratios found in England in the late seventeenth century, a period, when as far as we can see, registration there was good and the puritan discipline of the interregnum had been dissolved. Our calculations will tend to overestimate Scottish illegitimacy, but the distorting effect should be continuous and the constancy of illegitimacy ratios in the Lothians, Fife and the Central Lowlands, the area where the Church's authority was most readily accepted, suggests that the levels of distortion did not change. The falling levels of illegitimacy in the later seventeenth century in the two highland areas support this view, since it was in this period that church discipline became effective.

Our choice of parishes for a sample was based on the quality of the records rather than the centrality of a parish to its region. We were concerned that the regional structure, as we laid it down

---

15 Peter Laslett, Karla Oosterveen and Richard M. Smith (eds), *Bastardy and its Comparative History* (London, 1980), p. 14.

16 This level has been worked out for all the parishes which contributed to the study for the years 1858–60.

17 J. A. D. Blaikie, 'Illegitimacy in Nineteenth Century North-East Scotland' (unpublished Ph.D. thesis, Queen Mary College, London, 1987), ch. 4.

geographically, might obscure a social frontier, so we studied particularly the contribution of individual parishes to their regional totals to see if there were any that stood consistently much higher or much lower than the general regional level in their figures. For a few decades some were markedly higher than the rest of the region: this was the case for Forglen (north-east), Dailly (Ayrshire), Kilmartin (Western Highlands), and Kemnay (Aberdeenshire). By contrast Kilbirnie (Western Highlands) was usually lower. Alvie (Eastern Highlands), notable in the mid-nineteenth century for its high illegitimacy, was also higher for the three decades for which its register could be used. The parish with the most consistently high level of illegitimacy was Westerkirk (south-west). The ratios for Westerkirk and the south-west region as a whole are set out in table 3.

Table 3 Illegitimacy ratios for Westerkirk and the south-west

	Westerkirk	The south-west
1691–1700	11.2	4.3
1701–10	9.3	5.1
1711–20	15.1	4.3
1721–31	5.6	3.6
1731–40	9.8	4.1

The aberrant nature of this parish lasted for several decades and a shadow of the discrepancy continued into the 1850s, with a level of 18.4 per cent when the regional figure was 14.5 per cent. The minister of a nearby parish, Wamphray, remarked in the *OSA* that 'virtuous men are more frequent in the walks of agriculture, than anywhere else': he does not seem to have cast about much for his evidence.[18]

Westerkirk was an upland rural parish, large in extent but with a population according to Webster of only 544. The number of illegitimate births which would produce a high ratio would not need to be great. In such a setting a handful of illegitimate children in one decade might lead to the establishment of a structure of support, such as the availability of child minders, which would

18 *OSA* (1797) xxi, p. 458 (original edition).

reduce the economic sanctions against illegitimacy. Without there being any weakening of the formal constraints, as expressed by the kirk session, bastard-rearing could thus become less stressful for the girls concerned.[19]

Bastard-bearing might also have a particular continuity of its own. As a check on this we collected the cases which were 'repeaters' – always noted by the kirk sessions because of the enhanced penalties laid down for these. Some women had a second, third, fourth or even fifth bastard, but as the penalty did not increase after 'quadrilapse' the higher productivities were usually indicated by 'multilapse'. Peter Laslett writes that 'a rise in illegitimacy beyond a certain point is no longer a rise in the number of women who have bastards, but rather in the number of bastards borne by a minority of them.'[20] Our figures (see figure 7) show no such correlation for any of the Scottish regions; illegitimacy levels appear to have risen or fallen with no corresponding rise or fall in the number of repeaters. It is noteworthy, though, that the percentage of cases which were 'repeated' reaches a low level in the 1720s and 1730s (the period of most effective church discipline) and another in the 1760s and 1770s.

Laslett also postulates what he calls a 'bastardy prone sub-society', i.e. that the families of bastard-bearers were more likely than other families to produce further bastards, in successive generations. The surname structure makes it impossible to test this theory for most of Scotland. However, amongst the numerous remarks made by ministers about deviant women which we have collected, in only one was there a statement that the woman's mother had also borne bastards.

We found that the percentage of repeaters was consistently higher in the north-east (including Aberdeenshire and Caithness) than elsewhere in the country; aside from that there were no marked regional differences. In most regions there appears to have been a peak between 1690 and 1730, most often in the 1690s; in Fife and the south-west there was another peak in the

---

19 An explanation of this type might account for the high level of illegitimacy in a larger parish, Terling, in the opening decades of the seventeenth century, as shown in David Levine and Keith Wrightson, 'The social context of illegitimacy in early modern England', in Laslett et al. (eds), *Bastardy and its Comparative History*.

20 Laslett et al. (eds), ibid., p. 239. On p. 86 Richard Smith writes that it appeared 'that as the bastardy ratio went up the proportion of women producing more than one bastard went up at an even faster pace'. Laslett makes this point also in his *Family Life and Illicit Love in Earlier Generations* (Cambridge, 1977), p. 147.

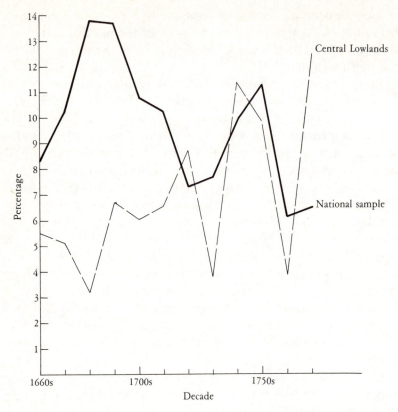

Figure 7 *Percentage of 'repeater' cases, national sample and Central Lowlands, by decade*

1750s. Otherwise, except for the Central Lowlands, there was a downward trend in the eighteenth century. Certainly by the 1770s fewer women than earlier were bearing more than one bastard. (See figure 7.)

Repeatership was usually between 5 and 15 per cent of the total cases of illegitimacy, which means that often the figures are small and consequently give very variable percentages. Nationally, and here the sample is of a fair size, they were rarely over 12 per cent, and in the 1760s and 1770s under 7 per cent. In the Central Lowlands, which did not share the general trend, the figure stood above 10 per cent only in the 1740s and 1770s. The figures are for the repeated births, 'relapse' or 'trilapse', etc. cases, so that the total of children born to mothers who repeated would be higher, somewhat over twice these figures for there were some higher parities. This has to be allowed for in comparisons of them with figures derived for England. In England the level of repeaterdom lies within the range of the different levels found by Richard M. Smith for various English parishes, which cover from 7 to 23 per cent of total illegitimate births, being to women who had more than one. David Levine, working on Shepshed figures, found that after 1750 35 per cent of bastard births were to women who repeated. Doubling our figures would not bring them into this range. We also do not find what Levine claimed, an association between proto-industrialization, that is the spread of intensive cottage industry, and repeating, for such industry expanded rapidly in Scotland after the 1740s when the level of repeaterdom was, in almost all areas, falling. There is a further point made by Laslett in his paper on the 'bastardy prone sub-society', that repeaters might be more mobile than other women, and so the level of traced repeaterdom would be held down.[21] This is not applicable in Scotland where the Church system was, at least until the 1770s, fully able to explore the past history of immigrants to a parish, and apply the correct penalty for repetition.

One further question which arose from the subject of 'repeaters' is to what extent these comprised couples who had stable unions, possibly even considering themselves married, albeit not in the eyes of the Church. This could have been particularly significant in Scotland, where, as shown in the last chapter, a powerful myth has held that 'handfast' and other irregular forms of marriage were prevalent and where the Hardwicke Marriage Act did not apply. As far as was possible we measured the number of repeaters pregnant by the same man and those pregnant by different men. In every one of the ten regions those pregnant by different men far outnumbered those pregnant by the same man. The large component of untraceable cases makes this impossible to quantify absolutely, but the consistency of the evidence is unmistakeable. To quote the figures from two very different regions: in Ayrshire out of a total repeater figure of 84, 23 were with the same man, 39 were with a different man, and 22 were untraceable; in the north-east out of a total of 160, 42 were with the same man, 62 with a different man, and 56 were untraceable. Longstanding unions were more easily traced and the transgressors identified than was the case with more casual unions, so we are confident that we have not missed any semi-marital relationships; our 'unknown' cases are

21 Richard M. Smith as above; David Levine, *Family Formation in an Age of Nascent Capitalism* (London, 1977), ch. 9; Laslett, in Laslett et al. (eds), *Bastardy and its Comparative History*, pp. 232–4.

likely to be liaisons with different men. The conclusion must be that while stable unions accounted for some repeaters (though when cited for fornication these couples did not claim to be 'married'), the majority did not fall into this category.

An important aspect of illegitimacy is the maintenance of illegiti- mate children. Morison's *Dictionary of Decisions* includes some cases of this. In that of Robert Oliver, a Roxburghshire day labourer, and Janet Scott, a woman of the same rank, in 1778, the man was deemed liable for support at three pounds a year until the child was seven, at which time he could either continue support until it was ten or else assume custody. In the case of Agnes Paterson, also a woman 'of low rank', against Alexander Speir, who possessed 'a considerable estate', the man was ordered to pay 100 pounds Scots (£8 6s 8d sterling) a year until the child was seven. In this case it was argued, but not accepted, that a boy would be earning at seven and a girl at ten.[22]

Most cases concerning child maintenance which came before kirk sessions did not involve the propertied class. In the earliest which we found (Alves, December 1661), a specific sum was not mentioned, but William Forsyth 'became willingly enacted and obliged to maintaine according to his abilitie & state of lyfe, the child called Issobell Forsyth procreated betwixt him and Janet Stenner in fornication'. A cautioner was produced to ensure he fulfilled his obligation, and the session appointed an extract of the act be given to the woman, 'that if the said William faile in performance according to his undertaking, she may have recourse to the Session for redress & assistance.' In another seventeenth- century case (Trinity Gask, September 1674), the minister reported that Janet Wedderspoon had come to him saying that Thomas Wandles, the father of her child, 'will give her nothing for the bairnes maintenance and she has nothing to nourish him with.' The man appeared before the session '& affirmed that for the present he had nothing to give her, but after harvest what he might spare of his fie should be given to her'. The session told the woman of the man's promise, '& knowing her indigency they appoynt for her weeklie two shilling scots during this harvest'.

In the eighteenth century there appears to have been some standardization in the amount payable. We discovered two cases concerning child maintenance in Kenmore (August 1733 and June 1736), and in both of them the man was expected to bear the

---

22 W. M. Morison, *Dictionary of Decisions*, vol. I & II, pp. 444, 438, 400.

expense of half the child's board. That this was not just a local custom is attested by a case which appears in Morison's *Dictionary of Decisions* for 1758: a woman had got a Justice of the Peace decision that the man should provide half the child's maintenance (50 shillings a year) until the age of ten.[23]

However, the standardization of responsibility cannot have been absolute, or there would have been no need for Alexander Fletcher and Janet McGrigor to have come before Kenmore session (December 1759) after agreeing to abide by the session's decision regarding the maintenance of their two bastard children:

The session after considering the affair ordain that for the two years and three quarters she has had the eldest child The said Alexander shall pay unto her fourty pounds scots money including thirty five shillings sterling which she acknowledges to have received already in part payment for said time for maintaining & cloathing the said eldest Child: and that in all time coming Alexr shall keep & maintain said Child without any trouble or expence to the mother: The session further ordain, that as to maintaining of the youngest Child, Alexander shall pay unto said Janet eight pounds scots, quarter about, for nursing & maintaining said youngest Child till he be six quarters old, after which time she the mother obliges herself to maintain & cloth her said youngest Child in all time coming without any trouble or expence of the father.

Although, as was seen in one of the seventeenth-century cases above, the mother of a bastard child could at times be considered a fit object for charity, in the same way as a widow or widower might be, sessions certainly did not consider themselves under any obligation to maintain bastard children. In Wemyss (April and June 1704), the session was informed that Margaret Hill, whose partner had fled, 'hath absented this paroch and hath left her child with a nourse which hath been burdensom to the session already'. A search was made for the woman, a matter for which the Church could use its espionage system effectively; eventually she was found. The session asked her what she was about, abandoning her child to be a burden on the parish. She insisted she had planned to return, but that 'whither present or absent she was not able to pay for the mentinance of her child. The child with the nourse being present the child was delivered to its mother and she told in plain

23 Morison, vol. II, p. 1357. The reason it came up before the court was that the woman had married, and the man was demanding the child be handed over to him; the judgment left her with custody. The pound Scots, used in some of these decisions, was worth a twelfth of a pound sterling.

terms she behoved to go work for a mentinance to herself and child & not be any longer burdensom or troublesom to the Session.'

The readiness of fathers to support their illegitimate children is discussed in chapter 7. The surprisingly high level of men accepting responsibility means that one argument about Scottish illegitimacy in the nineteenth century, that it varied with the ease with which a woman would find work and so support herself and her child, is of limited relevance in our period.

The recent work on English population history has associated the English fertility increase (both legitimate and illegitimate) in the eighteenth century with a delayed response to higher wages. This is now being modified by a closer concern for the changing level of job opportunities.[24] Scotland, as shown in chapter 2, also experienced a surge of economic growth from the mid-eighteenth century. There is uncertainty as to whether much of this occurred before the 1740s, but there is no doubt about the rapidity of change in the 1750s, 1760s and 1770s.[25] In the 1750s the tobacco trade moved into its most profitable stage and increasingly was able to use Scottish products in the return cargo. In the later 1750s the linen industry recovered from the setback resulting from the interruption of the export bounty, and expanded production enormously. In the 1760s there began in the south-east the changes in agriculture that were to make the agricultural revolution. T. C. Smout gives statistics which show these later decades as ones not only of economic growth but, in particular, of industrial expansion and, therefore, in a world with few labour saving devices, of proliferation of job opportunities.[26] We do not have the evidence to show whether legitimate fertility in Scotland was stimulated in the same way as it was in England,[27] but on our figures the economic developments apparently had no immediate effect on illegitimate fertility. It is clear that illegitimacy had risen considerably by the mid-nineteenth century, but by then a very different economic system obtained.

Ostensibly the Church, and the laws of discipline which it

24 Wrigley and Schofield, *The Population History of England 1541–1871*; R. S. Schofield, 'English marriage patterns revisited', *Journal of Family History*, vol. 10 (1985), pp. 2–20.

25 Valerie Morgan, 'Agricultural wage rates in late-eighteenth century Scotland', *Economic History Review* 2nd series xxiv (1971) has shown that rural wages rose markedly in the more developed areas between the 1750s and the 1790s.

26 'Where had the Scottish economy got to by the third quarter of the eighteenth century?', in Istvan Hont and Michael Ignatieff (eds), *Wealth and Virtue* (Cambridge, 1983).

27 Flinn, *Scottish Population History from the Seventeenth Century to the 1930s*, p. 277.

exercised, made no distinction of class, but the cases that came before the session were largely of those without property. Where the occupation of the woman was recorded it was most often 'servetrix'. Out of thousands of cases only a handful of women appear to have been of any higher status (whether such women were more virtuous, better guarded, or less likely to be found out is a moot point). The men belonged to a much wider range of categories. Many were fellow servants in the same household, but masters or sons of masters were also frequently cited. This does not necessarily mean they were of higher status in society, for children were often placed as servants in the houses of kinsfolk. However, there were in addition a number of cases involving men belonging to the gentry; the extent to which the kirk session was able to exercise discipline over them varied considerably from area to area, but to say that recalcitrance was more usual than submission would be a fair summing-up of the situation (see chapter 7).

Keith Wrightson has quantified the employment position of mothers and fathers of bastards in seventeenth-century Lancashire and Essex. He found that at least 28 per cent of Essex and 8 per cent of Lancashire fathers were fellow servants, and at least 23 per cent of Essex fathers and 14 per cent of Lancashire fathers were in a magisterial position vis-à-vis the mothers (masters, masters' kin or gentlemen).[28] We quantified this information for only one of our areas, the Lothians. Percentages varied greatly from decade to decade. In the 1680s at least 5.6 per cent of the men were fellow servants and 7.4 per cent were masters or sons of masters; from 1701–1710 10.3 per cent are known to have been fellow servants and 5.2 per cent masters or masters' sons; in the 1720s 4.1 per cent were recorded as fellow servants and 14.3 per cent as masters or masters' sons; in the 1730s the figures were 8.7 per cent and 17.4 per cent. In every decade a certain percentage of the total of fathers belonged to the same household as the mother.

The general conclusions of our research have been to show that for most of Scotland the rise of illegitimacy to the level it had in the mid-nineteenth century – as can be seen in table 4 – did not take place in the period of rapid expansion of domestic industry. The level of illegitimacy for the country as a whole was no higher in the 1770s than it had been in the 1730s. It is to the period of the

---

28 Laslett et al., *Bastardy and its Comparative History*, pp. 187/8. Wrightson also found that if couples were not actually serving in the same household then they were likely to be neighbours; this is not something which can be easily ascertained for Scotland.

Table 4   Illegitimacy ratios, 1760s and 1858–1860

	1760s	1858–1860
Lothians	1.0	7.3
Fife	1.8	5.4
Central Lowlands	2.5	8.2
Eastern Highlands	4.0	7.5
Western Highlands	3.9	8.2
Aberdeenshire	3.5	13.7
North-east	4.9	12.1
Caithness	7.6	7.3
Ayrshire	4.8	8.8
South-west	6.1	14.6
Whole country from selected parishes	3.6	9.5

The same parishes were used for both periods.

industrial and agricultural revolutions, or to the decades after these changes, that the increase must be attributed.

It is worth noting that though the figures in this table show a considerable difference for the different dates, they also show some persistence in regional rank order, with the Lothians and Fife low at both dates, Ayrshire and the two highland regions occupying a middle position, the south-west and the north-east high. The regions which conspicuously change rank are Caithness and Aberdeenshire.

A complementary aspect of sexual behaviour, also subject to church discipline was 'antenuptial fornication', i.e. pre-marital conception. Wrigley, discussing the high level of these in the England of the late eighteenth century, where some 39 per cent of first births occurred within eight months of marriage and the major part of these within six months has offered the idea that the European marriage pattern should be seen as 'a repertoire of adaptable systems rather than as a single pattern'. At this period in England, when the illegitimacy ratio was over 5 per cent, it would seem that between 50 and 60 per cent of women who bore children conceived the first out of wedlock.[29]

We decided, for comparison, to go back to all of the parishes where we had collected bastardy figures and collect comparable pre-marital conception figures. It will, of course, be asked whether the figures that can be drawn from KSRs for pre-marital pregnancy are complete. In the work by Wrigley and Hair for England pre-marital conceptions have been calculated from the intervals in OPRs between marriage and the baptism of the first child.[30] The need to allow for the inexactness of the concept of term has meant that only births at eight months of marriage or earlier have been considered likely to have been conceived before wedlock. Our material does not make this approach possible, for OPRs in Scotland tended to record not the date of marriage but the date of proclamation. But the discipline of the KSRs allows us to use the exact knowledge of the local community. Any birth taking place within nine calendar months of marriage would lead to persistent enquiry, and until the matter was settled, either by the session admitting innocence, or the parents doing penance, baptism would be denied to the child.

The use of calendar months ignored the fact that at different times of year nine of them can vary in length by as much as three days.[31] If the parents denied pre-marital intercourse midwives would be asked to inspect the child and state whether it appeared immature or not. In some cases enquiry would continue even after midwives had given good reason to regard the birth as premature. (The usual signs stressed by midwives were failure to suck and undeveloped nails.) Under these pressures many couples rapidly admitted to 'antenuptial uncleanness'. It seems unlikely that a couple would assent to the process of public appearances and a fine, to secure baptism, if they knew themselves to be innocent. The evidence is therefore fuller than that on which estimates have been made for England, since it includes those pregnancies which

---

29 E. A. Wrigley, 'Marriage, Fertility and Population Growth in Eighteenth Century England', in R. B. Outhwaite (ed.), *Marriage and Society*, (London, 1981), p. 157.

30 Ibid., p. 168; P. E. H. Hair, 'Bridal pregnancy in rural England in earlier centuries', *Population Studies* xx (1966), pp. 233–43, and 'Bridal pregnancy in Earlier Rural England further examined', *Population Studies* xxiv (1970), pp. 59–76.

31 Men claiming that they were not responsible for a pregnancy shared this rigid idea of the length of gestation. The insistence on measuring gestation from the time of intercourse was, by the mid-eighteenth century, out of line with medical knowledge. For instance, William Smellie, *A Treatise on the Theory and Practice of Midwifery* (London, 1752), vol. I, p. 126, gives the length of gestation as 'Nine solar months . . . from the last discharge'.

produced a child over eight and a half months after marriage. Both methods of investigation will, of course, miss births conceived just before marriage and which came late to term.

In spite of a General Assembly ruling of 1646 that antenuptial fornicators should receive the same punishment whether they married or not,[32] parishes did not follow a uniform pattern. In the eighteenth century the trend was towards insisting on only one appearance for the antenuptial cases, and a small fine. Sessions also used their own discretion in dealing with exacerbated offences. In Thurso (June 1692) James Bain had sworn he was not guilty of antenuptial fornication, but when his child was born, it was found 'by computation' that the child had been begotten before he had sworn; this was considered a heinous enough sin for the man to have to appear in sackcloth. In the case of William Moody in Forgandenny (January 1750), 'in regard the scandall was flagrant in the parish long before their marriage, the session were of opinion that both he and his wife ought to satisfie in the same way as all other ordinary fornicators being persuaded that nothing less could tend to Edification in their Case.' Conversely, Longside session decided that as James Davidson and Jean Bennet (March 1773) 'had been married before the Scandal became flagrant', it was sufficient to rebuke them privately instead of publicly.

One procedure which most kirk sessions gradually came to adopt was to demand consignation money from every couple who put up their names to be proclaimed for marriage, the money to be returned if nine months elapsed before a child was born.[33] Another ploy, if there was any doubt about a possible pre-marital conception, was for a minister to grant baptism of a first child only on condition that the father provided a cautioner that he and his wife would satisfy discipline if it should turn out they had been guilty of antenuptial fornication.

Though most sessions by 1750 had standardized public appearances for antenuptial pregnancy to one, with a financial penalty half that of ordinary fornication, Wemyss, in Fife, stood out for a long time against this practice. In August 1752, when the minister suggested inflicting a 'lesser Censure' on 'those who committed uncleanness before they married one another than on others who

32 A. Peterkin, *Records of the Kirk of Scotland, containing the Acts and Proceedings of the General Assemblies* (Edinburgh, 1838), I, p. 445.

33 For examples of sessional enactments see Dalkeith, October 1678, Auchterarder, July 1684, and Fordyce, August 1740.

did not marry those they committed uncleanness with', the session refused to entertain the idea. It was not until June 1769 that

the Session thinking on the complaint that has been often made to them that their Discipline as to Ante-nuptial Fornicators is severer than in all neighbouring Parishes & considering that it was not well proportion'd to have those who marry and those who marry not upon an equal foting resolv'd that from the first of September next those who are guilty of ante-nuptial Fornication shall have but one rebuke & that those who marry not shall continue as formerly.

The figures for pre-marital pregnancy obtained from the discipline are low, even in regions or at periods when bastardy was relatively high. In this they differ from those offered for England in the later eighteenth century.

It is our contention, discussed in greater depth in chapter 6, that as a general rule bearing an illegitimate child was not, as has been claimed for England, the result of a failed courtship, i.e. the woman becoming pregnant in the expectation that the man would marry her. A comparison of the statistics about women who gave birth to bastards with those who conceived a child outside marriage but gave birth to a legitimate child, bears out this contention. The figures are very different from those quoted above for England, for even in regions and periods of high bastardy ratios, the antenuptial conception ratio was low.

If the pre-marital conception ratios had been rising while the illegitimacy ratios fell, one might have argued that easier marriage was preventing some children being born illegitimate, but as can be seen, this did not occur in any of the regions and cannot therefore be put forward as the reason for falling illegitimacy ratios. For most regions though there is a rough similarity in the movements of the illegitimacy and antenuptial ratios, there is no close parallelism. For instance, both ratios reach their peak at the same time in Fife and in the Western Highlands, but in the latter case the graphs do not otherwise correspond. However in Ayrshire, and to a lesser degree in Fife, the two graphs have a good deal in common. In both cases the antenuptial level lies well below that of the illegitimacy ratio. The figures for these regions suggest that unmarried intercourse responded to some particular type of outside pressure, but that the prospects of marriage remained relatively static. What the graphs do not suggest is any considerable change in the availability of marriage, which would mean that women who in one period might be rightly confident of being able

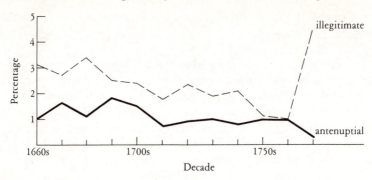

Figure 8 *'Illegitimate' and 'antenuptial' percentages of total births, Lothians, by decade*

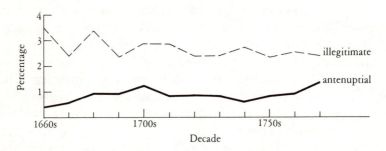

Figure 9 *'Illegitimate' and 'antenuptial' percentages of total births, Central Lowlands, by decade*

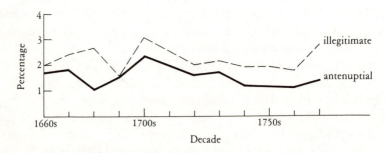

Figure 10 *'Illegitimate' and 'antenuptial' percentages of total births, Fife, by decade*

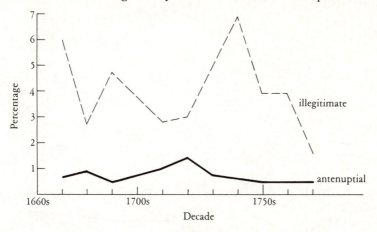

Figure 11 *'Illegitimate' and 'antenuptial' percentages of total births, Western Highlands, by decade*

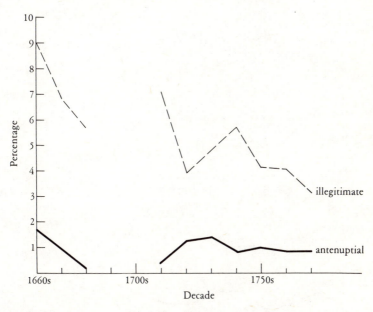

Figure 12 *'Illegitimate' and 'antenuptial' percentages of total births, Eastern and Central Highlands, by decade*

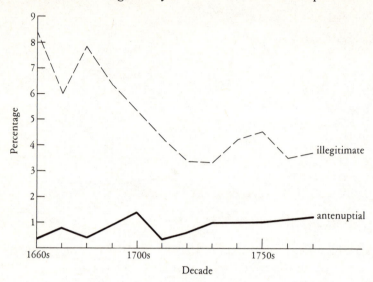

Figure 13 *'Illegitimate' and 'antenuptial' percentages of total births, Aberdeenshire, by decade*

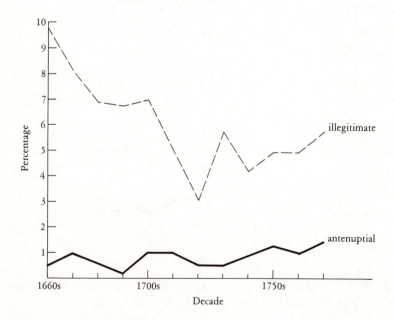

Figure 14 *'Illegitimate' and 'antenuptial' percentages of total births, north-east, by decade*

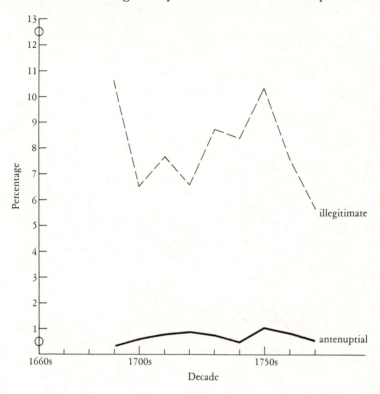

Figure 15 *'Illegitimate' and 'antenuptial' percentages of total births, Caithness, by decade*

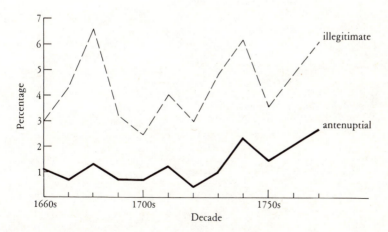

Figure 16 *'Illegitimate' and 'antenuptial' percentages of total births, Ayrshire, by decade*

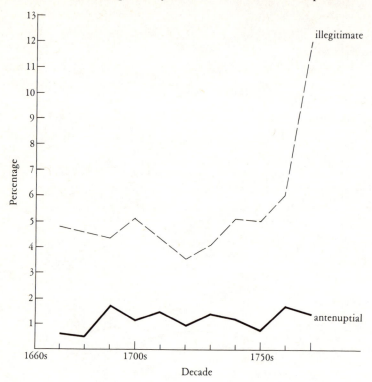

Figure 17 *'Illegitimate' and 'antenuptial' percentages of total births, south-west, by decade*

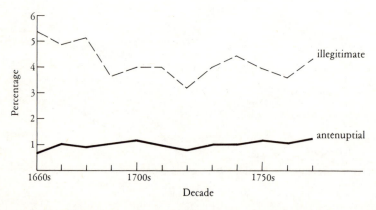

Figure 18 *'Illegitimate' and 'antenuptial' percentages of total births, national sample, by decade*

to marry before an unmarried pregnancy came to term, in another would not, for there is no sign of a general shift from one category to another.

The regions where antenuptial conceptions and bastards were within a few percentage points of one another were those which had consistently low illegitimacy ratios: the Lothians, Central Lowlands and Fife (figures 8, 9 and 10). The levels were by far the closest in Fife. Going back to the records, we find that here – unlike in any other Scottish region – a relatively large number of women gave birth to bastards not because they did not marry but because they married too late. We counted such births in our bastardy figures because the children were born illegitimate, but the Church considered the parents to be antenuptial fornicators because they achieved marriage after the birth of the child. We can offer no convincing explanation for this deviance from the usual Scottish pattern except, once again, to advance the argument of cultural differences between regions.

The figures above compared women who conceived a child before marriage with bastard-bearers, but in order to build up a complete picture it is also necessary to compare them with women who conceived their first child after marrying. In order to do this we have subtracted the bastards from the total estimated births for each region, to obtain a figure for legitimate births. We based our estimate of the proportion of first births in total births by counts based on the Old Parish Register of Kilmarnock. In this register the clerks, for much of the eighteenth century, recorded the 'parity' of the child. The figure set against each child was sometimes its place within the marriage, sometimes by the total of the father's progeny, but since the number of the marriage was also given, by collecting only the figures for first marriages we were sure of obtaining the parity in maternal terms. Of the births counted for three different periods, the proportion of firsts was approximately a quarter.

As figure 23 reveals, the national percentage of antenuptial conceptions among legitimate first births shows a definite but not drastic movement upwards from 3.1 per cent to 4.9 per cent. But this movement is the amalgam of the very different regional patterns shown in figures 19–22. The trend in the north-east and Central Lowlands is similar to that of the national sample, but both regions start below the national level and end above it. So does Aberdeenshire, where the general trend is broken by a sudden peak at 6.0 per cent in the 1700s. The Lothians and Fife both show a

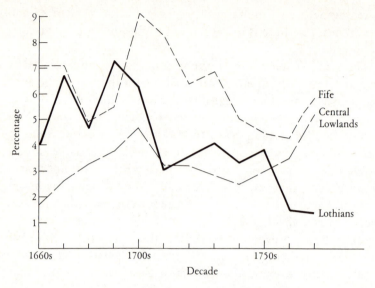

Figure 19 *Percentage of legitimate first births conceived before marriage, Lothians, Fife and Central Lowlands, by decade*

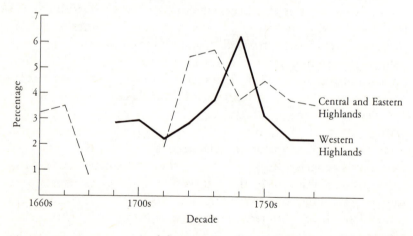

Figure 20 *Percentage of legitimate first births conceived before marriage, Western Highlands and Central and Eastern Highlands, by decade*

downward trend, but the Fife level is always relatively high. The figures for Caithness vary in a way which makes no discernible trend; the south-west is often above the national figure but also with no marked trend; by contrast Ayrshire had a marked upward trend from the early eighteenth century.

How far gone in pregnancy were the women in our antenuptial

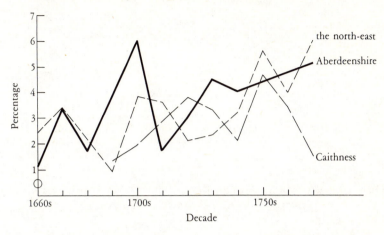

Figure 21 *Percentage of legitimate first births conceived before marriage, Aberdeenshire, the north-east and Caithness, by decade*

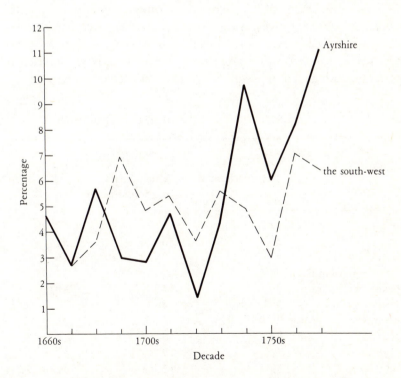

Figure 22 *Percentage of legitimate first births conceived before marriage, Ayrshire and the south-west, by decade*

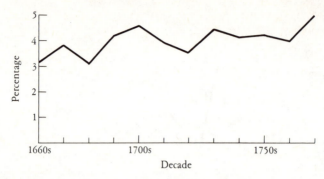

Figure 23 *Percentage of legitimate first births conceived before marriage, national sample, by decade*

cases when they married is not easy to learn from kirk session registers. The point at which sessions discovered the pregnancy may offer a clue. Information about this was available for 31 per cent of antenuptial fornication cases; the percentages are set out in table 5.

Given the system of consignation money, it might have been expected that the greatest number of discoveries would have been made when a child was born, but as can be seen, such was by no means the case. Visible pregnancy before marriage implies a woman far advanced in pregnancy, and it is noteworthy that nearly

Table 5 Discovery of antenuptial fornication

	percentages		
	Before marriage	After marriage but before birth	After birth
Lothians	31	9	60
Fife	36	13	51
Central Lowlands	56	9	35
Eastern Highlands	74	9	17
Western Highlands	25	14	61
Aberdeenshire	59	14	27
North-east	70	6	25
Caithness	42	10	48
Ayrshire	42	19	40
South-west	39	12	49
All regions	47	11	42

half of all these women fell into that category. This figure is particularly striking for the north-east and for the Central and Eastern Highlands, which provide a great contrast with the Western Highlands. That such a small percentage of women were denounced after marriage and before birth should not surprise; it must have seemed to most sessions easier to wait for the birth, when there could be no convincing denial.

The number of women for whom length of pregnancy can be calculated with any precision from information provided in session registers proved very low, only 148 out of a total of 1,961 (7.5 per cent). However, the percentages (see table 6) show a definite cluster between the fifth and eighth months.

Table 6 Percentage of antenuptial conceptions leading to births within each of the first 9 months of marriage

Month	Percentage
1st month	4.1
2nd	1.4
3rd	4.7
4th	8.1
5th	15.5
6th	21.6
7th	20.2
8th	18.2
9th	6.1

One obvious question is whether a contracted couple, i.e. one formally betrothed, considered this to be equivalent to marriage in licensing sexual intercourse. It is possible that this was indeed the case even though many of the births, as shown in table 6, were conceived well before marriage, for the interval between proclamation and marriage could be substantial. In May 1676, Wemyss session found that 'divers persones in this parishe after they give up their names for mariadge, Delayes the same verie long & comitts fornication betwixt Contract & mariadge.' At about the same period (August 1675) in Dalkeith, Alexander Tait and Maryon Purdie, who had been proclaimed for marriage, confessed antenuptial fornication but said 'it was after purpose and paction of marriage'. In Wemyss in January 1704, John Brown and Isobell Davidson, 'being asked when they were guilty answered the same night they were contracted'.

In Kinglassie (January 1759), George Aitkin, whose first child was born seven months after marriage, denied fornication. A week later he 'declar'd that by refusing antinuptial Guilt he only meant to refuse guilt before marriage in his heart and did not deny that he was guilty with Margaret Taylor before the proclamation of Banns and publick Celebration of his marriage with her'. The interesting thing is that some sessions at least (there is not enough evidence to claim this was general) clearly did consider fornication between contract and marriage to be a less heinous sin. In Kinglassie (September 1724), John Baxter asked to be allowed to make only one appearance since he was going to marry the woman with whom he had been guilty. The session would not allow this, 'it being Reported that the woman was with Child before Contract of marriage'. In Kenmore (September 1754), the session agreed to dismiss Duncan Buchannan and Cathrine Robertson with a sessional instead of public rebuke 'in regard the Guilt was Comitted betwixt the Contract and marriage'.

As a whole, though, table 6 gives an inconclusive answer to the question of whether most pre-marital conceptions were initiated after proclamation. It would need a very careful examination of parishes with high quality OPRs, as well as good registers of kirk sessions meeting frequently, to arrive at a clear answer.

Was there any way other than pregnancy that a session could learn about antenuptial fornication? In Dumfries (November 1685), John Burges and Janet Glencorse were actually found in bed together, but as they were willing to swear there had been no carnal dealing their public appearance was for their 'base and unseemlie carriage before marriage'. This bears out what has been said earlier in this chapter about ordinary fornication: if there was not a pregnancy involved, unless a couple were caught *in flagrante delicto*, the charge would always be scándalous carriage rather than fornication.

In an unusual – and sad – case in Dunbarney (August 1702), Robert Gourlie was cited for antenuptial fornication with Janet Archibald, not because she was pregnant (in fact she was claiming she had told people she was with child only to impel the man to marry her), but because the woman herself had alleged it. He was also cited because of 'their scandalous disagreement since their marriage'. Being asked if he had any carnal dealing with the said Janet Archibald, he confessed that he had, being enticed by her to come into her house one night after he had given over his work, & when he had some thought of laying by his purpose of Marriage with her; & being interrogate as to their disagreement since Marriage he confessed the same too, & said that he believed his unwillingness to marry her, his forsaid guilt with her, & her divulging of the same, togither with her untowardly disposition since they were marryed, might be the cause of the bad agreement betwixt them.

However, as indicated earlier, a charge of antenuptial fornication was nearly always the result of pre-marital conception. The rigid way in which the period of gestation was defined and the threat of this rigour is shown in the anxious notes recorded in the memoir of the minister of Penpont in 1694 about his recently acquired wife:

all the time of her being with child I was still afraid lest she a very young lass, being but yet in her 19 year through her rashness or carelessness of herself, should bring forth before the due time, which made me put my request . . . often to God . . . that so he might not open the mouths of the Ungodly.[34]

There was no kirk session enquiry or comment by the ungodly because in the event the couple had 25 hours on the side of respectability, but the minister's fears provide an insight into the ethos of his day.

Inevitably, there were many early births where a couple denied having had pre-marital sex. The usual procedure in such cases was for a midwife to pronounce on whether the child was premature or 'ripe'. The midwife's testimony was not the only yardstick which sessions used to judge guilt or innocence in such cases; if a cause could be given for an early birth that would be accepted as evidence. For example, in the case of Marion Rob (Logie, February 1697), whose child was born six weeks early, it was said that she 'had got a fall when she was with Child and was never well again after that fall till she was brought to bed'. In spite of lack of evidence about whether the infant appeared to be full-term or not, the session dropped the case. In Wemyss (August 1709), the child of Bernard Walker and Margaret Walker was born 27 days early, and they denied guilt. The man declared 'it was very well known

34 NLS, MS.3045, Diary of the Rev. James Murray.

she had got a stress which made her bring forth her child before the time.' The session clearly *did* know of this, and knew furthermore that there had been no reports of scandalous carriage between them, and therefore agreed to baptize the child. (However, it still insisted on the man's binding himself to satisfy discipline if evidence later came to light which proved him guilty.)

The midwife's testimony was not considered infallible. In Canisbay (August 1714), William Howat and Christian Rugg craved baptism for their child, born eight months after marriage. The minister reported he had had the infant inspected, and 'it was found to have all the signs of a timely birth'. The couple continued denying that they had had pre-marital intercourse, and there were no other presumptions of guilt, so the session referred the case to presbytery and when the couple continued to deny, their innocence was accepted. In Wemyss (March 1730), the child of David Tilloch and Elspeth Brown was born 27 days early. The midwife declared the child 'was as proper & full born as any child ever she received'. The affair was delayed, and two years later the man approached the minister again, craving baptism. When he continued to deny antenuptial fornication he was asked if he was willing to swear a solemn oath; when he did so the child was baptized.

Solemn oaths were used both in suspected antenuptial fornication cases and in ordinary fornication cases where a man denied paternity. The Church normally only allowed such oaths to be taken if it believed the man was innocent as he claimed. Having found so many references to such oaths in kirk session records, we were delighted to discover the following in Wemyss session register for August 1673, which provides the actual format and content of such an oath:

Compeired John Stirling befoir the pulpit and sitting there upon a stoole the whole tyme of the forenoones exercise and at the close thereof gave his oath The tenor whereoff follows I Johne Stirling with uplifted hand to heaven Doe declare before the Lord God, the searcher off hearts, As I shall answer unto him in the great day, wherein he shall Judge the quick & the dead, And render to every one according to thair works, That I never did comitt the act of uncleanness and fornication with Christian Pirie And iff this my declaration be not true, Then let me be seperate from the presence of God for ever, And even in this Life be ane example of Gods vengeance and wroth against all perjurie and uncleannesse.

The vigorous language of this oath, a form actually used, appears more effective as an instrument of coercion than the general purpose form officially prescribed.[35]

Sometimes sessions did not require an oath but simply used their common sense. In Cramond (June 1734), Margaret Fairholm gave birth to a seven month child and denied guilt. 'The session considering that there had been no presumption, save that she had brought forth her child about the seventh month after marriage, which is no extraordinary case; they thought fit to proceed no further in this affair.' In Kingsbarns (July 1749), David Campbell and Alison Lesles denied guilt after the birth of their twins four weeks early. The midwife declared that there 'was nothing more ordinary for a woman with twins than to bring them furth in the eight month'; the session allowed baptism to go ahead.

In marked contrast to the attitude of the sessions above was a case in Torphichen (May 1727) which shows a session determined to believe the worst. Mrs Taitt 'spouse to Mr John Tait Chyrugeon' gave birth to a child six weeks early. The minister believed the couple innocent and presented various reasons to the session: she had been ill of 'a violent Ague' for several months before she gave birth, she had 'met with a Fright' a few days before delivery, the child could not suck and had no proper nails on some toes, etc. However, the midwife thought the child was full term, and the session therefore insisted on the testimony of several of the women who had attended the birth. All declared they thought the child premature, and Mr Taitt solemnly declared his innocence, but the session decided that it required further evidence and called more of the women who had attended the birth. It was not until a letter was produced from 'Mrs Forrest' (i.e. Mistress, implying gentry status) which declared her belief in the child being born early that the session allowed baptism to go ahead. In the postscript to the letter Mrs Forrest added: 'I could have wished there had not been so much Din about it, it shews little Love to the Credit of the Gospel to put such Things in the Mouths of the wicked and Ignorant.'

---

35 The official form of oath is given in Steuart, *Collections and Observations*, p. 250: 'I . . . do declare before God and this . . . that I am innocent and free of the said sin of . . . of having carnal knowledge of the said C. D. and hereby call the great God, the judge and avenger of all falsehoods, to be witness and judge against me in this matter if I be guilty: and this I do, by taking his blessed name in my mouth, and swearing by him, who is the great judge, punisher, and avenger as said is, and that in the sincerity of my heart, according to the truth of the matter and mine own conscience, as I shall answer to God in the last and great day, when I shall stand before him to answer for all that I do in the flesh, and as I would partake of his glory in heaven after this life is at an end.'

There is a further category of women who must be looked at: those who were guilty of fornication before marriage but with men other than those they married. We did not count the issue of such liaisons as bastards, since by Scots law they were considered legitimate, even if the child would have been looked upon as a bastard within the community. We are not claiming this was a common occurrence, only that we were caught unawares by this group, whose existence we had not suspected. Out of a total of 1,961 pre-marital conceptions, 31 were known to have been fathered by a man other than the husband. Cases occurred as early as the 1660s and as late as the 1770s, and there was no region which did not have at least one such case. The highest number, seven, occurred in the Eastern Highlands, four of those in Kenmore parish in the 1740s. In Petty, another Eastern Highland parish, the session clerk recorded of one woman in 1765 that she was 'with Child by antinuptial fornication to her own husband', as though it were a surprise. No particular shock or horror was expressed at a woman bearing her first child to a man not her husband in any of the session minutes in this region.

Indeed, it was surprisingly rare for sessions in *any* of the regions to express any particular condemnation of such a thing happening. We found such expressions in only four of the cases, three of them in Ayrshire. In Grange, a north-east parish, in 1717, the session concluded that Margaret Dason 'was guilty of a remarkable wickedness in marrying with an other mans Child in her womb'. They were 'difficultyed in passing sentence against her, in regard the like had not happened formerly in this place in their time'. In the first of the Ayrshire cases (Kilmarnock, July 1698), Jannet McClunnochin claimed 'she never knew she was with child unto the said John Muir untill both her self and her husband William Aitken had found it moving and stirring in her belly, and so was removed with indignation at her disingenuity and dissimulation.' In another Ayrshire case (Kilbirnie, November 1760), Jean Sherret, married to John Blain, confessed that the child she brought forth six months after marriage was fathered by Hugh Orr. The session considered this case unusual enough to consult presbytery, and when she was publicly rebuked it was not just for her sin of fornication but also 'for her deceiving the man she was married to, by entering into marriage with him when she was with child to another man'. One is surprised not to find such sentiments expressed more often in such cases.

Somewhat less than a fifth of the women who bore children in our period conceived their first child out of wedlock. This figure is arrived at by taking the total number of fornication cases, removing from it the repeaters, adding on the number disciplined for 'antenuptial uncleanness' and taking the figure thus achieved as a percentage of a quarter of the estimated annual births in the parishes, an adjustment based on the OPR of Kilmarnock.

The national sample figures for the percentage of first births conceived out of wedlock are not quite static, moving between 15 and 23 with low points in the 1690s and 1720s. The notable feature is that there is no general trend except for the moderate fall in the seventeenth century. Differences within and between regions are much more marked, a fact to be expected since in these cases the samples are small. The two most dramatic sets of regional figures are set out, with the national sample, in figure 24. Both these

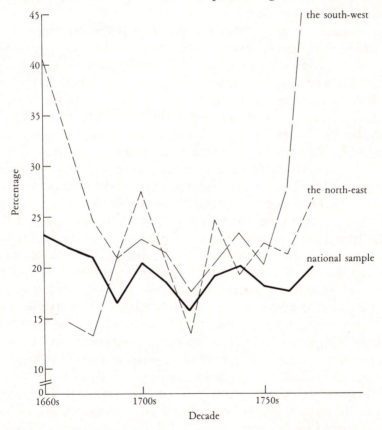

Figure 24 *Percentage of all first births conceived before marriage, north-east, south-west and national sample*

regions have periods of high level, the north-east at the start of the period and the south-west at the end, and in both these periods the level is mainly the result of high illegitimacy. In the Lothians, Fife and the Central Lowlands the level of first conceptions out of wedlock was always low, and so it was also for much of the time in the Western Highlands. Such trend as can be seen was always downwards in the Lothians and in Fife. In contrast the level was always fairly high in Caithness and for much of the time in the Eastern and Central Highlands. In Aberdeenshire and Ayrshire there was an upward trend.

What is striking about these figures is the relatively small part played in them by pre-marital pregnancies. These never provide as much as a third of the cases, and usually give less than a quarter. The share of these in total births has already been shown to be under 2 per cent. The majority of infants conceived out of wedlock were also born out of it.

The relatively static level of first conceptions starting out of wedlock in Scotland contrasts with that shown by Wrigley for England. Wrigley's figures show the percentage of first births occurring within eight months of marriage as about 15 in the late seventeenth century, when a further 1.4 per cent of births were illegitimate, rising to 35 per cent in the 1770s with a further 4.75 per cent illegitimate.[36] At this latter date, assuming a family size similar to that of Kilmarnock, between 50 and 60 per cent of first births in England, as already stated, were conceived outwith wedlock. The English figures, with the marked upward trend showing in both illegitimacy and bridal pregnancy, make it natural to see these two elements as results, for a significant part of the population, of a normal pattern of intercourse during courtship and the expansion of this part in the later eighteenth century, though they do not exclude other explanations. The low level of bridal pregnancy and the absence of a marked upward trend makes this an improbable explanation for Scotland. Only in Fife and Ayrshire, where there is a near parallel movement of the curves, as shown in figures 10 and 16, is the former explanation reasonable. Elsewhere it would be a more obvious interpretation of the figures to assume a fairly constant proportion of couples intending marriage entering on pre-marital intercourse, and a separate population with no immediate prospect of marriage responsible for the cases of illegitimacy.

36 E. A. Wrigley, 'Marriage, Fertility and Population Growth in Eighteenth Century England', p. 157.

6

Where, When and Why

The previous chapter summarized the quantitative evidence concerning illegitimacy in Scotland, but obviously there are many questions which cannot be answered by such data and which require a different approach. Fortunately, many kirk session registers went beyond the 'bare bones' of a case and provided us with fuller information, making possible the attempt an answer to such questions as: what were the circumstances in which these women became pregnant? Where and when did it occur? Why did it happen – were they raped, expecting the man to marry them, or just succumbing to persuasion or to vigorous courtship? Who were the men who got them pregnant – was it a casual relationship; what were the prospects of marriage; what were the circumstances of the seduction? In this chapter we attempt to resolve queries of this nature.[1]

Previously we stated that an accusation of fornication would normally be made only on the evidence of pregnancy (see chapter 5). It is worth emphasizing that kirk session registers also contain many cases which were deemed 'scandalous carriage'. This meant that a couple was caught in a compromising position – it might merely be their being alone in a house together with the door barred but not actually caught in the act, and that the woman involved did not give evidence of fornication by becoming pregnant. Such cases often took up an inordinate amount of time because endless witnesses had to be called to prove or disprove the allegation. We offer the following example.

In Kenmore in the Central Highlands (December 1750), a 'clamant Report of an unseemly Carriage' between Angus

---

1 Much of the material of this chapter was published in the *Journal of Social History* 22, March 1988, pp. 483–97, under the title of 'Girls in Trouble: the social and geographical setting of illegitimacy in early modern Scotland'.

McDonald, a married man, and Isobel Campbell, who had previously been his servant, reached the session. It was alleged that at a wedding the two had gone off together '& were afterwards found in the Cows Stalls in the Dark'. Not only that, but the following morning they were seen in the same bed, 'by which scandalous behaviour they gave great offence to every Serious Christian in the Neighbourhood'. The woman admitted going off with the man but insisted that she was not 'at any time off her feet but only Leaned with her Elbow upon the stall that was next the Door'. Asked what she was doing there with him, 'she could give no satisfying account but at last said that she was Craving him . . . for her wages he was owing her and being further interrogate if or not her head Cloathes came off and if her hair that was taped up came down she says she knows not but the Plaid that was about her head and her hair might [have] come down.' As for the events of the following morning she said he only 'stretched himself upon her Bed but did not touch her'. Angus McDonald was called, and his story was that he had been in drink the night of the wedding and did not recall what had happened. He denied being in her bed the next morning, 'but being told she confessed it he acknowledges he did lay himself down in it he again & again prevaricated & could give no good reason for their being together at all.'

In the weeks that followed, various witnesses who had seen the couple together gave their evidence. By February the session decided that 'as the Parties seem to think but little of the Scandal because the actual guilt of uncleanness is not proven against them, that this whole affair should be referred to the presbytery.' It was subsequently reported that the two of them had travelled together to the meeting of presbytery and spent the night in the same bed in a lodging house, 'by which it would apear they were two impudent abandoned Creatures.' This is not being quoted as a typical case of scandalous carriage – few couples were so brazen, and in this instance the presbytery ordered that they be treated as adulterers – but it does illustrate the attitude that one could resist accusations of fornication if not actually caught in the act or pregnant.

The Church manifested a strong disapproval of physical contact or demonstration, and such would always bring a risk of a charge of scandalous carriage. In Longforgan in 1685 the distaste for physical contact produced the ruling that 'no Brydegroom kiss his Bryde before the minister' on pain of a fine of ten merks. Even two people of different sex taking a walk together could lead to an investigation, the calling of witnesses, and even, if nothing more could be proved, a reproof. The level of intimacy which, in an English church case, could be claimed as 'honest courtship' would, in Scotland, initiate a detailed enquiry.[2] Of course, the Kirk acted only when information of unseemly conduct was brought before the session. It is possible that in some areas practices which obtained in the mid-nineteenth century, such as night courting and bundling, existed in our period but were not reported. It is, however, difficult to square the idea of such practices with the conspicuous evidence of active adherence by the populace to the standards of the Kirk.

Another type of scandalous carriage case occurred earlier in the century in Cramond (September 1707). Samuel Johnstoun was accused of unseemly behaviour with Agnes Bryce on the way home from Edinburgh. He declared that he and she, along with some others, drank a quart of ale, but that 'neither he nor she wer in drinke'.[3] 'Being desired to tell the truth whither there was any miscarriage between them by the way? he denyed, but said that she haveing a sore foot, satt down on the ground to looke it, & he satt down beside her, Being asked, If he kissed her & he answered, he did.' Two witnesses were called, and their versions were more suggestive. George Mure, a 60-year-old man, declared he saw the two of them at the highway side, 'and him between her leggs, and then he lifted up her cloathes & was Lying above her, he was not long above her, he pulled her up again & could not gett her kept up, she was so in drinke'. Mure's younger companion confirmed the story, adding that when he saw Johnston 'well up her coats, & Ly doun above her' he had caused Mure to call out to them in order to 'hinder them to committ sin'. The couple were convicted of scandalous carriage and ordered to appear before the congregation. Scandalous carriage may have been considered a lesser sin than fornication – and of course there was no pregnancy to contend with – but it nevertheless did warrant a public rebuke.

In a society where a wide range of activities between the sexes was unacceptable, there are puzzles about courtship practices. We found an interesting courtship case in Thurso (March 1722):

David Manson Sailor & Christian Nicol formerly delated of scandalous behaviour viz of walking together at unseasonable hours and particularly

---

2 M. J. Ingram, 'Church courts and neighbourhood: aspects of social control in Wiltshire, 1600–40' (unpublished D.Phil. thesis, Oxford University, 1976), shows considerable tolerance of physical familiarity between the sexes in the early seventeenth century.
3 A Scots quart was two and two-thirds the size of an imperial quart.

their sitting together one night a little above the Chappel of pennyland betwixt the hours of ten & eleven at night and he the said Manson sitting hard by her with his arms about her neck, both of them being cited . . . acknowledged what was delated against them to be truth . . . but at the same time they declare that the design of their meeting upon that night was to concert matters with respect to their contract & marriage and that they would not frequent one anothers company so much if they had not intended to marry very soon. The Session finding . . . that the foresaid Donald Manson sailor is in suit of her and that they actually Intend to marry and likewise considering that nothing can be proved against them but what may be allowable to persons that intend to marry do give up with this process.

What makes this case of significance is the fact that it was the only instance we found of a couple cited for scandalous behaviour who were let off any penalty because they were going to be married. It is possible, of course, that couples known to be contracted might have been allowed greater leeway and not be cited before the session for behaviour which would be considered scandalous in another couple; that is something we cannot know. It is certainly very clear, however, that a practice such as 'bundling', or courtship in bed, accepted in certain peasant societies, was firmly opposed by the Church of Scotland. In Kilfinan, in December 1721, the kirk elders learned that Duncan McCurrie and Isobel Midy had shared a bed while working at the harvesting in the Lowlands. McCurrie was called before the session and stated 'That he lay in Naked bed with Isobel Midy the tyme of their being in Lothian at the shearing in harvest last, that it was the Custom of the place for Neighbours and Country bairns to ly together and that there were many others who lay together as they did: he absolutely denyed any Carnal dealings with her.' She concurred and they were subsequently purged by oath of fornication. However, 'The Session Considering the baseness of the above practise of single persons bedding together, the offence given thereby to the Christian people and to be a warning to others for the future' appointed them both to make public appearances and be rebuked before the congregation.

Christian Barker of Wemyss (March 1755) was cited for indecent behaviour with a man who, she claimed, was courting her, and insisted that 'she would give over her Bed and sit by the fireside herself'. The session decided that 'her Excuse was only a sham and a shift' and ordered her to appear publicly. Admittedly this woman already had a bad reputation for having had strangers in her house, and the man was not known to the session. However, the very fact that, barring the Thurso case above, none of the couples cited for scandalous carriage even tried to claim courtship as a valid reason for their actions indicates that any kind of physical intimacy was considered unacceptable for an unmarried couple.

The absence of claims that marriage was promised has a direct bearing on the theory of 'failed courtship' in fornication cases. If girls who bore illegitimate children did so because they had expected their partners to marry them, then one would have expected this to have been the common defence under interrogation, particularly if the girl had been abandoned or repudiated. In fact, this is not so. Even the phrase 'under promise of marriage', which occurs in some places in the 1660s and 1670s, virtually disappears after that. In Wemyss, in January 1661, Geills Bred admitted fornication with David Beans, her servant, 'and being Inquired iff his filthines comitted was under promise of mariadge Answered negatively'. The man 'declaired he hade so often comitted the act of filthines with hir in hir own bed he could not give ane particular Accompt And being Inquired iff the samen was under purpose of mariadge Answered negative'. At a later date the question would not even have been asked. The use of the word 'filthines' may, at this date, indicate genuine revulsion to unmarried sexual activity on the part of the session. Promise of marriage followed by intercourse would have been recognised by the State but not by the Church as making a valid marriage. It is conceivable that the habit of not asking about promises arose from a desire on the part of the Church not to have to face the issue of two distinct laws of marriage. If this were the case we would expect that this policy would have been set out or mentioned somewhere on some occasion, but it is never discussed in our material. In all our 8,000 and more cases there is no reference to the definition of marriage by *verba de futuro*.

The relatively low number of fornication allegations made against elders and ministers, and the seriousness with which those made was taken, support the idea of a puritanical distaste for sexuality. But we have to remember that kirk session registers were regularly inspected by the presbytery, and their language may have been tuned to the assumed views of the higher court. Certainly, as shown in chapter 2, by the mid-eighteenth century, if not before, there existed a counter-culture in literature and comment of an openly bawdy nature.

In one case we encountered a woman alleging pregnancy in order to get a man to marry her. In November 1741, Margaret

Barbor of Rothesay claimed to be pregnant, but the man named as father denied guilt. The local community believed it was a pretended pregnancy, 'as a wheedle to noose him into marriage', and on 6 December the woman was examined by midwives who found no signs of pregnancy. It may be that a woman did think she stood a better chance of getting her partner to marry her if she were pregnant, but it would be unwise to argue from this one case (where the pregnancy was in any case fictitious) that women were likely to risk an illegitimate birth because of some vague hope of marriage.

The low level of pre-marital pregnancy, shown in chapter 5, makes it unlikely that any sizeable part of the population regarded sexual intercourse as a normal prelude to marriage. Figures 8–18 in chapter 5 (see pp. 160–4) bring out pre-marital pregnancy as a relatively stable component of births conceived out of wedlock. If intercourse had been seen as a normal part of courtship we would expect variations in the levels of pre-marital pregnancy produced by unexpected fluctuations in the economy.

There are popular beliefs, held in Scotland and elsewhere, about the role of intercourse before marriage, which have to be dismissed. One is the claim of the seigneurial right to intercourse with girls before or at their marriage, the so-called *jus primae noctis*, a theme associated with *La nozze di Figaro*. In spite of the fact that such an institution would have run counter to the ethos of the Kirk, it has been vehemently claimed as existing in Scotland by Tom Johnston in his *History of the Working Classes in Scotland*. Johnston uses, as support, references to statements by Boece, Buchanan, Skene and Boswell, but these authorities appear to be relying either on hearsay or on each other. The right, or practice, was also suggested scurrilously in the account of Scotland written by Thomas Kirke in 1679. These accounts place the practice far away and in the past, and so does the fictional description of it by George Mackay Brown. None of this so-called evidence has any historical validity, and the existence of such a right or practice anywhere in Christendom has been effectively demolished in the eleventh edition of the *Encyclopaedia Britannica*.[4]

The other myth is the popular belief that in peasant society there is a strong reason for a man to wish to be sure of an heir to his holding before he commits himself to marriage, and

---

4 T. Johnston, *The History of the Working Classes in Scotland* (Glasgow, 1922), pp. 12–13; Thomas Kirke, in P. Hume Brown (ed.), *Early Travellers in Scotland* (Edinburgh, 1891), p. 258; *Encyclopaedia Britannica* (Cambridge, 1911) xv, p. 593, 'Jus primae noctis'.

therefore antenuptial intercourse is taken for granted. Of course, a pregnancy was no insurance of masculine birth: the chance would be nearly even. In Scotland the level of antenuptial pregnancy was too low to justify belief in such a view, and Scotland was not a country with peasant rights in land. If there was a group of men likely to be concerned about an heir to a farm it would be the small landowners, the men for whom Sir Walter Scott coined the phrase 'bonnet lairds'. The distribution of this group varied greatly from region to region, and it formed a sizeable proportion of society in only a few counties, most notably in the Central Lowlands. In 1770 bonnet lairds owned 20 per cent of the land in Kinross-shire, 14 per cent in Stirlingshire and 13 per cent in Clackmannanshire.[5] It is striking that of all our regions the Central Lowlands had consistently the lowest level of antenuptial pregnancy.

If expectation of marriage was not the reason why many girls committed fornication, then why did they do so? Sheer proximity and opportunity form one obvious answer. A young man and a young woman serving together in the same household would be thrown together frequently, and the large proportion of cases involving fellow servants – echoing a trend found in England – shows that this temptation was indeed difficult to resist. The master and mistress of the household were supposed to keep an eye on their servants, but this was not always feasible, or, if feasible, not always carried out.

The world of our cases, for most of our period, was one of very limited material possessions. In Belhelvie, in January 1741, Elspet Davidson was pregnant by her fellow servant George Rheney. Their master appeared before the session, stating that it was being maliciously rumoured in the parish that he had made them lie in one bed together, and therefore he wanted them both to swear they slept in separate beds with a sufficiency of bedclothes on each. They acceded to his request, but at a subsequent meeting claimed that he had intimidated them into denying the truth, which was that on a very stormy night Rheney's bed had been too cold to sleep in and their mistress had told him to sleep in Elspet's, knowing full well what was likely to occur. The case dragged on for a long time, but the couple's statement was clearly the truth, or at least part of the truth.

Close contact with fellow servants of the other sex was not

5 L. Timperley, 'The Pattern of Landholding in Eighteenth-Century Scotland', in M. L. Parry and T. R. Slater (eds), *The Making of the Scottish Countryside* (London, 1980), pp. 137–54.

supposed to happen in bed, but the working life of many girls gave ample opportunity for seduction. In particular, the frequency with which girls were made pregnant by their master or their master's son shows how easy it was for someone with authority to create opportunities. Such liaisons need not necessarily be seen as coercion by a man in a higher social position, as many young people were placed in households of roughly the same social status as their own, very often the houses of kin. A man (even a married man) could always make opportunities for sexual intercourse with his servant.

Naturally there were also cases of couples who did not serve together, but who found – or made – opportunities. The question which then arises is where the act of intercourse actually took place. In common with Quaife's findings for seventeenth-century Somerset,[6] in most cases for which we have details it took place indoors rather than outdoors. Given the climate of Scotland, even in summer, this is not surprising. It might be in the house where the girl was employed if she was in service, or her father's house if she was not; it could be the man's house, or the house of a friend or relative. There may perhaps have been connivance in some instances, but for the most part it seems that a couple simply took advantage of an empty building. In Dysart (May 1669), when Elspet Whyte was asked where James Martin had had carnal dealing with her, she 'Answered in William Cunygham's house being posed wher was the folkes that belonged to the house Answerd that William Cunyghame was not at home and sume body cryed to his wife to goe to the yeard and in that tyme he lay with hir.' Also in Dysart, in February 1760, William White, the man named as the father of her child by John Ramsay's servant, Margaret Pringle, admitted that 'on the Friday after Leslie Mercat he went into John Ramsay's house when he knew that neither he nor his wife were within on ane ill design.'

Aside from houses, other indoor venues were stables, barns, byres and mills. There are statements such as 'in his barn' and 'in his brother's byre'. These were places where servants sometimes slept and also places where the risk of discovery might be small. Opportunities for intercourse were often seized during work. In at least one instance, that of Isabel Gardiner and William Suine in Dysart (October 1762), the two of them had been 'brewing in the Stable where his horse stood'. This apparently could go on until

6 G. R. Quaife, 'The Consenting Spinster in a Peasant Society: Aspects of Premarital Sex in "Puritan" Somerset 1645–1660', *Journal of Social History* XI (1977–8), p. 229.

very late at night, for 'she affirmed That many times he had been with her at the brewing business till two or three a clock (in the morning).'

Another instance of a sexual encounter at work comes from Wemyss, November 1721. It was alleged by Beatrice Turnbull here that, after the other workers left the workshop, Mr Orme, in charge of it, said 'Stay Beatrice, and I will give you the Receipt your father was speaking off for some iron. Then he shut the door, and strugled with her . . .'.

Mr Orme might choose to wait till the two of them were alone, but privacy was not seen as a necessary condition for sexual intercourse. It is difficult for people today to realize how rare it was in early modern society for most people to experience any degree of privacy. Whole households occupied single-roomed cottages, which lacked the furnishings to make partitions within them or to provide curtains for the beds. Three to a bed was a normal feature of life.[7] Intercourse could take place between a couple with a third person in the bed. (Of course, hard outdoor work might make the third person sleep heavily: certainly in several cases such people were found to be useless as witnesses.) In Dysart (August 1702), Margaret Simson 'acknowledged that she was frequently guilty of Adultery with the said Alexander Bans and that they were once guilty of it in Jannet Gordoun's House Janet Gordoun being in the bed with them in time of the action.' In Kilfinan (November 1744), John McLane denied Mary Smith's assertion that he had had intercourse with her at the Smith's house at the ferry of Otter, 'where the Landlord of the House Jo MacFarmling desired them to go to bed together.' Katharine Smith was called as witness but could not confirm whether or not intercourse had taken place, as 'after having lien down in Bed beside them [she] fell immediately a Sleep'. In Dysart (August 1767), Catharine Gilmour stated that 'when it was very late she & her Comerade went to bed, & that James came to bed to them a little aftere they had gone to bed – & then & there was guilty with her.' She subsequently added that 'James had been guilty with her both when her Comerade was in bed with her & asleep & also after she had got up in the morning she having got up before her &

---

7 It appears that there were gradations in status to different positions in the bed, the one nearest the wall being the most coveted position; cf. 'Captain Wedderburn's courtship', a ballad recorded by Jean Redpath, in which the man promises the woman the place in the bed by the wall. Presumably it was because the person on the outside would be the first one up, to unbar the door, stoke the fire, etc.

James.'[8] On the other hand, the fact that a third person had been in the bed at the alleged time was sometimes put forward as evidence of no misconduct suggests that some people felt that close contact with another person was inappropriate as a setting for sexual intercourse.

Outdoor work also provided many venues for intercourse, including, in Wemyss, 'at the water side of Leven', 'at the double dykes between Newtoun and Brankstoun', and 'in the Middle of Weems Mure'. In the Western Highlands the act often took place 'in the mountains'. As in seventeenth-century Somerset, sex was often the result of outdoor employment.[9] Distance from other workers gave opportunity. Beatrix Spittle, in Wemyss (February 1714), was guilty with George Bairner 'in the fields at a place called the horsehill the time the corn was stowing when she went with him to see what corn should be stowed [cut]'. In Dysart (April 1776), Janet Graham was guilty 'on a tuesday in May last pretty late at night, at the foot of the Pipers Braes, when she was agoing to wash to Mrs John Brodie'. In Kilfinan (May 1755), in the Highlands, Isabel Mun stated that 'their first Carnall Dealings were att the Peat-Moss, att the time they were Leading home the peats.' Also in Kilfinan (November 1744), Betty Stewart stated that Archibald Lamont had been guilty with her 'about the 22d May between Kildairg and Aird when she was thigging [acquiring] wood'. And in the same parish (October 1748) Dorothy McDonald claimed that Dugald McLauchlan 'had first guilt with her as they were attending some Cattle on the hills of Faylan'.

Travelling together to or from fairs or markets also provided temptation and opportunity. Helen Mackay (Kilmartin, February 1745) confessed guilt with Malcolm McBrian, smith, 'as they were both coming home from the first Foord Market upon a Friday' – which the session calculated must have been 27 July. Though the issue of drink was not raised in these cases, a visit to market would have included ale bibbing.

As one might have expected, all the cases collected of outdoor fornication occurred between April and September. However, as stated earlier, indoor venues were far more usual, and there is no discernible seasonal pattern to indoor cases.

8 The man claimed that he 'slept along with them all night – but that they had all their Clothes'. However, in July he finally admitted that the woman's story was true.

9 Quaife, 'The Consenting Spinster in a Peasant Society: Aspects of Premarital Sex in "Puritan" Somerset 1645–1660', p. 229.

Special occasions, marriages or traditional saints' days, which were still observed in spite of the efforts of the Church, all gave opportunities for contact, for drinking and for staying in other people's houses, or, alternatively, might lead to the absence of those who might prevent love-making. In Dysart, in December 1669, Joanit Archibald was made pregnant in 'John Dalrumpil's maltbarn . . . upon that day which John Williamson was married.' In January 1775, Barbara Miller claimed the first offence on 'the saturday evening before Kirkcaldie sacrament at the east side of James Horn's dyke', the second on 'the thursday before the king's birthday' and a later episode on 'the day of Gallowtown market'.

When looking at questions of opportunity and proximity it is necessary to realize that women were an essential part of the rural labour force in early modern Britain, and many tasks were age or sex-specific; that is, they would have allotted to them no more than the necessary muscle power and skill. From this it followed that it was in no way unusual for a woman to be working alone, or with only a man as companion, or to be sent on a distant errand alone. Housing was cramped, and if extra people arrived at a house they would share the beds already in use. These facts add up to a situation in which little effort was made to provide protection or chaperonage for women. In this the society of early modern Scotland differed from that of the mid- or late-nineteenth century, when there was considerable effort made by the upper classes to prevent servants having the opportunity for sexual encounters and when the respectable working class of the cities also endeavoured to protect and segregate the womenfolk.

There is little indication of disapproval of girls being in situations where there was a risk of vigorous seduction, though in May 1699 the session of Kells 'taking to their serious consideration the unnecessary and unseemly converse of some young women with strangers . . . on fairs and publick mercat days' ordered all young women 'to keep themselves at a distance from strangers and lascivious young men'. It is to be noted that the duty of separation was placed solely on the women, and even though the young men were labelled 'lascivious', there is no censure of them in the ruling.

Given the opportunist nature of many of the sexual encounters that led to illegitimate births, one might expect the economic changes of the later eighteenth century to have produced a marked change in the illegitimacy ratios. All Scotland, though to different degrees, was experiencing more frequent movement of people, accompanied by a desire for greater personal independence. In the

Lowlands there was a trend towards larger units of work, bigger farms, and industry organized on a wider and more regular system: in many places there were larger units of settlement as towns expanded and planned villages were set up. But larger work forces on the farms led to the use of labourers rather than living-in servants, and the demand for well-muscled labour and the need for more textile production tended to reduce the practice of men and women working together. There was also a marked increase in real incomes, and consequently more comfortable and better equipped houses. The box bed, which created internal divisions within rooms, was an important step towards some privacy, and the availability of more furniture and the creation of more inns both reduced the occasional need for bed-sharing between the unmarried of different sex. In the 1770s there is evidence of considerable unemployment and dislocation in the Lowlands, which may have frustrated some prospects of marriage.[10] Some of these various economic changes might be expected to enhance, and others to reduce, the opportunities for unplanned sexual intercourse. It may well be that the absence of an upward trend in illegitimacy, except in Ayrshire and the south-west, may stem from the fact that changes which increased the level of supervision successfully countered the effects of greater mobility.

In common with those of seventeenth-century Somerset,[11] girls in early modern Scotland were likely to claim that they had been guilty with only one man and on only one or two occasions. The second statement is more suspect than the first, given the statistical probability of becoming pregnant from one or two acts of intercourse, but it does indicate that such behaviour was considered more acceptable than frequent couplings. As the kirk session made no distinction in punishing a girl who had fallen only once and one who had done so on a number of occasions but with the same man, the pattern being striven for was clearly one set by the community rather than the Church.

A typical statement was made by Mary McNiel in Kilfinan (February 1751): 'it was about february 14th in Innins Barn in the Daytime and that they only had Carnal Dealings together once.' Or that by Beatrix Spittle, whom we have already encountered stowing corn, that 'she was never guilty with him nor any

10 Bernard Bailyn, *Voyagers to the West* (London, 1986), pp. 45, 198.
11 Quaife, 'The Consenting Spinster in a Peasant Society: Aspects of Premarital Sex in "Puritan" Somerset 1645–1660', pp. 232–3.

other person before or since that time.' However, Isabel Mun, previously noted as having fallen the first time when leading home the peats, was not able to make the claim of once only. She was able to give a clear account of a second fall, but then went on to say that 'as to the third time they had Dealings she Could not particularly Condescend upon. But that they met Several times which she Could not Call to memory.' Geills Bred and David Beans, quoted earlier, did not appear particularly ashamed of their behaviour, but the description of Mary Livison (Kilfinan, November 1751) making her statement suggests a consciousness of having broken the rules. After giving a precise time and place of guilt with John Mun she was asked 'whither or not they met but that time – att this she paused, but att Last told they had frequent meetings in the month of January but not after that.'

There was also a number of women who named more than one man as guilty with them at about the same time. Not surprisingly, this could lead to problems in identifying the actual father of the child. For example, in Blair Atholl, in August 1744, Ann Robertson alleged that Duncan Robertson was the father of her expected child. He admitted guilt in January 1745, at the same time that she confessed that she had also been guilty with Angus McDonald, and that McDonald was the real father. McDonald admitted guilt, but denied fatherhood. Altogether we found 28 cases of women who, when challenged to name their partner, admitted, either then or later, that they had been guilty with more than one man at roughly the same time. This must be seen as in a different category from the successive liaisons which led to repeating illegitimacy.

Any sexual encounter which was considered incestuous led to a much higher level of penalty. Young people were often placed in service in the houses of kin, and therefore it is not surprising to discover that a number of guilty couples turned out to have the same surname. Physical relations between cousins, however close in blood, occasioned no extra degree of disapproval by the Church. It was a different matter with relationships which the session considered within the prohibited degrees. Though the range had been reduced by the Reformation to the narrow list contained in Leviticus XVIII,[12] with an additional list of parallel relationships not specifically mentioned in that chapter, it still included affines as well as kin, on the assumption that the marital bond made a couple

12 J. R. Hardy, 'The Attitude of the Church and State in Scotland to Sex and Marriage, 1560–1707' (unpublished M.Phil. thesis, Edinburgh University, 1978).

one flesh. Indeed, all the cases that we have found where incest was part of the accusation and where the relationship was clearly stated, were cases of affinity, not of kinship. For the most part they involved sexual links either with brothers- or sisters-in-law or with nephews or nieces by marriage.

The risk of an accusation of incest with its very high penalty could lead to belated attempts to conceal the link. In Dundonald (August 1787), Margaret Porter claimed to have been raped 'by a stranger' in circumstances that the session rightly regarded with scepticism, 'considering how improbable this was that ane could find ane opportunity for ane rape in the day time in a road so frequented'. Further investigation revealed that the man involved was her brother-in-law. A typical description of the woman involved in a case is that in Kilwining, January 1784, 'a sister daughter of his deceased wife'.

Incest also covered cases where, by the Church's standards, affinity had been established by sexual relationship without any marriage. For instance, in Dailly (August 1731) Mary McBroom was alleged to be pregnant to a man lodging with her and her sister also accused him of her own pregnancy. The case was referred to the presbytery as an allegation of 'horrid incest'. Similarly in Pencaitland (March 1656), a man was referred to the presbytery for having got Agnes Wedderburn with child and having behaved with scandalous carriage with her sister Jean. This behaviour had not made the sister pregnant so it was merely 'a great presumption of incest'. In Blair Atholl, in December 1751, Katharine Stewart's proclamation of marriage with John Gow was stopped following an allegation of indecent behaviour with Alexander Gow, his brother. When Alexander admitted the fornication, the proposed marriage was called incestuous and banned. In a case of the preceding century (Pencaitland, March 1666), a mere allegation of scandalous carriage between a man and a girl some years before was enough to lead the session to block his proposed marriage to her sister on the grounds of possible incest. Agnes McLaren in Kenmore (December 1755) was in trouble over an affair with the man married to her sister, but since the affair preceded the contract of marriage it was not called incest. In August 1712, in Wemyss, by contrast, an old liaison with a man was considered to have created a relationship which caused fornication with his nephew to be incestuous: Katharine Henderson, a trilapse case, had committed fornication with the uncle of her first bastard.

These instances show how an 'incestuous' relationship could, in some cases, be the result of ignorance of one of the participants of the sexual activities of the other, and that most cases labelled incest were not the result of sexual activity within a common household. The absence of instances of incestuous relationships between near kin does not mean that the most likely forms of such incest, between brother and sister and between father and daughter, did not happen, but only that any procedure initiated by obvious pregnancy was unlikely to pick them up. Such incest of near kin occurs predominantly when the girl is young, and from what we know of physiological development in early modern society, is unlikely to have led to conception in girls under 17. Yet most young people left their parental home for service of one kind or another before that age – in Scotland usually between the ages of 10 and 14. Sexual encounters with these juveniles would not involve pregnancy. They would belong with other types of sexual irregularity, for instance homosexual intercourse, child molestation and bestiality, recorded only when direct evidence of the activity was produced. One KSR mentions a man emerging from behind a horse looking decidedly flushed, but lack of clear evidence meant that a charge of bestiality was not brought. In Penninghame, August 1706, the schoolmaster was accused by two girls of having laid hands on their private parts when beating them. He cleared himself on oath, and the session decided that the accusation sprang from a mixture of malice and the desire to be free of school. But the allegation, in September 1721, against William Young, schoolmaster of Dunkeld, that he had lain with several girls aged between seven and thirteen, and even abused a four year old, was sustained. He admitted the charge and was imprisoned.[13] We have to accept, however, in the light of the rarity of instances of such sexual aberration, that the evidence on which kirk sessions acted was likely to ignore these types of offence.

There were other possible elements in seduction, besides sheer male strength, which suggest some element of force or a lack of genuine consent on the part of the girl. There were several cases in which men appear to have taken advantage of infirmity, mental or physical, in women. In some of these the woman was labelled 'ane Idiot' or 'almost an Idiot'. In Belhelvie (September 1721, Janet Simpson was described as 'known to be ane Idiot and deprived of reason from her Infancy', which suggests that the word idiot might cover mental derangement as well as mental deficiency. For

---

13 Leah Leneman, *Living in Atholl, 1685–1785* (Edinburgh, 1986), p. 158.

Elizabeth Stewart in Banff (April 1702), the fact that she was 'almost an idiot' did not prevent her being criticized for 'very bad fame' and recommended to the magistrate for deportation. The alleged thick-headedness of some women meant that it was difficult for the session to be sure that the sinfulness of the event had been truly registered and therefore repented. Margaret Gilmuire in Wemyss (September 1705) was described as 'grossly ignorant and altogether stupid and under no sense of her sin', and Jean Auchinleck in Dailly, who got into trouble twice, was described on the second occasion (October 1746) as 'brutishly ignorant'. Cases in which similar allegations of mental defect or ignorance were made about men involved in sexual offences are very rare.

The other disability mentioned, presumably because it impeded interrogation, was being dumb. But Elspeth Robertson in Blair Atholl (January 1747) was able to communicate by pointing to the man and making signs, and Mary Laing in Ellon (May 1757) did the same with the aid of her mother-in-law (a term which in the eighteenth century described a stepmother).

In Dysart (August 1671),

William Huttone declared that his wife Annas Mathie lying in a roome above him, he wakened about 3 or 4 hours in the morning, & heard a noise above, upon which he arose and chapped at the door, & with difficultie won in: having got in, she would have had him first search the chamber, but being suspicious he raised up a feather bed lying on the floor, under which was John Corser, who desired him to hold his peace & he would give him a pynt of aill.

Aside from passing references like the above, we did not take note of married women who committed adultery. Our primary concern was illegitimacy, and even if it were well known in the community that a child's father was not the woman's husband, legally that child was not a bastard.

There were, however, women whose husbands had deserted them, and in such cases the session was not always certain whether to treat a case as fornication or adultery. In some instances the woman's allegation that her husband must be dead was eventually accepted. In Foveran (May 1695), Margaret Shepherd was able to produce a paper signed by the commissary clerk of Edinburgh stating that the husband who had deserted her some 15 years before was dead. By contrast, at Longside (December 1710)

Christian Dalgarno's statement that her 11 year absent husband must be dead was not allowed to be more than a strong presumption, and the case was labelled adultery.

This was an age before death certificates, and death could be accepted without formal documentation. In February 1677 in Ayr, Marion Cunyngham's husband, who had deserted 12 years earlier was considered to have died because some seamen had stated before witnesses that he was dead. Similarly, in Golspie in March 1747, Jean Bain was relieved of the accusation of adultery by some witnesses stating that her husband had died at Fontenoy. In Dalkeith (January 1697), Jannet Wilson's allegation that her husband had died two years before in Flanders was not proved – and indeed the fact that she then fled the parish would suggest that the claim was spurious – but her partner was allowed to appear for fornication only. Margaret Selton in Ellon (December 1673) was still considered an adulteress when she claimed that her marriage had not been consummated because of impotence. In Cramond (November 1715), Helen Duncan was fostering a child with milk resulting from an adulterous birth: the session considered that she should be made to pay towards the maintenance of her own child out of her fees, but here the concern seems to have been more financial than moral.

Apparently evidence of a spouse's death did not necessarily absolve the other from the guilt of adultery if it proved to be incorrect. This is shown in a case in the Court of Justiciary in 1673, where a wife had secured that a fraudulent testimonial of her death in Virginia reached her husband, who married again on the strength of it. By nine to six the judges held him guilty of adultery but then pardoned him. It is doubtful that a church court, even in the seventeenth century, could have taken such a severe line.

A much more common form of adultery was that between a married man and an unmarried woman. Its frequency almost certainly relates to the uprotected position of the unmarried female farm servant. It is clear that girls who consorted with married men did not expect that this would lead to marriage. As shown in chapter 3, while divorce, both for adultery and desertion, was recognized by both Church and State in Scotland, in none of the several hundred cases covering adultery or desertion which we have seen was the possibility even mentioned. The obvious difficulty that working people would have experienced in employing a lawyer, let alone the practical obstacles in the procedure of divorce for desertion, may account for much of the silence, but the total absence of reference to divorce, even to enquiries as to whether it had happened, suggests that there was an opinion current that it was not for the common people.

Apart from the attentions of upper class men to lower class women, most of our cases involved men and women of similar standing. There was, however, one anomaly; the case of Sipio Kennedy in Kirkoswald (December 1727), described as 'ye Blackmore in Culvan'. The session asked the presbytery for advice as the man was not a member of the church, though the session believed he had been baptized by an episcopal minister. Following the presbytery's recommendation, the man swore that he adhered to the Christian faith, and he duly made his public appearances before the congregation. There is no hint of racial prejudice in the recording of this event.

In most cases the women were, or at least appeared to be, willing participants in the act of sexual intercourse, but the possibility of rape obviously did exist. Scots law had been unwilling to concern itself with this crime unless the victim was propertied and had actually been abducted. In the matter of evidence it expected the victim to have cried out, and to have lodged a legal claim of rape within 24 hours. Our cases showed that seduction could be a fairly rough affair without the girl calling it a rape. In Lochgoilhead (October 1752), Jean Luck said the man responsible for her pregnancy was William Hind or Hay, 'she did not exactly know which', a travelling packman who was lodging at a nearby alehouse. She had gone to the house on

an Errand and saw him sitting at the fire with some Punch before him and that he gave her a glass upon some acquaintance she hade formerly with him at Lochgoilhead, and that she left them to goe home and that he followed her and caught her before she got home that she cried but his landlady's assistance came too late and found them only talking together at her father's door.

Cries notwithstanding, given the circumstances described, Jean Luck could hardly be classified as unwilling.

It was not unusual for statements to include an allegation that some degree of physical roughness had been used.[14] It seems that roughness, in the eyes of the community, was a normal part of life:

14 In Quaife, 'The Consenting Spinster in a Peasant Society: Aspects of Premarital Sex in "Puritan" Somerset 1645–1660', p. 240, 'Somewhat fewer than one in ten of the girls consented to sexual intercourse through fear or violence'.

rape meant real violence. In 1687 in Pittenweem the cries of a farm servant that 'Thomas Hog will not let me alone' brought her master, also called Thomas Hog, running upstairs. The handling of this case by the session in no way differed from that of a case of indiscreet behaviour. In February 1720 in Kilmarnock a normal case of unmarried pregnancy led the woman, Janet Stevenson, to allege not only violence, but that the man had forced snuff, or something like it, up her nose, and 'disordered' her for many days. Two other cases of clear rape came from the Eastern Highlands. In Blair Atholl, August 1751, Christian McFarland had reported to her family that she had been raped, and her father had told her to keep quiet about it: it was the evidence of pregnancy that led to its publication. Here it seems that rape in itself was a cause of shame. In Croy, in November 1761, witnesses assured the session that Ann Sinclair had been raped, and the session's comment was that she was 'more to be pitied than blamed'.

We also came across a number of cases of attempted rape. One is worth quoting at length (although it is not entirely clear how far the man actually went) because it presents such a vivid picture of horseplay between the sexes, including the actual words used by the participants. Anna Swannie complained to Canisbay session (August 1731) of James Groat's violent treatment of her. The main witness declared that on the day in question he had been pulling heather along with Groat and another man, Charles Banks, when they saw the woman and wondered who she was:

Charles Banks wager'd half of his dinner with the Declerant that he would not take a kiss of her Whereupon the Declerant call'd to her, inform'd her of his wager & asked a kiss to which she reply'd it was not usual for a young Rogue to kiss an old wife like her That then he softly laid her down & took one or two kisses from her But meant no harm.

After some more idle chat the woman had left them, and

was gone but a little way when James Groat said it was well Done to be with that Woman and Immediately pursued her That the Declerant called to her to take Care there was one following her when soon after they went out of his Sight who listening heard a Voice from the place he supposed they were Crying Murder murder That shortly after James Groat returning they asked him what meant he? What had he Done? To which he made a reply so horridly prophane that it Deserves to be Registrate no where but in Eternal Oblivion.

The session certainly did not treat such behaviour lightly. Although Groat denied actual guilt (i.e. penetration), the session, 'considering the odious nature of the sin itself, but especially the Dangerous Consequences which may ensue if it is not Exemplarly punish'd to the manifest hazard of Innocent Travellers whose Chastity is expose'd to the Insults of such heaven daring Villains', ordered him to appear publicly in sackcloth.

It will be noted that the woman in this case was in no way considered to have provoked the attack, and it is a universal feature of all the cases we collected that any attitude along the lines of 'she had it coming to her' is totally absent. One other example of attempted rape should suffice to give the flavour of such cases. In St Ninians (December 1724), Isobel Key told the minister that on her way home the previous night Robert Moir had attacked her and had only been stopped from actually raping her by some others coming alone. She testified before the session that Moir had

let down his Breeches & discovered his nakedness to her, & damned himself but he would ly with her, calling her damned Bitch & Jade; & that when she was outfoughten, by good Providence, the said John Mitchel & some others coming the same road from Down to Keir, she got out of his hands to them, & he was hindred from committing the act.[15]

We have concentrated in this chapter primarily on the women involved. It must be pointed out that the offence of fornication was seriously exacerbated if the man involved was actually a member of the kirk session, an elder (the system of eldership is described in chapter 1). In Dysart (October 1673), even though the elder involved with Isobel Moyes was intending marriage, he was suspended from office indefinitely for fornication. In Wattin (December 1758), Kenneth Sutherland, an elder, got his servant Elspet Corner into trouble and resigned. In Rothesay, Janet Auld's case of November 1738 led to the removal from office of the ruling elder, Duncan Lea, which shows the session prepared to take on a man of relatively high rank. In April 1758, in Alves, the session was astonished when Thomas Laing, elder, stood up and confessed that he had got his servant, Isobel Naughty, with child and sent her away. The session recorded its amazement, since it had had no other word of the affair, 'and scarcely knew what to say to Thomas' whom it described as 'a poor wretched old man'. When it

15 For other attempted rape cases see Longforgan, May 1718; Olrig, July 1723; Thurso, July 1723; Belhelvie, August 1754.

collected its thoughts on a subsequent occasion he was deposed.

The gentry class, from whom some of the elders were drawn, fell into rather a different category. The difficulties under which sessions could labour in bringing such men under their discipline are discussed in chapter 7.

There are few cases of women of the upper class coming before the sessions. In Rothesay, Bethia Beith (July 1706) was the daughter of a minister, and she was sinning within her own class with the son of the lord provost of Rothesay. Similarly, Ann Beith, also in Rothesay (June 1709), the widow of a burgess, was in trouble with an ex-baillie. In Thurso (January 1710), Elizabeth Sinclair, daughter of a late laird of Barroustoun, was in trouble with another man of lairdly background, and in Kingarth Mrs Elizabeth Stewart (February 1693), also involved with a laird, was allowed to stay in her own seat during her public appearances.[16] We have not found cases of women sinning with men of a lower social class, a negative fact which suggests that such women were in some way protected.

A final question must be addressed in this chapter, although our sources do not provide us with the means to answer it in any conclusive way. How were girls who gave birth to illegitimate children in this period regarded – not by the Church, but by the community in which they lived? Given the wide variance in illegitimacy ratios revealed for the seventeenth century in the previous chapter, it is clear that attitudes toward bastard bearers are likely to have differed markedly between regions.

Yet regional differences in the ratios are not so conspicuous as those shown by T. C. Smout for the later nineteenth century, nor are they as sustained.[17] It is true that there are some high figures in the seventeenth century, but these seem to reflect the difficulties still being experienced by the established Church in setting up its system of government in these areas. From the time that the Church can be seen to be in charge, no region shows the high levels experienced by the north-east and south-west after 1855, except for the south-west in the last decade of our study. We cannot find any persisting differences in the attitude to sexual activity outwith marriage in eighteenth century Scotland, but there are pieces of evidence on this subject which are worth considering.

16 'Mrs', i.e. 'Mistress', implied rank, not marital status.

17 T. C. Smout, 'Aspects of sexual behaviour in nineteenth-century Scotland', in Peter Laslett, Karla Oosterveen and Richard M. Smith (eds), *Bastardy and its Comparative History* (London, 1980), pp. 211–15.

The first is a specific case which came before Petty kirk session in June 1765. The story was that William Sinclair had been courting Jean McDonald when he had happened to meet up with a previous suitor of hers, called John McNicol, who told him that during the three years she had been a servant in his father's house she had 'made a practice of Bedding with him':

The above narration of McNicols had such weight & credit with Sinklair that he declined agreement with this young Woman in Point of Marriage – But declined to give his Reason – being tender of the Girls Character – Till at Length being urg'd much to give in his Objections, he made plain all his mind as above.

The two men and the woman appeared before the session. Jean McDonald

Complained of her being badly us'd by the affair & in order to Repair her Good Name begs of the Session to Take McNicols Oath whither or not he had ever committed Lewdness with her. She did not care to Require his oath if he had told Sinklair, or not, but if ever he was Guilty with her or not as no less would clear her of a bad Report.

The session agreed to this, and McNicol willingly swore 'That he had never any Carnal Dealings with the Girl either in the day time or nightime in his life.' The minister concluded by declaring to Sinklair 'that he had no Grounds of any further Objections against the Girl, and that now he might go forward in the intended Marriage when he pleased.'

Whether the marriage went ahead or not we do not know, but the above does act as an effective antidote to one particular notion that might have arisen from some of the material in this chapter. Chaperonage may have been lax and opportunities many, but we must not therefore assume that the loss of a woman's virginity was regarded as nothing to be ashamed of.

The second piece of evidence comes from a book by David Stewart of Garth. Although written in the early nineteenth century, there is no reason to suppose that the custom which he described was not a longstanding one:

For the illicit intercourse between the sexes, in an unmarried state there was no direct punishment beyond those established by the church; but, as usual among the Highlanders, custom supplied the defect, by establishing some marks of reprehension and infamy . . . . Young unmarried women never wore any close head dress, but only the hair tied with bandages or some slight ornament. This continued till marriage, or till they attained a certain age; but if a young woman lost her virtue and character, then she was obliged to wear a cap, and never afterwards to appear with her hair uncovered, in the dress of virgin innocence.[18]

The custom of indicating that a woman was not a virgin is interesting because by accepted doctrine the unmarried mother had purged her offence. It was expressly stated in a letter signed 'A Country Elder' in the *Scots Magazine* for 1757 that penance re-established a girl's character, and that she could expect to marry later. The chances of subsequent marriage for those who had done penance are, unfortunately, not discernible from our material, but that the view that character had been re-established was not simply a view of those managing Church affairs is shown by a surprised comment by Edmund Burt, writing in the 1720s, that 'When a Woman has undergone the Penance, with an Appearance of Repentance, she has wiped off the Scandal among all the godly, and a Female Servant in that regenerated State is as well received into one of the Families as if she had never given Proof of her Frailty.'[19]

It is a disappointment that there are other aspects of our subject for which we have no good information. For example, we cannot ascertain whether there were differences in the age of girls bearing bastards, between regions or over time. We have little information, other than negative statements of reproving kirk sessions, on courtship practices, which could have a bearing on illegitimacy levels, as T. C. Smout has shown for the nineteenth century.[20]

18 David Stewart of Garth, *Sketches of the Highlanders* (Edinburgh, 1822), vol. 1, p. 89.

19 *Scots Magazine*, August 1757; Edmund Burt, *Letters from the North of Scotland* (Edinburgh 1974), I, p. 195.

20 T. C. Smout, 'Aspects of sexual behaviour in nineteenth-century Scotland', pp. 211–13.

7

Response to Authority

The majority of women who became pregnant, men who fathered bastard children, and members of both sexes found guilty of scandalous carriage, profaning the sabbath, or breaching the peace, conformed to the rules of the Church by admitting guilt and making their appearances before the congregation. Baptism would not normally be granted to an infant until both its parents had satisfied discipline, or at least provided surety that they would do so (not just for sexual misdemeanours but for sabbath breaches and other offences as well). This was a powerful tool in the hands of kirk sessions, for there is no doubt that the majority of people considered baptism very important, even though it was not necessary for salvation by Calvinist dogma.[1] In Thurso, in June 1737, the father of an illegitimate child whose mother had died in childbirth begged that the child be baptized as 'no Woman would engage to Nurse the said Child while unbaptized.' There is also an indication from at least one case that conforming to church rules was important, not just in the eyes of the kirk but in the eyes of the community as well. In Foveran, in August 1749, it was reported that Mary Hay had been put out of her mother's family and would not be received into it again until she had satisfied discipline; for this reason she was allowed to make just two appearances.

Kirk session registers do not record the feelings of those who appeared publicly before a congregation; however, wives' feelings were taken into consideration in two cases of married men who had sinned. The father of Katharine Gow's child (Wattin, February 1763) was Thomas Calder, a married man. The presbytery recommended that the session 'deal the more tenderly with him on account of his Wife Mrs Calder who is a Woman of a reputable, blameless Character'. The second case (in Spott, November 1687)

---

1 It was normal only for a man to present a child for baptism, but we did find Kilmarnock session allowing some women to present bastard children themselves.

was not one of adultery as the man had got the other girl pregnant before he married. He asked if he could make his appearances privately instead of in front of the congregation 'because it will be A great grief to his wyfe if he should Appear in publict'.[2]

Although the degree of shame felt by individuals must have varied a good deal, yet some shame there must have been. And if the majority accepted this as the consequence of their misbehaviour, there was still a substantial minority who attempted to evade the consequences of their actions or who defied the Church's discipline. It is this minority who form the subject of this chapter. Resistance to authority can tell us much about the functioning of that authority and about the society within which it operated.

We can divide our resistance into two categories, although naturally there is some overlap. The first part deals with behaviour which was not primarily a defiance of church rules, but rather a desire to avoid the consequences of bastard-bearing. Even without the threat of church discipline, an unmarried woman might have denied being pregnant, fled the parish, attempted to abort the foetus, abandoned or killed the newborn infant. And the men involved might have denied paternity of an illegitimate child. The second part (see p. 219) involves members of both sexes who deliberately refused to conform to the rules of the Church.

It was not particularly unusual for a woman called before a session to deny being pregnant, but in most cases this was probably a panic reaction (or, perhaps, based on the hope that the apparent pregnancy really was not true), for such women usually confessed a short time after. However, Margaret Young (Kilmarnock, April 1693) denied she was pregnant on the same day as she later gave birth, which places her in rather a different category.

An accusation of pregnancy was normally the result of visible swelling. However, Jean Hay (Belhelvie, January 1672) denied the charge and said it was 'a more dangerous sickness'; about a month later, poor lass, she died 'of a hydropsia', which explains the mistake.

It was not only swelling which gave rise to gossip and speculation: anything resembling morning sickness in a young

---

2 The elders consented to this, though the minister was unhappy about it because it seemed to him unfair that the woman, who had been if anything less to blame than the man, had to make public appearances. As a compromise the session decided to impose a hefty fine on the man and to intimate this to the congregation.

woman could have the same effect. In Grange (December 1687), Margaret Thomson denied being pregnant and said her sickness was due to another cause. Her name did not appear again in the records, so clearly this proved to be the truth (unless she had had a very early miscarriage). Jonat Chalmers (Drainie, June 1679) went so far as to bring a bill of slander against the woman who had falsely accused her of being with child. However, Isobel Hislop in Dalkeith, who denied being pregnant on 9 September 1737, claiming she was being treated for 'a trouble upon her body', was in childbed on 25 September. In Kinglassie (November 1710), Janet Christie was alleged to have brought forth a child. She said she had simply been ill. Her breasts were examined and no milk was found in them, so she was cleared.

The inspection of breasts was the one sound means a kirk session had of establishing whether a woman had recently given birth or was shortly to do so. The eighteenth century was clearly not squeamish about mother's milk: the midwives who examined Margaret McTier's breasts for the session of Kirkoswald (March 1767) produced the milk in a glass for the elders.[3] For the most part, the mere threat of a breast inspection was enough to make a recalcitrant pregnant woman confess. (To refuse to submit to inspection was not a real option for it would have been taken as presumption of guilt.) Others waited until after the midwives had found milk before doing so. And at least if a woman really was innocent then the ordeal of having her breasts inspected would provide incontrovertible evidence that she had been falsely accused. As far as we can see from our records, the breast inspection was not held in the presence of the kirk session: this would have involved an improper degree of undressing, though, of course, everyone was used to seeing women nursing children.

It was, naturally, very much easier for a man to deny paternity than for a woman to deny pregnancy. Before blood tests were invented, there really was no certain way of proving that a particular man had fathered a child. In spite of this difficulty, kirk sessions certainly did not abrogate their responsibilities when it came to pinning down the man believed to be responsible for the pregnancy. In the first place, he could not be freed of the sin until he had undergone church discipline, and in the second place – as

---

3 An unusual feature of this case was that the milk was *not* considered proof of pregnancy. She had had a child about three years earlier and presumably went on breastfeeding for rather a long time.

was discussed in chapter 4 – he was expected to contribute to the child's maintenance.

Fairly often men denied guilt and/or paternity, but in most cases, within a comparatively short time they would admit the truth of the accusation. It seemed to us worthwhile to count the number of cases in which the man named admitted fatherhood within a month of the allegation. There is an element of potential error in this crude measure, for men might be out of the parish at the time of the allegation. But the percentages of speedy admissions showed some interesting features which suggest that as an index it is not meaningless. Figures 25–9 give the regional and national trends in admission percentages, and table 7 the average levels.

Table 7 Percentage of men, by region, admitting paternity

Region	Percentage
Lothians	62
Fife	61
Central Lowlands	60
Central and Eastern Highlands	70
Western Highlands	69
Aberdeenshire	75
North-east	78
Caithness	72
Ayrshire	46
South-west	42
National Sample	65

The major differences in level, as shown in table 7, are striking. All the northern and highland regions approximated to or went beyond 70 per cent admissions, the south-east and Central Lowlands stood near to 60 per cent, and the south-west and Ayrshire were under 50 per cent. The figures maintain a very steady level in the various graphs, showing that the averages for the whole period were not the result of haphazard changes, but persistently sustained. In northern and highland areas there is very little trend but in the south the trend was slightly downwards. This

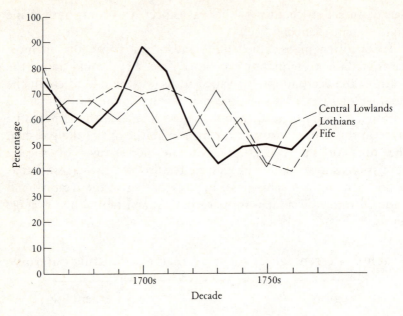

Figure 25 *Admission percentages, Lothians, Fife and Central Lowlands, by decade*

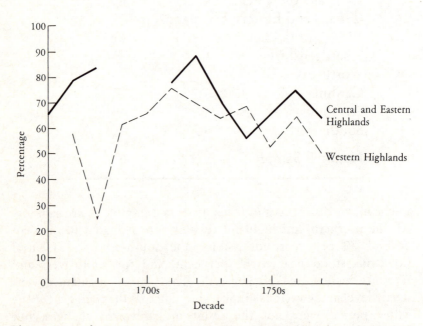

Figure 26 *Admission percentages, Western Highlands and Central and Eastern Highlands, by decade*

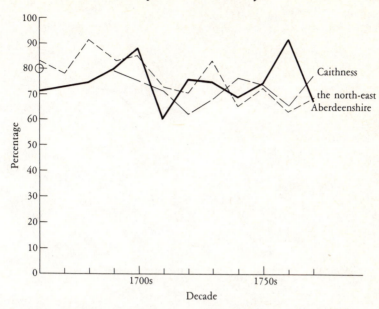

Figure 27 *Admission percentages, Aberdeenshire, the north-east and Caithness, by decade*

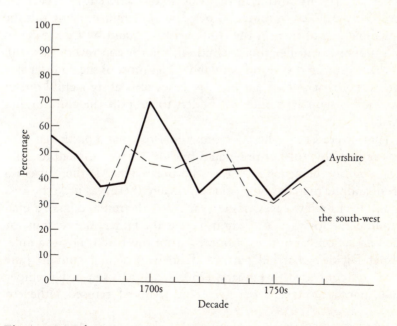

Figure 28 *Admission percentages, Ayrshire and the south-west, by decade*

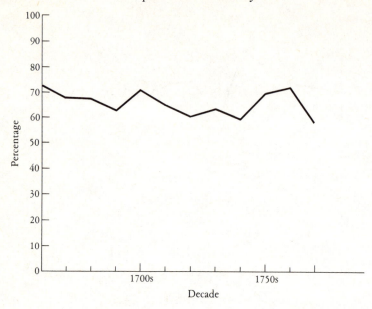

Figure 29 *Admission percentages, national sample, by decade*

is particularly interesting in the south-west, where it produces the level for the 1770s of under 30 per cent. The figures bring out the unwillingness of men in the south-west to stand by their women and support their illegitimate children, and the contrast of this with the behaviour in the rest of Scotland. Over most of the country it is safe to say that in two out of three cases of bearing a child out of wedlock, a woman would not be left to support the child on her own.[4]

There were cases where a woman insisted that a particular man was responsible for her pregnancy and the man continued to deny it in spite of being cited before the presbytery. If there was no proof and the man did not yield to pressure there was little the kirk could do. In a few cases, some years after the initial denial, a man would come forward and admit he was the father: the reasons for such an action cannot be fathomed from the KSRs. For example, Elspet Dickie's married partner (Belhelvie) denied guilt in June 1745 and confessed in January 1750. When accused in December 1766, Sarah Douglas's partner (New Abbey) refused either to

---

4 A minor point of interest is that in Westerkirk, the parish with consistently higher illegitimacy than elsewhere in the south-west region, 60 per cent of the men acknowledged paternity.

confess or to deny and fled to England. He returned and confessed in June 1772. In Banff, Isabel Mackenzie's partner denied paternity in September 1764 and confessed to it in November 1774.

It was not unusual for a man to admit guilt but refuse to admit paternity until he saw that the date of birth corresponded with the occasion of fornication. If it did not then he might feel himself justified in denying responsibility. Margaret Farquhar's partner (Wattin, January 1733) denied responsibility for her child because it was born ten days too early. However, the session considered ten days 'no matter of Debat' since it was common knowledge that he was the father. James Crawfoord denied being the father of Margaret Gow's child (Thurso, January 1740) because it was born 14 days early. The process was laid before two 'gentlewomen', who declared that it was quite usual for a first child to be born 12 or 14 days early. The session proclaimed the infant to be Crawfoord's.

The view of many men that they would be able to identify a child as their own by the date of birth was based on the common popular misconception that the normal term of pregnancy dated from the time of intercourse rather than that accepted today, that it dates from the last menstruation. They also held to a belief in very fixed lengths of gestation, calculated over nine calendar months, with complete disregard of the fact that calendar months vary in length. For some unknown reason, the question of timing featured far more prominently in the kirk session records of Western Highland parishes than anywhere else in Scotland. Sessions in that area were meticulous about pinning down the exact date of fornication, and men were prone to deny paternity if the birth date was even slightly off their estimate. Given the poor level of general knowledge about this subject indicated above, this could lead to some bizarre results.

However, even in the Western Highlands there were rules which prevented a man getting away easily with such a denial. Katrine Campbell's partner (Kilmartin, July 1749)

demurr'd a little as to his being Father, and alledging in his defence that the birth of the said Child did not answer his time of guilt with her by the space of fourteen days. He was then told that as he had acknowledged guilt with her, he must be the Father of the Child, according to the Rules of this Church provided she was willing to clear herself upon Oath six weeks before and after the time of their guilt from having any carnal knowledge of all other Men.

She did so and he then acknowledged being the father of the child.

Sometimes the woman would protect her partner, usually a married man in such cases. The commonest story told by a woman involved with a married man was that she had been raped by a stranger. Elizabeth Scot (Foveran, August 1763) had enough imagination to describe a precise location. The unknown man had 'jumped out from a benty bush betwixt John Nicol's and the Black Dog'. Sessions can usually be found in the right in their profound scepticism of all 'unknown man' stories.[5]

Whether or not her partner admitted responsibility, the woman was still the one certain to bear the brunt of any penalty or shame. Obviously it was also far easier for a man to flee the parish and lose himself elsewhere than it was for a pregnant woman, although some women did try. To some extent geography determined how feasible such a course of action was. The border area of Dumfries and Galloway was one which frequently saw women slipping over to England, or, alternatively, taking ship for Ireland, to have their illegitimate babies. Most of the women who fled appear to have done so out of blind panic rather than in a more calculating way, and they often returned shortly after.

Simply fleeing from one parish to another was rarely a solution, since if an unknown woman appeared in a parish the minister and elders would insist on knowing who she was and what she was doing there. Even running to a city like Edinburgh was no guarantee of anonymity. Ministers were remarkably skilful at tracking down runaway women, no matter where they went.

In Dysart, Fife, Elspet Still became pregnant by a married man, John Leith. She fled to Edinburgh, where she had the child. Then, after a letter from the minister reached Edinburgh, she fled again, this time to Montrose, where Leith's sister, Jean, gave the baby to another woman, on the pretext that its mother had died in childbirth. It was Jean who related this tale on 22 February 1691, but on 1 March Elspet returned to the parish, confessed, and submitted to church discipline.[6]

One woman who left on a more permanent basis was Margaret Innes. On 24 July 1670 she fled from Aberdour (where she must have been in service) to her parents in Belhelvie, Aberdeenshire, whence her father arranged passage for her on a ship to Holland.

5 For instance, Elspet Beak (Cramond, October 1673) was told that her story of a man, now fugitive, forcing her in the high street was 'most improbable lyke'.

6 When the session first cited Elspet 'John Leith did draw his sword, and offered violence to two of the elders, who were sent to bring her to the session.'

There is no record of her returning, and her father had to make public appearances before the congregation for aiding and abetting her.

Another possible course of action was to abort the foetus – or at least to attempt to do so.[7] It is impossible to quantify the number of women who attempted abortion because any who were successful would not appear in the records, while the unsuccessful ones denied doing so, and proof was not always forthcoming. It is possible that many women who might have considered abortion did not do so simply because they had no idea how to go about it. In Mauchline, Ayrshire, Marion Anderson (January 1691) said she was given herbs to drink to abort the child in her womb by a woman who claimed to have got rid of hers with the same. In Wigtown attempts at abortion were made by three different women in the space of six years (September 1714, June 1718, and October 1720), which suggests some local 'wise woman' to whom girls would resort. Dr Buchan's popular handbook, *Domestic Medicine*, states in the 1797 edition that abortion was 'daily advertised' by people prepared to assist with it. This statement does not occur in the original edition of 1767 or in either of the editions of the 1770s. It seems likely, therefore, that it was only towards the end of the century that such advertizements were made, and it is in any case unlikely that these had any practical effect outside the main towns. Newspapers, which presumably were the vehicle of the advertizements, cost a woman's day labouring wage, and did not circulate among the bulk of the population.

In Fossoway the same woman apparently attempted abortion on three separate occasions. On 21 June 1747, Margaret McCarter (also spelt McArthur) admitted fornication and named a married man who denied it. On 13 September she said she had 'parted with child' (miscarried) in mid-July and that the man had given her something which she took. In February 1755 she surfaces in the records again, witnesses alleging she was 'endeavouring to make away with the child in her womb'. The infant was in fact stillborn. On 2 May 1756 witnesses again alleged she was tampering with a

---

7 There is no clear evidence of any form of contraception in kirk session material. The only kind of 'birth control' available seems to have been induced abortion. Elspeth Dryburgh (Wemyss, October 1704), who was not pregnant, admitted to fornication. On 'being asked if she had used any means, after she was guilty, to prevent her being with child, could not deny but she had been guilty of such practise.' In this case it is not made clear whether she had ever been pregnant, but the implication is that she had taken steps to secure an abortion.

foetus. She denied this, and the attempt was clearly unsuccessful, for on 11 May the beadle caught her trying to abandon her infant at the kirk door.

The most common way of attempting abortion was to take drugs, herbs and 'physick'. Occasionally the terms used were specific. In Grange, in February 1732, Helen Graham claimed her partner had brought her pennyroyal and wormwood sage to make her part with child. In Dysart, Elizabeth Ogilvie (November 1756) alleged that her master was the father and that her mistress gave her the 'bitter apple' in a drink, which must have been a local name for some drug. She apparently also made Elizabeth lift heavy items of furniture. Elspet Cromertie (Canisbay, July 1751) allegedly asked to have a stone put on her back. Isobel Grig (Foveran, July 1679) was 'endeavouring to smoother and kill the child in her womb'.[8] It was reported of Elspeth Jamison (Wemyss, September 1709) that she was 'indeavouring to put back the birth and for that end had been seeking the saving tree from the gardiners and did leap over the bastealie'.

As will have been noted, some of the women accused their partners of procuring the means for attempted abortion. One cannot guess how often this was true (the men, not unexpectedly, denied it), but a genuine note is struck by Margaret Walker (Torphichen, September 1728). She said her partner gave her herbs which she refused to take; also he had insisted he would deny being the father and she had said to him, 'God will not let you deny it.'[9]

It was sometimes possible for a woman to carry a child to term without being noticed as pregnant and reported to the kirk session. This was a dangerous situation because it made possible the abandonment of her child as a foundling, or its killing. As the Church increased the efficiency of its discipline the social stigma of producing an illegitimate child may have become more fearsome. Though child abandonment was never a frequent event in any parish, there are signs that the case incidence was higher between 1680 and 1720 than either earlier or later: the raised level might explain the Statute of 1690, which laid down a presumption of murder on any woman concealing an unmarried pregnancy if the

8 A. Macfarlane, 'Illegitimacy and illegitimates in English history', in Peter Laslett, Karla Oosterveen and Richard M. Smith (eds), *Bastardy and its Comparative History* (London, 1980), p. 77, refers to the practice of tying the waist very tightly as a means of aborting the foetus.

9 He did initially deny guilt and paternity but admitted it a short time later.

infant should die. This copied English legislation of earlier in the century. Fountainhall remarked in March 1679 that 'it were to be wished that we had such a statute made with us' as the English one of 21 James I c.27, making it murder if the mother did not call for help in labour or if she concealed the pregnancy and death of the bastard.[10] However, Mackenzie stated in 1678 that 'the Law presumes so far, a woman who has born a bastard, and has conceal'd her being with child, to be guilty of Paricide, if the child be found dead.' The new law therefore merely enacted existing practice.[11]

This law was assumed to apply only to the unmarried, though its wording was more general. A girl accused of infanticide had only to be convicted of concealing her pregnancy and not calling for help in labour to be considered guilty of infanticide, unless she could produce strong evidence to the contrary. In England evidence from two counties shows that there was a change in opinion among the men who made up juries early in the eighteenth century. In Surrey, where there had been cases of infanticide every 18 months, in only one case after 1727 was there a conviction; with the failure of severity, prosecutions fell off. Any evidence of preparation for the birth, such as the collecting of scraps of linen, came to be allowed as evidence which would override the presumption of guilt.[12] But in Scotland severity continued longer, and seems to have gone even beyond the statute. In 1713 a girl who had told two people that she thought she was pregnant was convicted under the presumption, as was one in 1743 who had told the child's father under promise of secrecy. The nineteenth century commentator David Hume felt that some of the judgments were 'slovenly', not justified by rigorous standards of proof, and that, in particular, the courts had heard several cases at the same time, a process unlikely to lead to care and discrimination.[13] The latest execution under the statute was that of Anne McKie in 1776: after that, though the law continued to be stringently operated, the prosecution settled for banishment. In one case a married woman was convicted under the statute. She had concealed her pregnancy

10 Sir John Lauder of Fountainhall, *Historical Notices* (Bannatyne Club, Edinburgh, 1848), vol. 1, p. 224.

11 Sir George Mackenzie, *Laws and Customs of Scotland* (Edinburgh, 1678), p. 156. The Act is in *APS* ix 195.

12 J. M. Beattie, *Crime and the Law in England, 1669–1800* (Oxford, 1986), pp. 113–24.

13 David Hume, *Commentaries on the Laws of Scotland respecting crimes* (Edinburgh, 1986), pp. 292–9.

because her husband was on the run from the army and she did not wish it known that he was near at hand. In another, a girl was convicted even though her child had been seen alive after an unaided birth near an open fire; it had been subsequently killed by the fire.

The Church did not impose criminal penalties in the cases which it retained in its own hands, but it seems to have stretched the law in a different way, concentrating on the fact of concealment, which could be regarded as a repudiation of its discipline. In 1809 the change in legal opinion produced a statute modifying the law: concealment was still criminal, but the sentence was only two years' imprisonment, marking the view that it was neglect, not evidence of murder.[14]

Both in the issue of concealment and in the initial denials of some girls of pregnancy we deal in the unreadiness of some women to accept physiological changes as definite indications of pregnancy. Rural women in our period cannot have grown to maturity without seeing biological processes of reproduction, given the lack of privacy. The Kirk discouraged explicit sexual conversation, so observation may not always have been generalized into an intellectual system. Even in the much more sexually explicit and articulated world of today, with formal teaching of sexual matters in schools, it is possible for a girl not to understand how her body changes and why. It was possible that the hope of a girl that she was not pregnant might become translated into belief. In some cases the intention of a girl to admit pregnancy might be overtaken by the actual birth. We should not accept the legal opinion of the seventeenth and early eighteenth century that failure to disclose pregnancy was always a deliberate decision, and one usually made with criminal intent.

English historical research gives some support to the legal view that infant death in cases of concealed unmarried pregnancy was likely to be infanticide. Keith Wrightson has cautiously advanced an estimate, based on a study of Essex cases in the early seventeenth century, that infanticide then ran at the level of 2 per cent of illegitimate births, some of the child murder being by the father. A paper by R. W. Malcolmson suggests a higher level in the eighteenth century, and shows that in Staffordshire infanticide and concealment cases (which the author clearly thinks were

---

14 The modifying statute is 49 Geo. III c. 14. For late cases under the 1690 Act, see John Burnett, *A Treatise on various branches of the Criminal Law of Scotland* (Edinburgh, 1811), pp. 571–5.

bound to be cases of child killing) formed a quarter of the homicide trials.[15] The author points out that it was impossible for stillbirths, as a percentage of all illegitimate births, to be as high as they would be if the allegations of the accused were accepted. We should still recognize, however, in opposition to seventeenth-century legal opinion, that some concealed births were of children already dead, and that the circumstances of such births would enhance the risk of natural perinatal death. Concealment may not have been a deliberate policy on the part of the mother; a woman living away from her family might have no available person in whom to confide, and with a first birth might not have changed so drastically in shape as to encourage questioning.

The parishes we studied produced a total of 20 cases of either concealment of pregnancy or infanticide, and in two of the concealment cases no action was taken. The 18 cases where murder was alleged form approximately 0.2 per cent of our illegitimacy total. If we add to this the near 1 per cent of abandoned illegitimate children, foundlings, the number of women determined to get rid of their child is low, and much lower than these English estimates. There are various statements in the Scottish press which claim that infanticide was unusually common in Scotland.[16] These were simply based on impression, and are not sustained by even that most unreliable of quantitative material, criminal statistics. Our figures suggest the opposite. The local figures put forward for parts of England are so much higher than those found in this study that, even if some infant corpses had been successfully concealed – and Scotland had a considerable amount of wild hill country not susceptible of search – we still have to accept a far lower level of child murder in Scotland. In England the economic fears of an unmarried pregnant woman were strong, but she did not face the public shame almost inevitable in Scotland; her embarrassment would be confined to the effect of her position on those living near or related to her. In our cases the economic plight was less severe than in England. Church discipline coerced many of the fathers into admitting responsibility, as shown in table 7, and this meant agreeing to contribute to the support of the child. If a woman could not gain help from her parents or her man, a parish would give some relief while she was nursing her child. We do not have

---

15 Keith Wrightson, 'Infanticide in earlier seventeenth century England', *Local Population Studies* no. 15, 1975, pp. 10–12; R. W. Malcolmson, 'Infanticide in the eighteenth century', in J. S. Cockburn (ed.), *Crime in England 1555–1800* (London, 1977), pp. 187–209.

16 An example is the correspondence in the *Scots Magazine* of 1757.

comments about the willingness of masters to take on servants with children, but parishes assumed that once a child was weaned the mother did not need relief. In the first half of our period of study a woman moving to work in another parish would need to show a 'testificat' of conduct from her last parish of residence, and such a document would reveal her past, but if the sin was purged this would probably be no handicap to movement. There would, of course, be no chance of denying the child's birth in the parish where she had done penance, which, since it was that where the offence had been committed, was usually that in which she was already employed.

Malcolmson's study of English cases stresses the acute problems of a servant girl (for such the mothers almost always were) faced with pregnancy, loss of employment and inability to earn a living for lack of a character reference. The days of written references lay ahead, in the nineteenth century, though Kussmaul's work on English farm service shows that employers would make enquiries about a worker's general reputation at a hiring fair.[17] The picture given by Malcolmson seems to belong much more to the mid-nineteenth century, when most residential service in England was for domestic work, and thus more intimate than farm work, and by which time the management of household servants had become much more systematic. It is significant that he illustrates the predicament of a pregnant servant with a long quotation from George Eliot's *Adam Bede*, written in the later 1850s. In Kilmartin, in 1695, Malcolm McPhaiden claimed to have had intercourse with Mary McIndeora. His statement seems to have been an act of malice to prevent her family marrying her to someone else. He was said to have stated that he himself 'would not marry one himself with whom he fell in fornication'. In the Eastern Highlands and elsewhere there were some cases of antenuptial pregnancy where the father of the child was not the husband, and where the husband does not appear to have rejected either the child or the wife (see chapter 5). In the absence of memoirs or personal accounts by the type of woman likely to become involved in scandal, we should not accede to the idea that a girl's 'character' was permanently damaged by pregnancy, since most of the statements to this effect come from other countries or other periods than this.[18] We have already noted in chapter 6 the

---

17 Ann Kussmaul, *Servants in Husbandry in Early Modern England* (Cambridge, 1981), ch. 4.
18 e.g. K. H. Connell, 'Illegitimacy before the famine', in K. H. Connell, *Irish Peasant*

case in Petty, 1765, when a woman complained that a slander was hindering her marriage. There are a few other cases of similar complaints, but not enough for us to judge whether allegations of misconduct would normally be a handicap.

Our research revealed a certain number of concealed pregnancies in which, during subsequent investigation, the mother alleged that the child had been born dead. Where there was no good reason to contradict this only ecclesiastical discipline would be applied. For instance, in Drainie, in January 1674, Christian Millan, who did not call for assistance at the birth and was suspected of infanticide, was merely made to stand in sackcloth, and in New Abbey, February 1766, Mary Turner, who claimed she had had assistance, was referred to the presbytery. In some other cases the mother fled the parish. Where the child's body could be found and it appeared to have been born alive, and sometimes even when it could not be found, the woman would be imprisoned and tried for the criminal offence.

In March 1740, Margaret Jameson (Ellon) had denied giving birth but examination of her breasts convinced the session that this was untrue. She then claimed to have aborted at 16 weeks and to have thrown the body in a pool. The elders went with her and found it. It was stated by the midwives to be perfect, and she was sent to the prison in Aberdeen. A similar case in Dysart (February 1729), where Margaret Spence admitted throwing a female child down a well without checking whether it was alive or dead, also led to imprisonment, even though she changed her story and claimed it had been born dead. Anne Dempster (Kingsbarns, June 1750) persisted in denying having given birth even after milk was found in her breasts, but three months later the body was found and 'laid beside her in the prison'.

We do not know the end of all these stories. Grizzel MackGuffach (Fordyce, August 1746) claimed that her child had been born dead when its body was found buried in a cellar. Similarly, Agnes Mitchel (Torphichen, November 1737), who threw her child in a coal pit, claimed it had miscarried, but midwives said it was a full-term body. Janet Vaitch (Pencaitland, January 1691), who claimed

Society (Oxford, 1968), pp. 55–62, claims that in nineteenth-century Ireland a mother of an illegitimate child had very poor marriage prospects; M. Ingram, 'The reform of popular culture? Sex and marriage in early modern England', in Barry Reay (ed.), *Popular Culture in Seventeenth Century England* (London, 1985), pp. 129–65, states that a good reputation was of value in women for both sexes. For women it affected marriage prospects, for the married of both sexes 'sexual credit' was important in the middling social ranks.

that she 'saw a beast carrieing away the head' of her aborted foetus which she had put in a hole, clearly did not convince the session that the child had been aborted. Silence on the part of registers on the end result of these and other enquiries may come from the habit of registers of not bothering to record details when cases passed to another jurisdiction. KSRs were kept to record the Church's share in business, not to satisfy curiosity. Contemporaries, of course, would know the outcome of cases.

The Church's attitude to concealment was severe. At Inveresk in 1710 a blind woman, Anne Davidson, was before the session for fornication, but when it discovered that she had not disclosed her pregnancy 'till she was delivered', the session sent the case to the presbytery, which passed it to the Lord Advocate. It ended with her receiving lesser excommunication and being referred to the sheriff. There is no suggestion that the child had not survived, and Anne Davidson eventually claimed that she had been irregularly married.

There are other cases of Church severity beyond the letter of the law. In April 1725 Christian Will, in Wemyss, was cited for concealment along with her mother, who must have known of the pregnancy since they shared a bed. They claimed that they thought her trouble 'a gravel' and did not call in outside help during childbirth: a neighbour's accidental visit was thought to have prevented child murder, yet clearly the woman had assistance from her mother during the birth. In Dysart, in October 1772, Margaret Spence gave birth in secret but it is not clear that the child died; in any case, the Solicitor General, looking at the evidence, refused to start a process. In Wemyss, in February 1707, Bessie Swine was afraid to tell her mother of the pregnancy and so had no outside woman with her during birth. In all these cases the offence appears to have been simply concealment, not the murder of a child.

Among 8,429 instances of illegitimacy there came to light in our records 78 cases of abandoned children in the parishes studied. A disproportionate number of these abandoned children occurred in the late seventeenth and early eighteenth century. None were recorded for the Western Highlands and only four for the Central and Eastern Highlands. There were 11 in both the north-east and in Aberdeenshire. The highest figure was for the Lothians where 19 were mentioned. Abandonment of a child could be a means of killing it, though it may be unwise to deduce a murderous intention from an act induced by fear of discovery and desperation. That a child was found dead should not surprise in the case of one left in Cramond in January 1688, considering the time of year. One abandoned in the same parish in November 1733 was in such bad shape that the family it was boarded outwith by the parish insisted on a specially generous fee: however, it survived to enter apprenticeship at the appropriate age.

In Cramond, Dalkeith and Dysart foundlings were sufficiently numerous for the parishes at times to have more than one being supported. Ayr also had four in the period between 1661 and 1690, but as a town it might have been the place of deposit by rural mothers. Grange in the north-east had two foundlings to support in the 1720s, so had Eddleston in the Borders. But in most places foundlings were sufficiently rare for it to be normal to refer in the register merely to support for 'the foundling'. Because of this nomenclature there is usually no way of knowing the sex of the child.

The rarity of abandonment in the Highlands might indicate a society tolerant of single lapses by unmarried girls, or alternatively one where it was relatively easy for an unmarried mother to gain support. But it is also possible that geography played a part. In a society made up of small hamlets and joint farms, the only way to leave a child for others to find without being identified was to take it to another settlement or, preferably, to leave it at the manse door, which would ensure prompt care.[19] In the Highlands, particularly in the west, parishes were large and settlements far from each other. A nocturnal and secret march to deposit a child may have been simply too great an enterprise for a mother weakened by childbirth. On the other hand, the more ruthless procedure of abandoning the child in the wild to die would have been relatively easy: there may well have been cases of murderous abandonment of which we have no evidence.

Not all abandoned children came from impecunious women. In September 1766, in Ellon, a newborn girl was put down outside the manse with an anonymous letter to the minister and elders and a 20 shilling note. The letter promised more money from time to time and requested that the child be baptized. But the child was not well provided for, apart from money, for the women who nursed and reared it had to be paid immediately to get a blanket for it. The interest of this case is that the abandoning parent could write. It is

---

19 It was usually the minister who reported to the session the existence of a foundling, which suggests that he was the first member to know of it. A minister would be the best informed in the parish on who had recently lost a child and would be able to nurse another: for this reason leaving the child at his door gave it the best prospect of survival.

possible, of course, that here it was the father rather than the mother who left the child. In Torphichen, in September 1702, the session considered it sufficiently proven that the child laid down in the parish a year earlier belonged to the daughter of a local landowner. It asked the minister to write to her mother, 'the Lady Pottishaw', asking her to take the child and reimburse the session its expenses in maintaining the foundling. In October it was reported that she had done so. In Yester, in 1668, a small local landowner was concerned that a foundling might be attributed to his wife and asked for a testimonial that the lady had recently been seen in good health.

Kirk sessions, faced with a foundling, were very concerned to trace the mother. In this they were inspired first by religious need, for only an active attempt to bring home responsibility to, and induce penance in, the offender could justify the claim of the congregation to be part of the visible church. There were also financial considerations. A foundling was expensive to support, for the parish had to pay the opportunity cost (a recompense for opportunities lost) for the woman who nursed it and who was thereby restricted in what other gainful work she could do, and because a parish would usually continue to support the child until it could be sent to service at some age between 10 and 14.

While foundlings were still unweaned a session would have to pay generously for their nursing and care, but after that the method of support usually adopted was to hand them over for care to an elderly woman already on relief with some small extra monthly allowance and occasional funds for clothes. The parish would also pay their school fees until they could read and were conversant with the Bible. A parish might resume care, giving support and medical aid, if an apprenticed foundling fell ill, or material help if he was neglected by his employer. The same method was used for the care of destitute orphans, and both types of children would eventually merge into the normal labouring ranks of the poorer part of society. Occasionally, though, a session took a less generous approach. During the famine of the late seventeenth century the session of Perth decreed (May 1700) that a girl foundling of five years was old enough to beg for her living, and stopped supply.[20]

Together the concern of both God and Mammon made it

---

20 The session's words (May 1700) were 'Which Child being now come to the length of five years and upwards, The Session thinks she may travel and shift for her Self at the begging and ordains no more to be given her.'

necessary to try and find the mother, particularly since in locating her a session might be able to prove that the child was the responsibility of another parish. In November 1670, in Dalkeith, Margaret Thomson admitted abandoning her child there because it was the parish of the father, who had refused to accept paternity, driven her away with threats, and then fled himself. In April 1749, Janet McAlester in Kenmore left the parish before the birth of her child. Some years later the minister of Kirkintilloch was in a position to point out that the child, abandoned, had been supported by his parish. Isabel Maxwel (Wemyss, March 1740) in 1737 left her child in Dunfermline, because she had no milk, but was sufficiently concerned to check up on its survival over the next few years.

In 1758, Daviot parish in the Eastern Highlands spent one pound and six shillings tracing the mother of an exposed child. There was the woman of Fossoway caught in the act of leaving her child. In 1772, the parishes of Dysart and Kennoway were taking legal opinion as to whether, in the case of a child abandoned in Dysart whose mother had been identified but not found, it could be proved that the mother belonged to Kennoway. St Ninians, in 1729, knew that its parishioner Agnes Dobie had laid down her bairn at a door in Linlithgow, and Forglen, in 1722, knew that Christian Reid had fled the parish, abandoning her child in Turriff. In 1707 Cramond was so certain that the mother of a foundling belonged elsewhere that it persuaded the presbytery to organize a search and located her a month later in Linlithgow. In most of these cases we do not know what clues were followed in the detective work. But one common ploy when an abandoned infant was found was to have a midwife examine the breasts of all unmarried women in the parish for signs of recent childbirth.[21]

So far, the cases considered have been ones where the main motive was avoidance of penalty, formal or informal, rather than outright rule-breaking, and the motive was, predominantly, fear. But there were also members of both sexes who deliberately defied the rules of the Church.

Church discipline was never meant to be purely punitive; great pains were usually taken to make certain that offenders understood the nature of their sin and truly repented. It is not at all unusual – particularly in the early period – to find sessions refusing to

---

21 At Udny this cost the parish five shillings, a small charge compared to the support of a foundling.

absolve men or women after the requisite number of appearances, because it was considered they had not truly comprehended the wrong they had done or were not penitent enough. Sometimes a session would criticize a woman as too stupid to understand her offence and so not capable of penance. More rarely was a man so described. In Dalkeith, March 1670, Robert Liviston confessed to fornication but 'being very stupid and insensible of his sin The session ordained him to be put in prison till he give surtie for his satisfaction and penance.' There were also linguistic problems in some areas. Janet Sinclair, in Canisbay, October 1726, did not understand English, which meant that the minister could not 'deal effectually with her conscience'; and in Alves, February 1762, the session decided not to cite a woman involved 'as she neither speaks nor understands English'.

More common was the issue of whether penitence was real. In February 1768, the session of Kinglassie refused to absolve Margaret Morton, a relapse, because she showed 'no sense of Shame in her Sin and particularly that she had been expressing Passion and resentment at the rebuke and no Sorrow for her repeated Scandal.' Attitude was all-important, and it does not seem overly cynical to suppose there must have been at least *some* hypocrisy on the part of certain guilty parties. Those unwilling to humble themselves before the session suffered for it.

In Torphichen, a man and his wife were guilty of antenuptial fornication and it was a relapse, as the woman had already borne him a child. The elders reported to the session that

they conferred with Archibald Glen & his wife; And that the said Archibald took it in good part; but that his wife being told by William Nimmo that her last fall with her husband before marriage was a sin; she commanded him to be silent, and he having enquired, whither she bid him hold his peace, for any fault of his own, or because he was commisionat by the session? she replyed. There had been over much of that allready, and Therefore he would doe well to be silent, else there would be worse of it.

The session considered her carriage 'most offensive and Insolent'. This occurred in 1704, and the session pursued the couple for years afterward; in 1707 they were referred to the presbytery, and not until 1708 were they considered sensible of their sin and absolved.

An unusually detailed description of a woman's involuntary response and the session's reaction appears in Forgandenny session minutes in April 1743. Margaret Anderson had been found guilty of incest, and the punishment decreed for her was that she must stand in sackcloth outside the church door between the ringing of the second and third bells. The session called her in and told her of this,

But in intimating this their sentence as Shee was humbled in Sackcloth she uttered the following Words Namely oh I cannot stand there to make a Fool of myself upon which she was immediately removed and therupon the Session, being deeply wounded and exceedingly grieved at such an Expression she had dropt as savouring rank of a proud & unhumbled Heart & Spirit, resolved to delay taking her upon her publick Appearances till such time as they had ground to believe shee had such a sense of her sin as to deserve all the Punishment which they at least had thought proper to inflict on her Body, and to acquaint the Presbytery of this her insolent Behaviour.

She was called in and

informed what great offence by such an Expression she had given to this Session Upon which she wept most bitterly and declared that what she meant by such an Expression was That being very weak of Body at the Times she would not be able to stand so long without falling down and thereby would make a Fool of her Self but did not think the Session was dealing too harshly with her and did not in the least intend to give them any Offence.

The following week the minister informed the session that the woman had expressed her sorrow to him for offending the session and her willingness to do as they ordered. For his part, the minister, 'tho' he was very much stunned at the time of her dropping the Expression which had offended them he was now satisfied she did not intend thereby to offend them or show a Contempt of their Sentence.' The session was still determined to refer her to presbytery, but a week later an elder who conversed with her reported that 'he was really of Opinion shee was acting a sincere Part for that amongst severall Expressions she had in their Conversation together he could not but remark this one, which she uttered with a great Deal of Concern, Namely That if it would please the Lord to forgive her her sin shee would never forgive herself.' The session decided not to consult presbytery after all.

There was a postscript to this case in October of the same year:

It was represented to the session that Margaret Anderson was complaining that she was not able to stand without at the porch door betwixt the ringing of the 2d and 3rd Bells as heretofore she usually had done for most of the Sabbaths she had compeared by reason of the coldness of the weather The Session agreed to ease her of this Appearance without at the porch door as taking no Pleasure in the punishment of her body further that as a Mean it might be blessed of the Lord for afflicting her Soul.

It was also Forgandenny session (May 1743) which resolved not to allow fornicators to continue public appearances unless they gave evidence of being humbled for their sin, 'because it was but too evident that the most part who were left of God to comitt such sins lookt upon their publick Appearances as a kind of Satisfaction & Atonement for their Crimes and thereby perverted the very Nature & Design of them as being only a Mean to bring them to a sense of and shame for their sins.'[22]

The most usual form of defiance of the Church's rules was a refusal to appear publicly before the congregation. Men did this far more often than women, but cases of women refusing to appear are by no means uncommon.[23] Sometimes the session prevailed on them to change their minds; those who proved incorrigible were deprived of church privileges, and a sentence of 'lesser excommunication' was pronounced against them (the sentence of greater excommunication was used very infrequently). Often, some years later, an excommunicated man or woman would ask to have the sentence lifted, after agreeing to undergo the discipline decreed by the session. With so many of the important community rituals and events tied in with the Church, exclusion must have been a very real deprivation.

We did, however, find evidence of at least one whole community who defied the Church for some years. The salt industry was very important in parts of Fife, and the kirk session of Dysart waged a longstanding battle to stop the salters profaning the sabbath by working their pans on Sundays.[24] In May 1745 a salter, guilty of antenuptial fornication, craved baptism for his child. The session

22 As chapter 2 made clear, this was unusually late in time for a session to be expressing such sentiments, which are far more typical of the seventeenth and early eighteenth century than of the 1740s.

23 For examples see Dalkeith, June 1776 and Torphichen, August 1778 and June 1779.

24 See January and February 1724, September 1725, and March 1740.

minutes recorded the fact that 'for some years past the salters have been denyed Church priviledges by reason of working their pans upon the Sabbath day', but that this 'scandalous practise being now left off by them', the man was allowed to be admitted to church privileges.

The language used about women who did not conform was strong. Janet Sinclair (Banff, June 1725) was 'a vile abandoned prostitute'; Janet Aberdeen (Ellon, March 1738) was 'reported to be a Strumpet'; Janet Strouk (Dundee, September 1743) was 'a notorious common Prostitute'; Margaret McIntosh (Croy, June 1760) was 'an old practitioner in wickedness'. In March 1714, the minister of St Ninians discovered that the testificat presented by Margaret Frazer was forged. He wrote to the minister of Kilwinning,the parish where she came from, and the reply he received was that the woman was 'a great whore'. Whether or not these women were genuinely prostitutes or not is unclear. The larger Scottish towns certainly had prostitutes in the eighteenth century, but we cannot be sure whether the women so commented on were prostitutes or simply promiscuous.

In the rare cases of women whom a kirk session considered to be virtually beyond redemption, recourse could be had to the secular courts. In February 1701, Rothesay session referred Anna McTimus, a relapse case, to the sheriff depute, who intended to keep her imprisoned and to have her head shaved in the public mercat (i.e. market) place. In one region, Caithness, the sessions themselves used physical sanctions. In March 1716, Christian Machugh, a trilapse case, was ordered by Wattin kirk session to be put in the 'jougs' (i.e. an iron collar) for half an hour before service, and later was ducked, shaved and exiled. Thurso kirk session also used the 'jougs' for several sabbaths on Jannet McKinla in October 1716 for 'notorious prophaneness'. In December 1701, the action there about Barbara McKean was even more drastic. She was to be 'convoyed from the pit by the executioner with a paper hat on her head to the stool, her head to be shaven by the hand of the hangman'. After that she was to be seen out of the town by the hangman and promised a ducking if she appeared again. Here the session made use of the town's officials for the physical treatment. In Wattin, in October 1704, Jean Guna was called 'a vile person unworthie of entertainment in a Christian society' and handed to the baillie for corporal punishment; and in Thurso, in March 1705 and April 1709, Elspeth Murray and Mary Sinclair were handed over to the magistrate for corporal punishment. What was expected was made explicit in October 1724 over Jannet Barrie: the magistrate was recommended to 'scourge her out of town' as a lewd woman. Some of the drastic actions were carried out not directly by the session but by a town council, which was accustomed to exercising physical discipline. Thus, in Ayr in the 1770s, prostitutes were passed to the council which would exile them and scourge them.

So far we have dealt almost entirely with women, yet in fact it was men who most consistently and successfully resisted the Church's authority, in particular, 'gentle' men. Resistance was not confined to gentry, however, and promiscuity among men was not labelled as it was for women. In 1649 the synod of Lothian and Tweeddale was handling the case of a man guilty of 'septilapse' in fornication, but made no particular criticism of him.[25] Similarly, when a man was involved in more than one unmarried pregnancy at the same time, this would lead to no special comment. But even if sessions were not openly denunciatory, they would wear down refusal to acknowledge their authority, and in the end achieve apologetic or evasive replies. In Kenmore, in December 1752, Archibald Campbell, named as father of Cathrine McNucador's illegitimate child, acknowledged 'that he said to Anne Dewar . . . his former partie, when she was urging him to marrie her, That said Cathrine . . . and half a Dozen more girls were with Child to him at the same time; he was gravilie rebuked for thus scandalizing himself and others, and for making so light of the sin of uncleanness.' Campbell ended up claiming that his remarks about Cathrine were 'a Joke to try what his Mother would say'.

We have discussed the connection between the gentry and the changing attitudes of the Church in Chapter 2. Here we look at the problem which kirk sessions faced in bringing landowners under their discipline. In 1719 and 1720, Alexander Robertson of Webster Straloch got three different girls pregnant without ever appearing before the session. In Caithness even a relatively minor member of the aristocracy, the 9th Earl of Caithness, did not submit to church discipline. In Thurso, in December 1712, it was recorded: 'the session considering the Earls frequent falls into fornication, and that he has not as yet given any satisfaction, and is still contumacious, recommend it to the minister to advise with the Earl anent his case.' (Needless to say, the minister got nowhere at

---

25 James Kirk (ed.), *Records of the synod of Lothian and Tweeddale* (Stair Society, Edinburgh, 1977), p. 291.

all.) Caithness was an area of many small lairds, and these lairds were responsible for quite a high proportion of pregnancies. In particular, the members of a clearly related group of families combining financial with sexual irregularity, the Sinclairs of Mey, Rattar, Murkle and the Earls of Caithness, who were backed by no greater landed wealth than the others, made a major impact on kirk session material. There was also George Sinclair of Forss who displayed the same mixture: in 1728 his younger brother was advising him to find an heiress as a wife as a means of escaping from debt, but he never married and in 1729 he was delated for relapse in fornication.[26]

In Rothesay kirk session register (May 1693) Issabel Austine named as father of her child the laird of Kaimes. Certain elders were ordered to speak to the laird 'discreetly and meekly'. The laird did in fact admit paternity in a letter craving baptism for the infant, but although he promised to make the requisite public appearances, when the time came he reneged on his promise. This is not atypical: in many cases it was clearly not a desire to avoid responsibility for the child which motivated these gentlemen, but rather the wish to avoid publicly humiliating themselves before men of lower rank. In Ratho (July 1698), Christian Goodale named as father of her child Alexander Foulis, laird of Ratho, and she was given 12 pounds for a quarter year's maintenance of the child; but when two elders called on Ratho he refused to meet them, saying 'I have nothing to do with you'. In Dumfries, in July 1701, James Murray of Conheath denied being father to Bessie Maxwell's child, and continued denying it as late as 1706, although she said he had maintained it for the first three years of its life.[27] In Dalkeith, Anne Taylor named the Earl of Aboyne (July 1723), and said he had taken the child from her and 'sent it to the Nursing'. There is certainly no record of the Earl's ever appearing before the session.

Although for the most part it seems to have been taken for granted – however much deplored – that men of gentle birth would consort with servant women, in Canisbay (March 1735) Sir James Sinclair of Mey was 'admonished to avoid the Company of Base Women which besides the Sin and Guilt would reflect Dishonour upon him.' In December 1692, Cramond kirk session received a

26 John Henderson, *Caithness Family History* (Edinburgh, 1884).

27 Dumfries and Galloway was another area of small lairds, and, again, some of these were responsible for a disproportionate number of pregnancies. James Murray of Conheath himself was named as father by two other women in Dumfries.

letter from Sir William Paterson of Granton saying that his
gardener had begot a child with his servant maid, and asked to have
the child baptized. The gardener submitted to church discipline
although the woman fled. Such a case is, however, rather unusual;
more typically the household of a gentleman who did not himself
submit to church discipline tended to feel they could behave
similarly. The difficulty which the kirk session of Wemyss had
with the Earl of Wemyss and his staff over the years illustrates this
point vividly.

In July 1706 Anna Thomson named the 4th Earl of Wemyss as
the father of her child; he denied this. During the previous autumn
she had been cited several times for having been alone with 'the
Black who serves the Earl of Wemyss', although she had
continually denied this. The session did not believe the Earl was
guilty with her and rebuked her for 'scandalizing a person of his
Lordships quality'. Paternity was never established. In December
1711 Anna Thomson was pregnant again; on this occasion the
alleged father was the Earl of Wemyss's factor.

In December 1713, Elspeth Simmers named the same Earl of
Wemyss. The session asked her 'what evidence could she give to
prove the same, for would any believe that a person of his quality,
sense and education would be guilty of uncleanness with her a
common coalbearer?' – which seems rather naive on the part of the
session. Her reply was that a number of people were aware 'that
she was familiar with my Lord'.

The alleged father of Margaret Middleton's child (already born)
was John Gordon, 'accomptant' to the 5th Earl of Wemyss. On
27 February 1729 it was reported that they 'had been suspected of
living in a criminal correspondence together; but nothing ever
could be found, as a Just ground of procedure against them'.
On 9 April it was reported that she had confessed to the minister of
Burntisland. Bringing her over from Burntisland to Wemyss
caused difficulties because her father would not put up bail and the
Earl of Wemyss refused to concern himself in any way. Finally, by
mid-April the session had Margaret in Wemyss, but was worried
about keeping her as she had already made one attempt to escape.
It was decided that the prison was too near John Gordon's house
to be safe, and the session prevailed on Baillie Brown to keep her
for just one night. That night Gordon started a 'tumultuous Riot at
midnight having come with a partie, to have carried off the woman
in a violent manner; but was happily prevented, taken prisoner and
thereafter sent to Kirkcaldy prison'. Margaret Middleton was also

imprisoned, but on 21 April it was reported that, with the help of accomplices, she had escaped.

Aside from the echoes of a more lawless age, these stories certainly demonstrate how difficult it could be for a kirk session to impose discipline if the local landowner did not support it. And, as a postscript, the Earl's next 'accomptant', Mr Adolphus Hay, was named as the father of Margaret Ross's child in July 1735. He at least did appear before the session and admitted guilt with her, 'but said he, I must look about me before I own the child.'

Our material gives numerous indications that men of the upper class held to some sort of dual standard of morality in terms both of class and sex. The rarity of fornication cases involving women among the better off implies some form of protection for them. There was no serious attempt to enshrine duality in law. Divorce, for instance, was by civil law available equally to both sexes, though its effect on property was not equal. Among the common people some male offenders appear to have held a dual standard of morality, but in this period this attitude did not receive Church support.

About 20 years after our period ends, the Reverend J. L. Buchanan noted that a woman 'if she is pregnant by a gentleman, is by no means looked down upon, but is provided in a husband with greater eclat than without forming such a connection.'[28] This is another useful illustration of differences in attitude between the Church and the community.

We found in one session register the transcript of a letter which a pregnant girl, Margaret Smith, received from a young gentleman, Benjamin Forbes, 'son to Edinglassie' (Foveran, October 1748). As an expression of confused feelings of affection, dismay, moral obligation and self-implication on the part of a member of the gentry class, it could hardly be bettered:

Margt I received a Note from you concerning your being with Child, which I'm sorry for, however your best is to leave the Town and go up the Country among your Acquaintances, for my Mother will be unsupportable if she find you out to be with Child in her Service. Since you lay the Blame on me, I can't help it, but since

28 J. L. Buchanan, *Travels in the Western Hebrides from 1782 to 1790* (London, 1793), p. 110.

you do, if you have a Boy you'll call his Name Findlay. I'm just going to sail, so you'll best take my Advice and leave the Town.

I am,

Your Friend

Benjamin Forbes

P.S. If the child be mine it's been gotten when asleep, however, when I return to the country shall find the certainty of that, and take Care of it, if it be mine. Adieu.

Benjamin clearly feared his mother more than he feared the session.

Once initial wrath had abated, it is likely that the Forbes family would have provided some sort of aid to Margaret. But there are cases of girls deserted by men in landed society who were confronted with hostility and could not withstand the strength of the upper class in using the law. In 1712, a Selkirkshire woman wished to write to the mother of her lover, but was illiterate. She obtained help from William Pringle, a Selkirk tobacco spinner, who wrote to Lady Broadmeadows at her dictation:

Madam this is to lett you know thatt this child thatt I am with is to your son and none els.

Madam I am very, sorry thatt such a thing should have been butt if you should have been never so angry it is worstt is myne and nott his for if I was going to Death I never a man in the world butt him So he needs nott take it to denayell for their is non the father of this child but him.   This is from Betie Jenkison.

The response of the family was to bring a case against Pringle before a Justice of the Peace and have him jailed for two weeks and fined 12 pounds Scots for a criminal libel.[29]

Much of this chapter places women as the victims of a system which, however much the Kirk might strive for equal treatment of the sexes, brought home the penalties of unmarried sexual activity more inevitably on them than on their partners. But not all women should be seen as victims: one or two were, by any standard, bad girls. A case from Dunbar illustrates this. There was a room attached to the kitchen of the house of Provost Fall, where his

29 SRO, SC 63/10/1.

maidservants slept, and one of these, Janet Penman, was the mistress of a man of some quality, Harry Knox. When she became pregnant in 1738 Knox and his friends discussed with her how to place the blame away from him. After considering attribution to a man who had joined the army, and to another who had died, they settled on a young tailor, James Pringle, who was in love with her. But Pringle was not prepared to accept guilt, and the session chose to believe him rather than Janet.[30]

A common theme of recent writers on Scottish society in the eighteenth century is to emphasize the high degree of control which the landed could exercise over their tenantry. There was no general established tenant right, so that tenancies were either 'at will', which gave security for the current year, or by lease. Landowners had baron courts which settled farming issues and minor criminal business, but which also supplied methods by which the brisk payment of rent could be enforced and actions by the peasantry which injured a landowner's rights or property penalized. Landowners often had the right to appoint the minister, could exercise considerable influence over the appointment of a schoolmaster, and, through their obligation to pay stipend and schoolmaster's salary, as well as the costs of repair of church and manse, could indicate displeasure in ways which were very uncomfortable for the parish. They could be extremely dilatory in payments to which they were committed by statute. Legal decisions in 1750–1 made it very difficult for a parish to quarrel with a laird in the courts.[31] It was also open to a landowner, provided he belonged to the established Church, to be an elder, and in such a case he would usually represent the parish in the higher courts.

Yet the cumulative weight of our material suggests that kirk sessions, whether graced with a landowner's membership or not, had in practice more effective authority over the mass of the people than had the landowners. Some historians consider that the Church experienced a decline in power during the eighteenth century. In formal terms this was so, but so long as the mass of the

30 Systematic questioning eventually produced confessions. The case went twice to the presbytery, which supported the session in making Knox do penance. He was allowed to stay in his seat for it, but not allowed to defer it to a time when the congregation would be small. When he offered the alternative of money the session said that it was not in its power to accept.

31 Rosalind Mitchison, 'East Lothian as innovator in the Old Poor Law', *Transactions of the East Lothian Antiquarian and Field Naturalists Society*, vol. 19 (1987), pp. 24–7.

population assented to Calvinist theology and the particular Scottish interpretation of it, the Church remained the dominant influence on society. We have indicated the ways in which some offenders attempted to evade penance and responsibility. This was almost impossible for women, and perhaps not surprisingly, our material shows very few making any attempt at evasion. For men the denial of guilt would not restore to them a clean reputation unless they were prepared to go on oath: by refusing to take an oath they could avoid financial responsibility. What is to us the most striking feature of our research is that over two-thirds of the men, in spite of some initial resistance in many cases, accepted discipline and responsibility. The Church, by its authority, was able to go a long way towards equality of treatment of the two sexes.

Conclusion

The initial, simple intent of our research was to see whether the later nineteenth-century pattern of illegitimacy in Scotland, with a relatively high national level and particularly high levels in the two regions of the south-west and the north-east, obtained in the early modern period. This has been answered in a somewhat puzzling way. At national level illegitimacy was not particularly high in the earlier period, and there was no clear trend upwards. The regional picture is unexpected. In the south-west there was a clear upward trend from the 1750s which could well have led into the levels of mid- and late nineteenth century. In the north-east there was no such trend. Illegitimacy and pre-marital pregnancy, both relatively high when our enquiry opened, had diminished, and in particular the level of illegitimacy, though not particularly low, was nowhere near the level of the nineteenth century. Whatever explanations can help in the understanding of the nineteenth century customs in these two regions of high illegitimacy they will clearly have to be different from one another. In the case of the north-east we have to accept a sharp discontinuity.

Our figures may be distorted by being drawn entirely from rural areas and from fairly small towns, and not at all from the main cities. Before 1755 the great bulk of the population was rurally based, and even by 1780 towns did not possess more than 20 per cent of the population, so the emphasis of our material is reasonably representative for Scotland as a whole. But the cities of Edinburgh, Glasgow and Aberdeen might have supplied figures with a different emphasis.

Our research has supported fully, and enlarged to cover our period, the statement made by T. C. Smout for the nineteenth century that there is 'no shred of evidence to show that couples thought that by living together they were thereby married . . . or that their children were not illegitimate.'[1] Certainly the Church operated a different law of marriage from that which obtained in the State's courts, but there could be no ambiguity about the marital status of any couple. This is the inescapable conclusion from the materials we have displayed in chapter 4. If there was not good documentary evidence of marriage the kirk session would call upon the couple to declare that they married each other. Marriage by habit and repute, recognized by the State courts, though to a considerable degree explained away by legal historians, was a very rare occurrence among the common people. The normal way in which cohabitation by any newcomers to a parish would be reported to the kirk session, and the detailed knowledge available about the circumstances of locally based people, would make it very difficult to acquire the reputation of a married couple without having been through a marriage. Not surprisingly, one of the few cases we have arose during the disturbed state of the country in 1745. Despite the ease and informality of irregular marriage, couples could not have been in doubt as to whether it had occurred. The Church did not tolerate any system of so-called 'common law marriage' or 'consensual union', and only in exceptional circumstances could a couple continue in a stable but unmarried union. So the definitions of legitimate or illegitimate for births were clear. In this our research, besides bearing out Smout's statement, gains further support from recent work on the south-west region.[2] In spite of the gap of 75 years between our material and that produced by civil registration, there can be no change in the definitions.

There has often been expressed a popular belief that extra-marital or pre-marital sexual activity was a form of fertility testing. This has even acquired academic credence.[3] It gains no support from our evidence. The theory is usually worded in the form that the man wished to check on the ability of a woman to bear a child. From what is now known of infertility it would be truer to say that the practice, if it existed, was one by which the couple established its compatibility in fertility. In any case, the small scale of the

1 T. C. Smout, 'Illegitimacy – a reply', *Scottish Journal of Sociology* 2 (1977), p. 98.

2 We are indebted to Rory Paddock, of the Department of Economic and Social History, Edinburgh University, who is studying illegitimacy in the late nineteenth century in two parishes of south-west Scotland, for the information that there is no sign there of consensual union.

3 Ivy Pinchbeck, 'Social Attitudes to the Problem of Illegitimacy', *British Journal of Sociology* 5 (1954), pp. 309–23, claims that fertility testing was common in Scotland, but provides no evidence for the statement.

element of bridal pregnancy, and its very stable nature, are counter indicators. If the practice had been general we would not find the level so low. Any particular component of fertility motivated from particular social reasons would be expected to change markedly as the peasantry in the eighteenth century became more sharply differentiated between tenants and the work force.

With regard to the various theories about the general rising trend of illegitimacy in the late eighteenth century and the early nineteenth century we have less of an answer to give, which is inevitable since, except for Ayrshire and the south-west, our figures do not show such a rise. Since economic growth was exceptionally rapid in Scotland between 1750 and 1800 the absence of an upward trend in illegitimacy is a negative fact of great interest. During this half century domestic industry, particularly textiles, became an important addition to family resources for much of the rural population, and also created a full-time industrial work-force. The nature of rural labour changed, as the class of subtenants or cottars was reduced to the status of simple labourers and farm servants, though the pattern by which the adolescents of both sexes left home for farm service early in their teens continued. But some of the work units to which these young people went had, before 1800, become too big to be regarded as true families. The past pattern of farmers boarding the labour force within the farm continued, but took a new form in the Lothians. Here the new large farms of 'improved' agriculture needed servants in numbers too great for them to be accepted as residents within the farmer's family. They were often housed in separate farm quarters. Those married were in cottages, and the others in separate parts of the farm house.[4] Later, in parts of Scotland, bothies, i.e. separate cottage dormitories for the unmarried farm labour force were introduced, and these might also be available for married men who had been forced to leave their wives and children in a nearby town. The period of an upward movement in illegitimacy in the Lothians, existing for too short a period to be clear as a trend, may be the start of a longer movement and reflect these changes, but without a longer run of good figures we cannot be sure.

The nineteenth century saw established a system by which the demographic features of the rural population were determined by the labour requirements of the employers. This was already to be

---

4 Alastair Orr, 'Farm labour in the Forth Valley and southern Lowlands', in T. M. Devine (ed.), *Farm Servants and Labour in Lowland Scotland, 1770–1914* (Edinburgh, 1984), p. 32.

found in some areas in our period.[5] By the 1790s the *OSA* provides a wealth of impressionistic studies of the social effects of economic change, even though in only a few places could the industrial revolution be seen to have begun. The expansion of domestic industry had reached the stage of making local paid work a very fluctuating affair, through sharp changes in demand, so employment for many was uncertain. By contrast, the demand for agricultural labour was very stable, dropping only slightly in areas where root crops were not suited. The increase in the urban sector and its activity provided new jobs in transport and made many acquainted with aspects of city life. William Creech in his impressionistic letters which make up the *OSA* report for Edinburgh has some disparaging things to say about the level of morality in the city, and in particular claims a 60 fold increase in brothels and a 100 fold increase in prostitutes between 1763 and 1783.[6] This sort of assertion is probably better witness of his lack of numeracy than of the true state of affairs. Other sources from the eighteenth century, such as the Boswell diaries, certainly do not give the impression of a shortage of streetwalkers in the 1760s. As an indication that commercial sexual outlets had become more available we might accept Creech's view.

The system of farm labour in Scotland did much to ensure the security of the work force, and this fact may have a bearing on the continuation of existing cultural norms. Wages may seem low in relation to the work and skill demanded but mostly they were paid in kind and so the real income of farm servants was insulated from sharp price changes. The system of long hires made at the hiring fair meant that the farmers chose the labour they needed, and that it was clear to those not hired that there was no place for them in the local farming world. The expansion of industry in and near the towns took up the surplus labour.[7] As a result the greater part of the rural population did not experience sharp fluctuations in its prospects. But there were rural industrial workers and they experienced greater insecurity. In the 1750s the export difficulties of the linen industry created unemployment, and in the 1770s the combination of financial insecurity and bad harvests caused severe depression.

5 Malcolm Gray, 'Scottish Emigration: the social impact of agrarian change in the rural Lowlands, 1775–1875', *Perspectives in American History*, 7 (1973), pp. 95–174.

6 *OSA* vi (Edinburgh, 1793), p. 611–13.

7 T. M. Devine, 'Farm Service in the Agricultural Revolution', in T. M. Devine (ed.), *Farm Servants and Labour in Lowland Scotland, 1770–1914*, pp. 1–8.

Some of these features, but only some, may go some way to explain why there was so little upward trend in illegitimacy. The picture offered by Tilly, Scott and Cohen of an increase in that part of the population normally experiencing sex before marriage, so that births which, in an earlier generation, would have taken place in marriage were now illegitimate,[8] does not appear to be relevant here. The low and steady regional levels of pre-marital pregnancy suggest that the section of the population experiencing sex as a prelude to marriage did not change noticeably.

The low level of pre-marital pregnancy, which destroys the idea of widespread pregnancy testing, does not, all the same, appear to have meant that bearing or being a bastard was the source of a stigma outside that section of society where there was land to inherit. Fordyce session in 1714 passed an Act, in other words a ruling, declaring that in future mothers as well as fathers should be named in the baptismal register 'for distinguishing Lawfull children from bastards', but since women in any case kept their unmarried name in Scotland the child's status would still not be obvious. We have found a solitary instance of a career handicap associated with bastardy in the case of a boy refused membership of the cordiners' incorporation in Glasgow on the grounds of bastardy,[9] but such a disqualification appears to have been rare. Certainly in the nineteenth century it was the complaint of those who commented on rural illegitimacy in the north-east that there was no stigma attaching to the child or to the mother.[10] From the many statements quoted from different people by Cramond on illegitimacy in Banffshire to this effect, one will suffice: 'men seem to marry a woman who has illegitimate children without any feeling of repugnance.'[11] There is the interesting statement by Stewart of Garth from the early nineteenth century, quoted in chapter 6, that highland girls convicted of fornication were expected to wear the head-dress, a cap, of a married woman, but

8 Louise A. Tilly, Joan W. Scott and Miriam Cohen, 'Women's Work and European Fertility Patterns', in Robert T. Rotberg and Theodore K. Rabb (eds), *Marriage and Fertility* (Princeton, NJ, 1980), pp. 219–48.

9 James Fergusson, *A Treatise on the present state of Consistorial Law in Scotland* (Edinburgh, 1819), pp. 182–7, the case of John Napier.

10 e.g. George Seton, *The Causes of Illegitimacy* (Edinburgh, 1860); see also T. C. Smout, 'Sexual behaviour in nineteenth-century Scotland', in Peter Laslett, Karla Oosterveen and Richard M. Smith (eds), *Bastardy and its Comparative History* (London, 1980), pp. 206–8.

11 W. Cramond, *Illegitimacy in Banffshire* (Banff, 1888), p. 49.

since all that this did was to associate them with those married it can hardly be seen as a stigma.[12]

We cannot offer any evidence on Shorter's thesis that rising illegitimacy was the result of women claiming independence and self-determination. Neither, of course, can he. Nor is there any evidence to support his idea of a change in sexual behaviour from 'manipulative' to 'expressionist'.[13] Women had not been able to manipulate men into marriage in the earlier part of our period, for there was no practice of 'shotgun' weddings, and they remained unable to do so. There does seem to be a general demand among men for greater freedom and independence, manifesting itself in the later eighteenth century. It informs the radical movement of the 1790s, but more significantly appears often expressed in the emigration of the 1770s to America. Tenants, often men of substance, were removing themselves and their families from an agricultural system where landowners had the right to labour services, and the county government to work on the roads.[14] Women did not hold any but small farm units and this view is not expressed by them. On personal, rather than economic or political, self-determination there is a considerable amount of evidence all through our period of study, showing that women were not subservient to men in the important task of decision making. We have found a large number of occasions on which the actual words used by women can be read and evaluated. Women considering marriage clearly acted, as the Kirk expected them to, as mature and independent individuals. The legal dominance over them by fathers or husbands did not prevent them from being outspoken, even if it meant that they had to submit to physical violence. Of course, women with status produced by wealth or by professional skill – the wives of landowners and midwives are obvious examples – would be expected to have and express their own opinions, but there are numerous instances of women holding their own and persisting in their opinions who had no claims or respect based on status.

In any case, our evidence leads us to assert that there has been far too much discussion which has assumed that illegitimacy must be explained in terms of the motivation only of the mothers. It is usual, when historians discuss fertility within marriage, for them to

12 David Stewart of Garth, *Sketches of the Highlanders* (Edinburgh, 1822), vol. I, p. 89.
13 Edward Shorter, 'Illegitimacy, Sexual Revolution and Social Change in Modern Europe', in Rotberg and Rabb (eds), *Marriage and Fertility*, pp. 85–120.
14 Bernard Bailyn, *Voyagers to the West* (London, 1986), pp. 517–19.

consider the production of children as the result of a decision by the couple, but for fertility outwith marriage to look at women only. It must be stated crudely that conception, within or outwith wedlock, is not parthenogenetic, and that unless we are to see the entire male sex as invariably set on seduction we must enquire into the motives and deliberations of both parents. The assumption, now usually tacit, of total male depravity, seems to be a survival of the common nineteenth century approach to sexual morals. A dual standard in both power and morality was then accepted, even if not usually voiced by churchmen. Men had the economic and political power, and for them some level of sexual promiscuity was to be regarded as normal and acceptable. Women were labelled 'finer' and 'purer' than men, but in need of protection since their morality was constructed on the weak base of ignorance and unaroused sexuality. Any sexual experience except within marriage was, for them, a major fall from grace. On this substratum of thought were based the various efforts of churchmen to reduce the high levels of illegitimacy characteristic of the north-east: societies, sermons, romantic literature and bullying by the poor law, were all aimed at persuading girls to retain their chastity, while little similar effort was aimed at the men.[15] That this view of the input of the two sexes to sexual activity was not confined to the nineteenth century is shown by a statement of the Moral Welfare Committee of the Church of Scotland in 1972, that 'the promiscuous girl' was 'the real problem'.[16]

For the eighteenth century, and even before 1700, the strikingly high level of 'admissions', that is of speedy acknowledgement of paternity by the men named by pregnant girls, as shown in chapter 7, is a refutation of this later standpoint, as well as a tribute to the steady pressure of the Church towards equality of treatment for the two sexes. Almost two-thirds of the men named admitted responsibility within a short time. Some, not yet named, even accompanied their partners to the session's enquiry. More acknowledged their paternity later, sometimes as soon as they could be got hold of, sometimes after several years' denial. In Aberdeenshire and the north-east the admission rate ran at three-quarters of the whole. When allowance is made for men who could

---

15 J. E. D. Blaikie, 'Illegitimacy in nineteenth century North-east Scotland' (unpublished Ph.D. thesis, Queen Mary College, London, 1987) shows many of the efforts, including the Onward and Upward Society. See also Alfred C. C. List, *The two phases of the social evil* (Edinburgh, 1861).

16 Callum Brown, *The Social History of Religion in Scotland since 1730* (London, 1987), p. 230.

not be traced, men who had died and those not under the authority of the Church because they were in the army, the level of acceptance of responsibility is impressively high. There may have been some unscrupulous Lotharios around, but the evidence is that men who fathered illegitimate children for the most part accepted the discipline of the Church; this meant that, though they had an easier course to run than did the women, they did not get off lightly.

Of course, men who did not mind staying permanently under an unproved suspicion could ignore the Church's enquiries. The striking thing is that, except in the south-west and, to a lesser extent, in Ayrshire, not many chose to take this line. The morality of the Church, and its methods of enforcing it, were accepted, 'internalized' by both sexes. Some small minority experienced sexual intercourse before they had gone through marriage. A larger minority, but still not a large number in the eighteenth century, fell victim to the temptations resulting from close working association and lack of supervision. Most of those who so 'fell', all the women and the greater part of the men, had to suffer economically for this lapse, in the case of the men by paying often more than half their annual money wage for the support of the child for several years, and in the case of the women by similar financial burdens and the involvement of care. In many cases it is to be assumed that the family of the woman housed and helped support the child. Public penance and fine (except that the fine might be modified for extreme poverty) hit both parents.

This conformity is more striking in that it continued through the period when couples were ceasing to conform to the rules of the Church on the way in which marriage should be conducted. The surge of irregular marriage from the 1720s, in those areas which had access to this facility (as shown in chapter 4), is evidence that obedience to the orders of the Church was not automatic, and that couples distinguished between rules of basic morality and those of good order.

There is little evidence in our material to support the idea of a trend towards secularization in Scotland. It is true that at the end of the eighteenth century the Church was withdrawing from the system of public penance, but that change seems to have come from the acceptance of a more individualist strain of theology. The struggle between evangelical religion and the more conventional adherence to a legally defined set of rights was to dominate Scottish politics in the 1830s and 1840s and force the Disruption of

1843. Even after that devastating reduction of its numbers and support, the Church of Scotland still had a dominant part to play in welfare and in the discussions on the social problems of urbanization.[17]

The most conspicuous result of our research is the gulf between the figures for illegitimacy ratios (set out in chapter 5) for the period before the 1780s and those which became available after the start of civil registration in 1855 even though there are similarities in the rank order of the various regions. Our general information on population, particularly on the size of parishes and their annual levels of births, becomes firm in the 1750s with Webster's census, and continues to be well documented by the ministers' comments in the *OSA*, so we can be sure that this gulf is real. Since we have not been able to carry out quantitative research in the 75 years gap between 1780 and 1855, we cannot offer a worked-out explanation for the shift upwards in the general level of illegitimacy, except to point out that by 1855 Scotland had fully experienced the economic change of the industrial revolution and its social consequences, which included the capitalized reorganization of agriculture, and had also shared the general British trend to sectarian division and evangelical individualism. The powerful sanctions of dogma had weakened as hard-line Calvinism was modified in some confessions, and the unified organization of the Kirk had been replaced by a fragmented structure. The Church of Scotland, the Free Church and the various minor sects which had joined together to make up the United Presbyterian Church shared between them the bulk of the protestant population, but there were also Methodists, Baptists of both the Scottish and the English persuasion, Haldaneites, Congregationalists and Quakers, as well as the rare communions of Unitarians, Glassites and Irvingites. Irish immigration had drastically increased the significance of the Roman Catholic community, and, in particular, enhanced its numbers in the Lowlands, as well as having increased the episcopal component of protestantism. Fragmentation made it possible for churchmen to put the blame for what it saw as a social evil on the adherents of other bodies, but this common response to statistics did not need a highly fragmented structure, as is shown by the readiness of the Free Church leaders to put the blame on the now defunct 'Moderate' party.[18] It was common, even in small parishes,

17 Ibid., pp. 196–8.
18 K. Boyd, *Scottish Church attitudes to Sex, Marriage and the Family, 1850–1914*, (Edinburgh, 1980), ch. 3.

for there to be sizeable communities not of the established Church, and this meant that the option of a change in religious allegiance was open to those unwilling to face private church discipline in the stricter communions. It was sometimes alleged by the Free Church that illegitimacy levels were lower in its communion than in others, but apart from its domination of the highland area, where illegitimacy continued low, this, if the claim were true, might have been the result of girls with bastards seeking an easier route to baptism than that offered by this Church. Similarly, the apparently high level of bastardy in some Catholic parishes through the nineteenth century may have been the result of the fact that the priests and population of this communion had a higher regard for baptism than for dogma.[19] If the inevitability of church discipline had been an element in limiting extra-marital sexual activity in the early modern period, this had ceased to be the case by the mid-nineteenth century.

But it would be unreasonably particularist to emphasize the change in the structure of the churches. Society as a whole had undergone a major transformation. It had moved from a system of direct social control by lordship to one of control by economic forces and of influence, sometimes control, by organs of the State. People by the 1850s were almost as likely to live in towns as in the countryside. Most were employed in units of work which were based on concentrations of capital, whether in the form of large scale industry or of large farms. The labour needs of such units were specific and the rewards of labour restricted, so that a deep social gulf separated the people who controlled work from those who supplied the muscle power. Certainly the Scottish economy had been expanding rapidly in the last 30 years of our study, but this expansion had been mainly within the existing structure of economic units, and only to a small degree marked by the creation of new units and new types of work. By contrast, the industrial revolution is not misnamed. It would not be surprising if patterns of human behaviour had also altered considerably, but we are not in a position to label and assess the particular types of pressure which would lead to such changes.

Nor are we in a position to make more than general suggestions about the particularly drastic change in the levels of illegitimacy in the two areas of the north-east and the south-west which so caught the attention in the later 1850s. In the north-east we might see a

19 Alasdair Roberts, 'Aberdeen baptismal registers, 1782–1836', *Innes Review* 31 (1980), pp. 24–5.

return to the pattern of behaviour existing in the mid-seventeenth century, when over 40 per cent of first births were conceived out of wedlock and the illegitimacy ratio stood at 9.8 per cent. When the Church abandoned public penance, and as it found itself no longer able to pursue all cases effectively, values of an earlier age could recur. It is worth noting that work on one particular north-east parish, Rothiemay, possessed of an exceptionally good OPR, shows that illegitimacy there began to rise after 1811, in other words with the onset of agricultural improvement, but that bridal pregnancy had started to increase in the 1770s.[20] Certainly the employment practice of the large farms in this area took a ruthless approach to its labour needs: since not much was wanted in the way of female labour the farmers employed mainly unmarried men. The decision of a farm worker to marry might well necessitate a decision to leave farming altogether. Few jobs carried the right to a cottage, and the shortage of cottages prevented marriage. Eventually illicit sex may have proved irresistible. But it is also claimed that there was little attempt, by parents or employers, to exercise supervision over the behaviour of young people, and that night courting was taken for granted.[21] These suggestions do not meet the rise in bridal pregnancy, and this feature suggests a different interpretation of marriage than that accepted in our period. Of course, a high level of bridal pregnancy would be likely to send up illegitimacy too, for intended marriages might not occur through unforeseen difficulties or the change of mind of one of the partners.

There is evidence of relatively high illegitimacy in other communions in the north-east. The Catholic population of Tomintoul had an illegitimacy ratio of 16 per cent in the years 1808–11, and of 23.5 for 1817–21. By the 1840s the level was 35 per cent.[22] In looking at high nineteenth century illegitimacy ratios it should be remembered that the difficulties and embarrassment created by an unmarried pregnancy for the mother, when levels are low, may no longer obtain when they are high. A mother would leave an illegitimate infant, once weaned, with parents or with a sister. Children reared in the miscellaneous families of different parentage would see such a household

20 Blaikie, 'Illegitimacy in nineteenth century North-east Scotland'.

21 Malcolm Gray, 'Scottish Emigration: the social impact of agrarian change in the rural Lowlands, 1775–1875'.

22 Alasdair Roberts, 'Illegitimacy in Catholic Upper Banffshire', *Scottish Journal of Sociology* 3 (1978–9), pp. 213–24.

structure as normal. Those who were able to confine their procreative life within marriage would be regarded as fortunate rather than as virtuous.[23] The high and persisting illegitimacy of Westerkirk in our study may represent such a state of affairs.

In the south-west the relatively early up-swing of illegitimacy suggests that we should not look to the movement of agricultural improvement for an explanation. In this area improved farming, only beginning in our period, did not call for large farms. Farmers made their profits from dairy farming, for which such units were inappropriate. Dairymaids were skilled and valued workers. The two classes of farmer and labourer were more closely related than elsewhere in Scotland. It was possible for an aspiring man to move from the status of farm hand to farmer, by use of share-cropping arrangments.[24] A study of late nineteenth-century illegitimacy in two parishes in this region places it mainly among women working as farm servants.[25]

Our figures show that illegitimacy in the south-west was rising fast before improved farming took over. They also show that the men of the region did not readily acquiesce in church discipline: the low level of 'admissions' all through our period (see table 5, chapter 7 and figure 28) is one of its striking features. This is also the region producing most of the instances in which a woman refused to name the father of her illegitimate child. Altogether, even in the eighteenth century it stands out for the unwillingness of the population to abide by the rulings of the Church.

This may surprise some people, for this region is associated with presbyterian resistance to the church policy of the restored monarchy of 1660. But it is a mistake to see this resistance as specifically presbyterian; as many of the genuine adherents of the presbyterian system recognized, the demands of the Covenanters of this region ignored the system of church authority which was expressed in the church courts, classifying majority decisions, when unpalatable, as 'carnal'. The covenanting extremists were demanding that they alone should decide what was to be the government in Church and State: this was not an adherence to Calvinist dogma, or to presbyterian polity, but rather a demand for

23 Blaikie, 'Illegitimacy in nineteenth century North-east Scotland', ch. 3 gives instances of such households; Smout, in Laslett et al. (eds), *Bastardy and its Comparative History*, p. 206 points out that in some parts of the south-west illegitimacy appeared to be hereditary.

24 R. H. Campbell, 'Agricultural labour in the South-West', T. M. Devine (ed.), *Farm Servants and Labour in Lowland Scotland, 1770–1914*, pp. 55–70.

25 Verbal communication from Rory Paddock.

minority rule. It was coupled with a readiness to resort to violence. Galloway was also the only area of lowland Scotland where there was any organized form of resistance to agricultural innovation and reorganization, specifically to enclosure, in the eighteenth century.[26] It seems fair, therefore, to see the south-west of Scotland as an area with a long tradition of resistance to authority, and to accept that a relatively high level of illegitimacy and an unwillingness of both sexes to bring home responsibility for bastards to their fathers, was part of that resistance.

Apart from the wayward behaviour of the south-west of the country, Scotland's experience makes an important point in the discussion of the motivation of early modern society in sexual matters. We see here a nation learning to contain sexual impulse mainly within the narrow range of opportunity that society made permissible, out of genuine acceptance of religious doctrine. This containment lasted through a period of rapid economic change in the eighteenth century, but did not survive the industrial revolution.

26 J. Leopold, 'The Levellers' revolt in Galloway in 1724', *Scottish Labour History Journal*, 14 (1980), pp. 4–29.

Appendix: A List of the Parishes Used for Quantitative Work

These parishes form the basis of our quantification, but the KSRs of other parishes have been used to illustrate particular points. We do not cite our material by its catalogue references in the SRO because since the time of our original research many of the registers have been moved to regional archives. However, we have given the parish name, and the month and year for the information used, which will enable those who so wish to trace the register involved through the SRO. In many cases the SRO still carries a microfilm copy of the material transferred.

Lothians

Cramond, Dalkeith, Pencaitland, Spott, Torphichen.

Fife

Kingsbarns, Dysart, Wemyss, Kinglassie.

Central Lowlands

Dunbarney, Dunblane, St Ninians, Falkirk, Muiravonside, Trinity Gask, Longforgan, Auchterarder, Logie, Gargunnock, Fossoway, Muthill, Forgandenny, Fintry.

Central and Eastern Highlands

Petty, Croy, Kilmadock, Alvie, Moulin, Kenmore, Blair Atholl.

Western Highlands

Kingarth, Kilmartin, Rothesay, Kilmory, Gleneray, Inveraray, Golspie, Kilfinan, Kilbrandon, Lochgoilhead, Durness.

Aberdeenshire

Longside, Belhelvie, Kemnay, Ellon, Foveran.

North-east

Grange, Fordyce, Forglen, Alves, Drainie, Banff.

Caithness

Thurso, Wattin, Olrig, Canisbay.

Ayrshire

Ayr, Kilmarnock, Kilwinning, Mauchline, Dailly, Sorn, Kirkoswald, Straiton, Dundonald, Dalrymple, Kilbirnie.

South-West

Dumfries, Westerkirk, Applegarth, Kells, Penninghame, Minnigaff, Glencairn, Wigtown, Eskdalemuir, Stranraer, Colvend, Troqueer, New Abbey.

Index